CW00362827

Praise for
THE END OF ISRA

"Heschel wrote that *the prophet's word is a scream in the night. While the world is at ease and asleep, the prophet feels the blast from Heaven.*

"It's not just that Bradley Burston saw what only few others could see, it's that he found the courage to share it—urgently, honestly, relentlessly.

"Burston has been a voice of moral clarity for decades. If only more had listened... we might not be where we are today. And even still, he wouldn't stand for us giving up hope—and so the struggle goes on."

—Rabbi Sharon Brous
Author of the forthcoming *The Amen Effect: Ancient Wisdom to Mend Our Broken Hearts and World*

"Bradley Burston has warned for years that Israeli Jews would never be truly safe until Palestinians are free. Now Jewish safety and Palestinian freedom look further away than ever.

"Still, his essays don't counsel despair. They model wisdom, decency, and hope."

—Peter Beinart
Author, *The Crisis of Zionism*

"Bradley Burston is 'the kind of person who loves Israel and hates occupation,' in his own words about another Israeli. On every issue Burston touches, his passion for Israel, its beauty and potential and tragedy, bursts out of these pages.

"His writing reflects his fierce and intimate devotion to Israel, alongside unflinching observations about what's going wrong, and how it could be better.

"Burston's collected works represent an essential warning cry, a fine and complex tableau, and a roadmap to a better Israel."

—Dr. Dahlia Scheindlin
Political scientist and author of *The Crooked Timber of Democracy in Israel (2023).*

THE END OF ISRAEL

ISRAEL

DISPATCHES FROM
A PATH TO CATASTROPHE

The End of Israel:
Dispatches from a Path to Catastrophe

By Bradley Burston

© Copyright 2023 Bradley Burston

ISBN 979-8-9891347-0-0

These pieces first appeared in a *Haaretz Newspaper* column called A Special Place In Hell. They are reprinted with kind permission.

The writings in this book were originally published in HAARETZ and are solely owned by Haaretz Daily Newspaper Ltd.

Any use of the writings without the prior written consent of Haaretz Daily Newspaper Ltd. is strictly prohibited.

All rights reserved. No part of this publication may be reproduced, stored in a retrieval system, or transmitted in any form or by any means—electronic, mechanical, photocopy, recording, or any other—except for brief quotations in printed reviews, without the prior written permission of the author.

Cover and book design by Skyler Kratofil.
Front cover photo: Varda Spiegel,
"Priced To Move At The Jaffa Flea Market!"
Back cover photo: Jim Hollander

Published by Fryman Press

THE END OF ISRAEL

DISPATCHES FROM
A PATH TO CATASTROPHE

Bradley Burston

Fryman Press

For Vee, who lives by the truth.

TABLE OF CONTENTS

A WORD OF CAUTION

How are things here, you ask.
Things here are past insane.

The dispatches collected here are not pretty. They are a study in loss. They detail the decline and fall of a nation which questioned - even before the horrific war still unfolding - whether this year's Independence Day would be its last. An Israel where the delusional and the fanatic were sovereign. A land which, the biblical book of Numbers warns us, eats its inhabitants alive.

The people of the Holy Land are easy to love. They are easy to vilify. Every one of them has known too much cruelty and trauma, too many hopes hijacked and strangled, to be anything resembling normal. It is no wonder that they are so often impossible in exasperation. The wonder is that any of them – in fact, so many of them – meet hatred with hope.

It is no wonder, as well, that they sculpt the truth. That they filter facts through tribal fealty, family lore, unaddressed grievance, selective hearing, post-traumatic stress disorder both inherited and ongoing. I, though American born and raised, am no different from them.

I ask just this: that you take their outlook, and mine, with one Hebrew caveat turned on its head: *Chashdehu v'Kabdehu.* Suspect them, but respect them.

INTRODUCTION

I'll make this quick. Over time, you come to realize that any aspect of the Holy Land can be explained either in tens of thousands of words, or in one sentence. The same is true of the tragic and brittle and vicious figure who has overseen the end of Israel, Benjamin Netanyahu.

So this is what this book is about: Once, not long ago, a leader with great resources of potential and power faced a choice – bravely stake your legacy to a vision of an historic and just peace, or contort and sacrifice your country for the sake of your personal political longevity.

He chose. Israel lost. End of story.

PART ONE: WHAT HAMAS KNEW

Hamas knew that a fearful, spiteful Israeli leader, in hock to undeterrable authoritarian fundamentalists, could degrade and demoralize and ultimately put an end to a Jewish state in ways which Hamas could never hope to approach.

Hamas had learned that its own tools and goals – the obliteration of a two-state solution, the imposition of a fundamentalist-dominated illiberal regime, eventual absolute, single-religion rule over all of the Holy Land – were increasingly mirrored in Netanyahu's choices of fanatic allies and anti-democratic, maximalist, effectively suicidal objectives.

Hamas came to know this Netanyahu - blinded to his own faults by arrogance, ambition, and an insecurity bleeding into paranoia – vastly better than he knew himself.

Hamas knew that from the late 2010s on, Netanyahu was satisfied that with bribes and, every few years, with a violent military "mowing of the lawn" in Gaza, he had succeeded in containing Hamas.

By then, Hamas knew that all it needed was a bit more time.

FIVE LAST WORDS

MAY 20, 2021. Two and a half years before the war.

How are things here, you ask. Things here are past insane.

Over the border in Gaza, families are farming out their children, separately, to other families, so that if one of our highly explosive "smart" bombs demolishes a house they happen to be in, not all of their children will be killed.

On our side of the border, where Hamas has rained rockets on Israeli communities which Benjamin Netanyahu cannot be bothered to care about, and hasn't cared about for the eternity for which he has held office, some families have begun doing the same thing.

The whole nation of Israel knew we'd lost this war the night it started. When the rockets reached Tel Aviv, something very powerful shattered to shards. It was Israel itself.

Everyone knew it at once. Some Israelis hated the idea, others saw it as a blessing in disguise. After all, even if Israel had already lost the war, even if parallel lynch mobs of Israeli Arabs and Israeli Jews were out for rival blood; even if in Israel synagogues were torched and

a Muslim cemetery desecrated and sacred texts firebombed to ash,
Netanyahu's death grip on power had been rescued. By Hamas. And
by the Jewish scumbag fascist supporters of terror whom Netanyahu
had spent recent months coddling and courting and campaigning for.

And not for the first time.

After all, it was the toxic cocktail of Jewish terror and Hamas
violence that first brought Netanyahu to power more than a quarter
of a century ago. The fervently right-wing Israeli who gunned down
Yitzhak Rabin, followed by a shocking spate of Hamas suicide
bombings of public buses in major Israeli cities, paved Bibi's come-
from-far-behind electoral path to Balfour Street.

That's how Netanyahu likes his people. Shattered. Furious.
Fearful. Paralyzed.

I don't want to live one more day in Netanyahu's Israel.

He just came on television, standing there with his campaign
smirk and his smug, drunk-on-his-own-wonderfulness baritone
bellow, a warplane serving as his background prop. "They've sustained
blows they did not expect," he crowed, referring to Hamas. "And I
have no doubt that we've sent them backward a good many years!"

The Big Fool says to push on.

For years and years and years, all that Netanyahu wanted us to
hear was Iran, Iran, Iran.

Now we know why.

The only thing he's ever been really good at, was taking Israel
apart from the inside. It wasn't just starving the health care system,
the schools, the social nets. It wasn't just acquiescing to every whim
of his vital-vote ultra-Orthodox supporters, even to the point of
calling off the police and turning a blind eye to abjectly dangerous
actions that have resulted in scores of Haredi deaths.

He had other plans, concerns of greater urgency. He was
grooming us, all of us – including those of us who hate him – to
keep him in charge.

Along the way, he's been terrifying and privatizing and molding

Israel's news media into submission, into exactly what he needs. So that people here wouldn't, couldn't, see what he's actually gotten away with. Any more than people here can see what we're actually doing in Gaza. To Gaza. To human beings. To children.

What we do know is that he's done to the shaky, defective constructs of democracy in Israel precisely what he has done, yet again, to Gaza. He knocked on the roof with a brief warning, then he brought it all down.

The minority that votes for him – at this point a minority is all he needs to stay in power forever – sees all this as a good thing.

He raises up racist, misogynistic, homophobic, Kahanist gang leaders to the status of partners in government? Grants them immunity from the law? Sure, why not? Israel loses, but what counts is that Bibi wins.

Denigrate and delegitimize non-Jewish Israelis and treat them as steerage-class citizens? Undermine all nonviolent Palestinian activism in the West Bank, kneecap the more moderate Palestinian Authority while finding inventive ways to shore up and bribe the Hamas regime in Gaza? Promise security but leave millions of Israelis without access to bomb shelters? All in a day's work.

Pulverize a building housing foreign media outlets? A masterstroke. A Bibi-ist fantasy realized. Bibi has groomed us well. The media is the enemy, treacherous, leftist, anti-Zionist. Bring it all down.

One more thing. Turn the Likud into an increasingly dictatorial political force, in some ways a version and, yes, a partner of Hamas? I don't want one more day of it. Not it and not him.

One fine day, may it come soon, this will no longer be Netanyahu's Israel.

Those first days of this war, when I saw the images of children killed in the fighting that Netanyahu could have avoided altogether, I had no words. But now I do. Five.

Fuck Hamas. And fuck Bibi.

Early on - when Hamas leaders saw that Benjamin Netanyahu would exploit violence and domestic disunity for political gain, and that he would work as passionately as they to render impossible a just peace between Israeli and Palestinian states - Hamas knew that he was their man.

THE RIGHT'S FEAR OF PEACE
WILL BE THE DEATH OF ISRAEL

FEBRUARY 3, 2010. Thirteen years before the war.

SHEIKH JARRAH, Jerusalem

As the grandson of anarchists, I've always had a soft spot in my heart for fanatics. Expressions of extremism, and passionately reasoned, exquisitely twisted world views make me feel, how shall I put this, at home.

So it was with a certain relish that I approached the cover story of a recent issue of *Commentary*, "The Deadly Price of Pursuing Peace," written as it was by a talented colleague and friend, Evelyn Gordon

The thrust of the piece, which *Commentary* Editor John Podhoretz understandably calls "groundbreaking," is that Israel's international standing has plummeted to an unprecedented low - and the number of Palestinians killed by Israel has concurrently soared - specifically because of Israel's having done much too much for peace.

"The answer is unpleasant to contemplate, but the mounting

evidence makes it inescapable," she writes. "It was Israel's very willingness to make concessions for the sake of peace that has produced its current near-pariah status."

The essay has the seamless, compellingly elegant, hyper-lucid, parallel universe logic of a hallucination - or a settlement rooted in the craw of the West Bank. Until I read it, it was difficult for me to comprehend the current runaway-freight recklessness of Israeli authorities and a certain segment of the hard right, bolstered by shady funding from abroad.

It was hard to fathom why Israeli police in this quiet hollow of the Arab half of Jerusalem, would choose to openly flout and violate the rulings of an Israeli court. I was unable to grasp why they would manhandle and arrest non-violent demonstrators, among them the executive director of the Association for Civil Rights in Israel - for protesting the official expulsion from their homes of more than two dozen Palestinian families here, driven out and into the street, so that subsidized and sheltered settlers could move in.

It was beyond my understanding why an Israeli government which views the idea of a Palestinian Right of Return as tantamount to annihilation of the Jewish state, would set a legal precedent [arguing that homeowners who lost their property as a result of the 1948 war should be allowed to return to that residence] which paves the way for just such a right.

Just as I was clueless as to why the Knesset was to vote Wednesday on a bill that would make providing aid to asylum seekers fleeing African genocide – granting them shelter, medical care, food - a crime subject to up to 20 years in prison.

Or why there were vigorous new campaigns to increase gender segregation at the Western Wall and on public buses, and why women have been arrested and interrogated on suspicion of having worn prayer shawls while praying on their side of a barrier raised so that they would no longer be able to watch their sons' bar mitzvah on the men's side.

Or why a sudden and ferocious campaign against human rights organizations and charity work agencies in Israel is coinciding with new human rights outrages against Palestinians and foreigners, some of them unable to leave, others forced to.

It was not until I saw the title of the *Commentary* piece that it all made sense.

The right is terrified of peace. And, in the end, the right's fear of peace will be the death of Israel.

They are afraid of peace, in part, because it threatens the core of what has come to replace other values as the goal of Judaism: permanent settlement of the West Bank. But that is only a part of it.

They are afraid of peace because they are afraid of the world. They dismiss fellow Jews who want to see a two-state solution - a majority of Israelis - as unrealistic, as living in a bubble. The name of the bubble these moderates live in, however, is planet Earth.

The right, meanwhile, wants to wall off Israel as the world's last remaining legally mandated Jewish ghetto. A place where all the rules are different, exit and entry, citizenship and human rights, because the residents within are Jews. A place where non-Jews, dehumanized as congenital Jew-haters, are rendered invisible. A place which, if suffocating and insufferable, still seems safer than the scary world outside.

A place which, because of its walls and its politics and its cowardice, is losing its ability to function as a part of the world, reveling in cheap-shot humiliations of key foreign ambassadors, deliriously proud of its sense that of all the world, including most of its Jews and Israelis - only the Jewish right sees the real truth.

This braid of thought was venomously endorsed this week both by an uncharacteristically Kahane-sounding Alan Dershowitz, and the obscenely infantile Im Tirtzu movement. According to them, where Cast Lead [a 2008-2009 war in which more than 1,100 Gazans and 13 Israelis were killed] was concerned, the real war criminals are [war crimes investigator] Richard Goldstone and [then-New Israel

Fund president] Naomi Chazan - two people who are open about their love of Israel, and who have worked their whole adult lives for its well-being.

The fears of the right are not mere devices of rhetoric. The risks of making peace are real. Every bit as real as the risks of failing to make peace.

It all comes down to belief. It comes down to the kind of country the believer wants Israel to be. And for that reason, there is a civil war going on for Israel's soul.

It will not be weaponry that decides this war, but courage. People who care about the direction that Israel is moving, and whose watchword is moderation, would do well to choose one facet of the fight, and join. One place to start, is to support the New Israel Fund and the groups it supports.

Another place to start is this one. At the weekend, challenging the threats of rightist thugs and law-scorning police, the weekly demonstration on behalf of the Palestinian residents of Sheikh Jarrah doubled in size. The police backed down on their vow to break up the protest, and the Kahanists barely showed.

If non-violent peace activism scares the right to this extent, there must be a great deal of power in it.

After all, most Israelis can sense that if peace is to be the enemy, more dangerous even than the threat of war, this is one doomed ghetto.

Things have reached such a devastating point, that for the first time in recent memory, even [then-defense minister] Ehud Barak is beginning to get it: "The simple truth is, if there is one state" including Israel, the West Bank and Gaza, "it will have to be either binational or undemocratic," Barak told the Herzliya Conference Tuesday.

"If this bloc of millions of Palestinians cannot vote, that will be an apartheid state."

The fear of peace has left Israel as a country which is prepared for nuclear warfare but not for non-violent protest on behalf of

Palestinians. The fear of peace, and the blackmail of the right on behalf of settlement, has contorted Israel into a body which, unable to countenance the perils of treating the sickness of occupation, will eventually be killed by it.

Israel's defense minister, for one, is convinced.

"The lack of a solution to the problem of border demarcation within the historic Land of Israel – and not an Iranian bomb – is the most serious threat to Israel's future."

Over the years, Hamas came to realize how little Benjamin Netanyahu's lack of interest in the welfare of the Palestinians living in Gaza was matched by his astonishing lack of interest in the security of the Israelis living along the border with Gaza – either because many of these Israelis were peace and democracy activists and other leftists who, Bibi knew, would never vote for him, or because many others were lifelong Likud voters who, he liked to assume, would vote for him no matter what.

Hamas watched and waited, probed and studied, feinted and attacked, signaled moderation and adapted, constructing underground fortifications like nowhere else in history - all geared to luring Netanyahu's Israel into playing into its hands.

By October of 2023, Hamas knew that for the sake of his "judicial reform," Netanyahu had waved away dire warnings of the danger of a multi-front war, ignoring the advice of his military chiefs, even announcing - until he he nearly set off an actual civil war - that he would fire his defense minister for urging a pause in the "reform" for the sake of Israel's security.

Hamas listened and learned. By the time Netanyahu chose the hardline "reform" over its legions of critics in the military - by the summer of 2023, when Netanyahu was quoted as saying "The country can get by without a few [protesting Air Force] squadrons, but not without a government" - the path to catastrophe was open and clear.

HAMAS WANTED AN ISRAEL IN MOURNING. HAMAS GOT ITS WISH.

JULY 22, 2014. Nine years before the war.

A little while before the air-raid sirens started, I was walking home with groceries. I saw a woman who works at the bakery, crossing the street. She was wearing sunglasses which looked borrowed. There was a cigarette where the unfettered smile had gone.

She didn't see me. She was leaving work after only a few hours. She walked as if carrying a load equal to her own weight. She was carrying nothing. No one had to ask where she was headed.

A funeral.

I can't tell you anything about this war that you don't already know. I can only tell you what it feels like to me.

It feels like the weight that woman is carrying.

This is week three of the war. Gaza is an unstaunched bleed. A place which has long set a standard for human misery, is worse off than ever.

We named this war after a cliff [*Mivtza Tzuk Ei'tan*, literally, Operation Steadfast Cliff]. As if we hadn't learned long ago that every war is a cliff. As if we wouldn't realize, once we'd stepped off into it, what that feels like. It feels like falling.

Maybe that's because, on the way down, war seems to sharpen the focus, even as it blurs the vision.

Neither peoples wanted this war. For many of us, the temptation is to place responsibility for the killing and the crimes on one side alone. But we are in this together. Both sides could have prevented this through diplomacy. Both sides, giving in to hardliners, believed they could get something they wanted through war.

Hamas, as a start, wanted to see an Israel in mourning. Hamas has got its wish.

Much of Israel is in quiet mourning over an unthinkable possibility: That this horrible reality is the way things are going to be, off and on, forever.

Having exacted horrific, if largely unintended, civilian casualties, Israel cannot simply opt for the application of ever greater force.

But with a government divided in its goals and held at permanent gunpoint by the hard right, our leaders offer neither hope nor new ideas.

On both sides, extremists have had their way with the peoples of the Holy Land. On both sides, extremists have done everything they can to see to it that there can be no peace based on two states, nor any peace here at all, ever.

How do you know an extremist? Here's one possibility: By their inability to abide the presence and the humanity of the other side.

"We will continue to batter the homes of the Zionists until the last Zionist leaves Palestinian land," Hamas official Mushir al-Masri said last week. "All of Palestine, from the sea to the river."

At nearly the same time, Likud lawmaker and Deputy Knesset Speaker Moshe Feiglin published an article titled «My Outline for a Solution in Gaza,» in which he wrote, «Subsequent to the elimination of terror from Gaza, it will become part of sovereign Israel and will be populated by Jews. This will also serve to ease the housing crisis in Israel.»

On both sides, the funerals continue. On both sides, we mourn, we seethe, we want to believe that this war will actually accomplish something. We suspect, also, that it will not.

On both sides, we wonder why the other side does not tell their extremist leaders to go to hell, so that the people can be left alone to live.

But the other side does not, perhaps, in the case of the Gazans, because they hate us much more than they blame them. And we are no better.

At some point, certainly too late, perhaps endless years and wars and children's lives from now, people here may finally come to learn the underlying geometry of this land and this conflict. It goes something like this:

This small place cannot hold just the Israelis, or just the Palestinians. And, since neither will go anywhere else, it's only really big enough to hold both of them.

There's another lesson, too. We reduce it to math, to body counts, to casualty graphs and condemnations. But one look at a small child during an air raid, or one long walk to a funeral, is enough to prove it:

The blood of the non-combatant stains the hands of everyone here. Every one. Both sides. It doesn't wash off.

Beginning in March, 2018, Gazans held a series of weekly demonstrations called the Great March of Return along the border with Israel. The mass protests, which began as a grassroots expression of non-violence, called for lifting Israel's military blockade of the Strip, and instituting the Right of Return to present-day Israel for Palestinian refugees and their descendants who fled or were expelled in 1948.

Though the protests initially raised hopes for an accelerating trend of non-violent protest, groups of young men, in the main Hamas and Islamic Jihad activists, began approaching the border fence, in some cases trying to dismantle it. At some points they threw Molotov cocktails and rocks at the soldiers. During this period, militants sent firebomb kites and incendiary balloons over the fence, setting off large fires at Be'eri and other kibbutzim. IDF troops responded with various means, including live fire, and the confrontations resulted in hundreds of Palestinians killed and thousands injured.

The catalyst for the worst single day of casualties was Donald Trump's decision to move the U.S. Embassy from Tel Aviv to Jerusalem. The ceremony was held on May 14, the eve of the anniversary of Israel's founding, and of the date on which Palestinians commemorate the Nakba, the catastrophe, marking the exile of more than 700,000 Palestinians during the '48 war.

WHAT KIND OF MAN GRINS LIKE THAT, WITH THE DEATH TOLL 10 PER HOUR?

MAY 15, 2018, NAKBA DAY. Five years before the war.

What kind of man is this?

What kind of man says these things? Does these things? What kind of man grins like a kid in a candy store, knowing that in Gaza, the death toll is rising by ten Palestinians every hour?

Knowing that just outside Gaza, thousands of Israelis are under grave trepidation for their families, their neighbors, their future.

Okay, he was busy at the time, helping the Trump administration formally – that is, in a high-spirited holiday mood —dedicate a U.S. embassy in Jerusalem.

But what kind of man talks like this, at a time like this?

"Dear friends, what a glorious day!" Benjamin Netanyahu gushed, barely able to contain his glee. In fact, unable. "Remember this moment!"

As Netanyahu spoke, the casualty count mounted, eventually reaching 60 dead and well over a thousand wounded, many if not most by IDF sniper fire.

What kind of man, well-read, well-spoken, aware of irony wherever he sees it, chooses just that moment to tell this kind of anecdote:

At the age of three, Netanyahu told the crowd, recalling his boyhood near what is now the embassy, "I would approach this place right here, but only so far, because my mother told me, 'You can't go any further.' This was near the border. It was exposed to sniper fire. That was then. This is now, today."

What is this man made of? He does not think like other people. He has a vision and a way of operating which are his alone. He has hopes and wishes and dreams and goals for himself and for Zionism which he has harbored for the length of his decades-long career.

And now, in the space of barely a week, his every Zionist and personal wish list just came true.

Days after the prime minister was televised worldwide lobbying against the Obama administration's Iran nuclear deal, the crowning foreign policy achievement of the president Netanyahu hated with open and undisguised passion, Donald Trump pulled the United States out of the agreement.

The next day, on May 9, Netanyahu's status and apparent freedom of movement took another leap upward, as he held talks in Moscow with the unrivalled power broker in Syria, Vladimir Putin.

Within 24 hours, one of Netanyahu's most cherished life goals – bombing Iranian installations – had come at least partially true. Ascribing to Tehran a late-night rocket barrage targeting the Golan Heights, Netanyahu launched Israel's largest air offensive in Syria since the 1973 war, striking at nearly all of Iran's military positions there.

But Netanyahu was only getting started.

This is a man who found in 2016 that he could gain popularity by openly siding with IDF medic Elor Azaria, who, on his own initiative, carried out a field execution against an incapacitated terrorist.

This is a man who then found he could further enhance his

power by undermining his own army chief and firing his defense minister, because they insisted on prosecuting Azaria for violating the IDF's rules of engagement.

This is a man, that is, who has found he can benefit from the deaths of Palestinians – provided he can titrate the killings to what an increasingly sympathetic press calls a "reasonable'" level.

This was a man who for months this year pointedly turned aside the pleas of senior army brass, who repeatedly urged Netanyahu to act immediately to address a crippling humanitarian crisis in Gaza – lest the Strip boil over into mass unrest. They gave ample evidence of the dismal plight of Gaza's two million residents, driven to new depths of desperation by high unemployment, infrastructure collapse and lack of opportunity.

Netanyahu's response? Banning officials from using the term "humanitarian crisis."

What kind of man is this? The kind who turns aside any contacts with Hamas, which more than once before the current wave of Gaza protest and bloodshed began, made overtures to discuss a *hudna*, or long-term cease fire.

This is a man who for years failed to act seriously on warnings by the state comptroller and others, that the fence bordering Gaza was inadequate to the threat of being breached and overrun in the event of mass demonstrations.

This is a man who failed to act on clear forewarnings that the army was ill-equipped and under-trained to confront and repel tens of thousands of protesters by non-lethal means.

We know what kind of man this is.

This is a man who finds himself praised for the level of violence in the military's response in Gaza.

On Monday, citing a news bulletin in which *The New York Times* wrote "Israel responded with rifle fire to a mass attempt by Palestinians to cross a border fence, killing at least 28," an admiring Ann Coulter, an icon of the pro-Trump American hard right, tweeted:

"Can we do that?"

In a macabre win-win, here is a man who only benefits at home when Israel is condemned abroad.

Here is a man who would do anything to avoid peace talks, and who has over the past year seen the issue of Jerusalem taken "off the table" by Donald Trump, the issue of territorial compromise taken off the table by his hardline, pro-annexation coalition partners, and the issue of refugees effectively taken off the table by his diversionary insistence that African asylum seekers be expelled at nearly any cost. This is a man who, addressing that embassy crowd on Monday, was euphoric.

It was not only his loyalists who exhorted Israelis to put aside their feelings about the deaths in Gaza and, in the words of Likud cabinet minister Ofir Akunis, "regardless of their political leanings, every Israeli must celebrate with us today."

On the other side of the aisle, Avi Gabbay, head of the opposition Zionist Union [the Labor Party], chimed in with "This is a very important holiday for the state of Israel and the Jewish people as a whole."

As for Gaza, Gabbay added, "What's going on there is very, very troubling, but we have no alternative. In this situation, first of all we must win."

Netanyahu could even take some comfort in an unusually sympathetic press, including, in some cases, appreciative coverage in unlikely outlets.

CNN, for example, which in the past has come under criticism from pro-Israel activists, invited Gil Hoffman of the right-leaning *Jerusalem Post* as a guest analyst during the ceremony.

"Things are going in the right direction," Hoffman said. "The embassy moving and the Iran deal being cancelled are steps in the right direction toward the moderates winning, over the extremists."

What kind of man is this newly, dizzily ebullient Netanyahu? The world has yet to come to grips with the directions and confluence of

Trump's sudden new world order, but the prime minister is basking in it, even as blood and fire remake the Gaza border, and the army warns that we are closer to war than at any time since 2014, when the last conflict with Hamas took place.

And as for the rest of us? I'm trying to remember a time when this place was more depressing. I can't.

PART TWO:
THE RIVIERA OF THE DAMNED

In his brief first reign as prime minister and in his endless second, Netanyahu inherited two key policy initiatives regarding Israel's future with the Palestinians - in 1996, the Oslo peace process toward a two-state solution, which he would be instrumental in killing, and, in 2009, the intended-as-temporary, three-year-old military blockade of the Hamas-ruled Gaza Strip, which he would render permanent.

LET THEIR PEOPLE GO

MAY 12, 2006. Seventeen years before the war.

In all of the Holy Land, there is no area more beautiful than the Gaza Strip. And none more accursed. It is the Riviera of the damned. The cruel Club Med of the eternally passed over, the pitied, the left to drown.

This week, a number of schoolchildren were caught in the crossfire of a gun battle in which Hamas and Fatah vied for the upper hand. The children lost. Eight were wounded in the exchange of fire. Later that day, an official of Shifa Hospital in Gaza City noted that at least four people suffering from kidney diseases had died in the Strip in April, after the cash-starved Palestinian Authority Health Ministry cut budgets for dialysis treatments. Some cancer patients have stopped receiving chemotherapy, the hospital has a dwindling two-week supply of medicines, and it cannot afford to repair medical machines when they break.

If that were not enough, the next day, Gazans were told that fuel could run out soon, after the Israeli company that supplies petroleum

products to the Strip, citing a succession of unpaid bills, threatened
to stop supplying it.

Should we care? We should, and not only because we live on the
slopes of Vesuvius, and there's thick black smoke issuing from
its summit. Not only out of quietly terrified self-interest, that is,
not just because today's misery can be tomorrow's murderous
desperation.

We should care because there are people living next door to
us whose normal daily life is built of the kind of hardships one
sees after a natural disaster. No work, no money, little food, open
sewage, disease, depression, hope too scant, shelter too primitive,
services too meager, death too soon, the horizon too empty, the
future worse than no relief for an unbearable present. We should
care because we will travel to the ends of the earth to help people
suffering tragic loss, large-scale traumatic injury, destruction of
their homes, their livelihoods, but as far as Gaza's concerned, a
few meters from our doorstep, good riddance.

We have left it to the wolves.

We were right to have left it [in then-prime minister Ariel
Sharon's abrupt withdrawal of thousands of settlers and soldiers in
2005]. But we were wrong to have done it the way we did.

We hurt and abandoned and embittered our people who lived
there and whom we expelled.

We hurt and exploited and, yes, abandoned the Gazans
themselves, who lived in a colony we called part of the Land of Israel
because we were unwilling and unable to run it as what it was, a colony.

And now we are hurting and abandoning them as what they have
become, what we have, in fact, made them, our neighbors.

"Stop right there, you've got it wrong," we console ourselves.
"These people want to kill us. These people want to throw us into the
sea. They won't even let us help them. Besides, we can't even manage
to feed our own people - you want to take care of them, too? And just
when we've finally washed our hands of them, after all these years?"

"They brought it upon themselves," we tell ourselves. "Let them stew in their own juice. They elected murderers to lead them."

"Let them go hungry, let their electricity be cut off, their water." "Why should we help them," we ask ourselves, "when their own brothers screw them, and have done so systematically for decades - the Egyptians, the Lebanese, the Jordanians, the Syrians, the Kuwaitis - the Arab world as a whole has let them rot - forced them to rot - evolved and adhered to an entire ideology explaining why the Gazans must be kept as a symbol of Zionist-induced suffering. For their own sake."

"Why should we feel responsible when the Saudis, the Emirates, could have used a sliver of a fraction of their stratospheric oil revenues to solve Gaza's problems, when the expenses of one week of the fruitless, decision-less 10-year Iran-Iraq war could have helped turn Gaza around. Their own brothers won't lift a finger, why should we?"

Forget, for the moment, what the right says. Consider the limousine left. There are a number of reasons why the disengagement from Gaza was and remains so popular in the svelte sections of Tel Aviv, Herzliya, and, for that matter, the Upper West Side. One of them is surely this: We don't want to think about those people anymore, and now we think we no longer have to.

"Mah li u'lezeh?" What does this have to do with me? The most unpleasant answer is this: Because we are still occupying them.

We occupy them, fundamentally, by deciding for them who should rule over them, and by deciding that we have the right to set them straight.

This is, of course, the cue for the right-wing chorus from abroad to dismiss this as the usual leftist drivel, and to point out the obvious:

Really, though what are they to us?

Well, here's the worst of it, especially for those of us who believe in in the Bible:

They are our family.

They are the relatives we cannot stomach, the cousins we have disowned, the kin we pretend are unrelated, the blood relations we act as if never existed.

They are certainly as ornery as we, as unforgiving, just as likely to think that we are all their enemies, as we are to think the same of them.

But they are also human beings, children of Abraham, trying to raise children and keep them from being shot - either by us or their own - keep them fed, perhaps even, one day, have an actual childhood.

It's about time we saw this price that we've paid for weathering the *Intifada* [the Second Palestinian Uprising, 2000 – 2005]:

Hamas has hardened our hearts. Islamic Jihad suicide bombers have robbed us of much of our compassion. Every Fatah Al Aqsa gunman killing innocents has blinded us to the Palestinians who aren't wearing masks, the vast majority.

Over the past six years, we made a conscious decision to stand up to their bombings, not to buckle under to the maiming and murder of our children, not to change our lives just to suit them, not to let the Palestinian fanatics win.

But this has cost us something very profound in the national soul. Suddenly, even leftists welcome the idea that you can't make peace with these people. Even leftists now embrace unilateralism, which, at its root, gives a whole new meaning to the tired adage of the right, that There Are No Palestinians.

We have to realize that our hearts have been hardened, and do the right thing: Let these people go. Even if they're still being used as pawns by their own leaders, their own brothers.

Even if their own people won't let them go, it's time we did.

We have to stop occupying them, find entirely new ways to start helping them, involve the international community as a presence for large-scale relief, start seeing them as what they actually are, human beings, trying to get by in one of the worst places on earth.

We must, as well, swallow our fears of international intervention and find a way to involve the international community in helping to stop attacks against us. We are no less deserving of life, nor of protection from killers.

The challenge of being a Jew in Israel today is to stand up and say, I'm willing to stay here, defend myself, and still find a way to help those in distress just over the fence - even if I find their leaders horrendous and the fanatic fringe among them abhorrent.

It's a challenge that moral people in the world face as well, the same international community for whom talk of concern for the Palestinians is so seldom matched by action.

Gaza, by rights, should be paradise, not hell on earth. These people are right next door. They are in our blood. Their future, whether we like it or not, is ours as well.

ISRAEL'S TEN WORST ERRORS OF THE DECADE

NEW YEARS EVE, 2009. Nearly 14 years to the war.

In the Mideast, dreams can only end badly. Not because messianic messages are, in and of themselves, bad dreams, but because of the nature of this place, the history which is as much imagination as it is record, as much sacred hallucination as it is shared memory. And because the dreamers of this place fail again and again because they are under the illusion that they are realists.

The decade just passing is one in which Middle East dreams came to die. It began, appropriately, with an Israeli leader [Ehud Barak] who saw his place in history as dependent on imposing a peace plan on the entire Arab world, and a Palestinian icon [Yasser Arafat] who saw his place in history as dependent on saying no.

In no decade of the modern Middle East has the roll of failure been so democratic. The titans Arafat and Sharon fought their battle to the death, and both lost. Bill Clinton, Ehud Barak, Hassan Nasrallah, Ahmed Yassin, hilltop youth, Al Aqsa Martyrs, Yossi Beilin, the Yesha Council, even Jimmy Carter - all dreamed Icarus dreams and realized, only too late, that in the brilliant sun of the Holy Land, wings of feathers and wax reveal their true selves, which is to say, nothing more than feathers and wax.

It was a decade framed by a fundamentalist Palestinian belief in salvation through suicide and a fundamentalist Israeli belief in salvation through brutality.

The decade ends as it began, clueless, hopeless, exhausted. For having lived through this, we are, all of us, somehow much more than 10 years older, yet none the wiser. In fact, what passed for our wisdom had died with our dreams. Socialist collectivism, rabid Revisionism, Reagan-Thatcher neo-conservatism, none of them has anything to teach us.

The Palestinians are ideological orphans as well. Ten years ago, they were promised that the armed struggle would cause the Jewish state to collapse like a spider's web. Ten years ago, they might have had a state of their own. Now they can barely breathe.

For both peoples, the lessons of this decade are unbearable. No Greater Israel, no Peace Now, no Wholly Palestinian Palestine, no Two State solution. Perhaps this is truly what the messiah has decided to settle for: a situation in which every single inhabitant of the land is to some extent miserable.

In this regard, there is perhaps no better time than this to review Israel's 10 Worst Mistakes of the Last 10 Years:

1. **The Siege of Gaza**—The stated goal of the siege was to undermine Hamas and to goad Gazans into rejecting Hamas rule. The effect of the siege has been to focus and intensify Palestinian anger against Israel, increase Gazans' dependency on Hamas social welfare arms, enrich Hamas coffers through tunnel taxation and foreign donations, and sap Palestinian support for Fatah, which, through its back-channel encouragement for the siege, is seen as a betrayer and a boot-licker in the eyes of many Palestinians.

2. **The Siege of Gaza**—The blockade was ostensibly a means to stem the influx of weaponry into Gaza. In practice, with shipments the size of automobiles flowing through the tunnels, the Hamas arsenal has grown ever more sophisticated, now believed to include Iranian-manufactured rockets capable of striking Tel Aviv and Ben-Gurion Airport from the Strip.

3. **The Siege of Gaza** - In the eyes of the world community, the overwhelming collective punishment - and the relative silence of Israelis in response - has gutted Israeli claims to the moral high ground. It has undercut sympathy for Israelis living within Qassam [rocket] range. It has kept open the moral wounds of the Gaza War, cramping rebuilding efforts, enshrining universal unemployment, and ensuring agonizing homelessness as the coastal winter gathers full force. Israeli officials have quietly taken steps of astounding insensitivity, arbitrarily barring such goods as school supplies.

4. **The Siege of Gaza** - The siege has been presented in the past as a means of pressing Hamas to release Gilad Shalit [an IDF soldier captured by Hamas within Israel and kidnapped to Gaza in 2006]. Not only does he remain captive, the terms of a prospective deal appear not to include lifting the siege. The siege has been presented in the past as a means of pressuring Gazans to end rocket fire. But rocket fire only increased after the siege was put in place. Finally, Cast Lead, the Gaza war a year ago, might have been prevented altogether, had Israel adhered more closely to the Egyptian-brokered Hamas-Israel truce agreement of June, 2008, and lifted the siege more completely in response to a drop in rocket fire.

5. **The Siege of Gaza** - The siege works to the detriment of U.S. support for Israel. In February, Secretary of State Hillary Clinton signaled anger at Israel over obstacles to humanitarian aid entering the strip. The message came

soon after Senate Foreign Relations Committee Chairman John Kerry, visiting Gaza, learned that Israel had blocked shipments of pasta, ruling it off the list of permitted humanitarian aid items.

6. **The Siege of Gaza** - The fact that the siege has failed so completely in achieving its stated aims, reinforces the impression that its real purpose is punitive.

7. **The Siege of Gaza** - The siege places Israeli officials in jeopardy of being charged with violating the Fourth Geneva Convention and other international codes, as outlined in detail in the Goldstone Report [a UN fact-finding mission established in 2009 to probe violations of human rights and international law related to Israel-Gaza violence]. Referring to the siege, paragraph 1335 of the report states that: "From the facts available to it, the Mission is of the view that some of the actions of the Government of Israel might justify a competent court finding that crimes against humanity have been committed."

8. **The Siege of Gaza** - With the siege under the direct aegis of Defense Minister Ehud Barak and his deputy, Matan Vilnai, the moral failings of the siege could prove the coup de grace to an already foundering Labor Party.

9. **The Siege of Gaza** - The siege threatens to destabilize the rule of Hosni Mubarak in Egypt, posing a potential threat to Israeli-Egyptian peace and Israeli security.

10. **The Siege of Gaza** - The siege corrupts the moral values of all Israelis, who, whether or not they are aware of what is being done to the people of Gaza, bear ultimate responsibility for all acts being carried out in their name.

YOU DON'T KNOW ME ANYMORE, LORD.
NOT AFTER GAZA

SEPTEMBER 1, 2014. Nine years to go.

This year, we're starting from scratch, Lord. It's almost Rosh Hashanah, and You don't know me anymore. Not after Gaza.

I thought things were bad a year ago. And the year before that. Turns out, I didn't know a thing.

More than anything, I still need to know what actually happened in the war this summer. And, despite my best instincts, I still don't really want to know.

This morning I took down the *machzor*, looking for some form of hope in the Rosh Hashanah service. This is what the prayer book opened to: What is read, and what is repeated, before the ram's horn is blown for the first time.

> *Min Hameitzar* – From the narrow strip, from the terrifying, dark, claustrophobic walled-off place, from the space whose very name is My Distress ....

This year, we read aloud the name of Daniel Tragerman, beloved of his family, four years old, child of God, descendant of Abraham, killed in Kibbutz Nahal Oz. May his blessed memory be, in time, for peace.

Karati Yah – I called to You, Lord. I called You. There was no one else to call.

This year, we read aloud the name of Kamal Ahmed al-Bakri, beloved of his family, four years old, child of God, descendant of Abraham, killed in Gaza City. May his blessed memory be, in time, for peace.

Annani BaMerchav Yah – The Lord answered me, and set me free, answered me and put me in a place of openness, spaciousness, freedom.

This year, we read aloud the name of Aseel Muhammad al-Bakri, beloved of her family, four years old, child of God, descendant of Abraham, killed in Gaza City. May her blessed memory be, in time, for peace.

Koli Shamata – You've heard my voice. You heard me when I cried.

This year, we read aloud the name of Anas Ibrahim Hammad, beloved of his family, four years old, child of God, descendant of Abraham, killed in Rafiah. May his blessed memory be, in time, for peace.

Al Ta'lem Oznecha L'ravchati Lshav'ati – When I cry out, don't just shut Your ears to my plea for relief, the sound of my breathing, my sighs, my cry for help.

This year, we read aloud the name of Khalid Suleiman al-Masri, beloved of his family, four years old, child of God, descendant of Abraham, killed in Rafah. May his blessed memory be, in time, for peace.

I don't know the truth, Lord.

I do know that all of this could have been avoided. But it wasn't. And we are all responsible.

I do know that all this could have stopped sooner, and these children left alive. But it wasn't. And they weren't. And we are all responsible.

Tuv Ta'am VaDa'at Lam'Deini, Ki BaMitzvotecha He'emanti – Teach me good judgment and knowledge, teach me to be sensible and fair and reasonable and understanding, because I was once, I have been, a believer in your commandments.

This year, we read aloud the name of Do'aa Mustafa Al Mahmoum, beloved of her family, four years old, child of God, descendant of Abraham, killed in Rafah. May her blessed memory be, in time, for peace.

Wherever we find ourselves this Rosh Hashanah, in whatever synagogue or open field or home we happen to be, an additional 450 children will be sitting beside us, uninvited. They will behave themselves. They will make not a sound. They will neither squirm nor feel restless. But we will.

They were alive last year, and now they are dead. And we are all responsible.

As the influence of hardliners grew in Netanyahu governments, military offensives – many of which might have been avoided by diplomacy – became more frequent. At the same time, settler leaders and other staunch opponents of any future Palestinian state began to see Hamas as an asset, a means and a justification both to avoid any resumption of moribund peace talks, and to refrain from a campaign to address the desperate social welfare needs of a Gaza Strip bombed, shelled, and blockaded by Israel.

RAIN AGAIN.
A TRULY JEWISH STATE WOULD
HELP REBUILD GAZA

NOVEMBER 4, 2014

What makes a country like Israel, Jewish? Is it demographics? Is it the kind of statistical majority that the government cites to defend a bill to hunt down, fence off, and deport non-Jewish refugee African asylum seekers who have committed no crime? Is it exclusion? Is it the kind of law that, according to Benjamin Netanyahu, would define Israel as "the nation-state of one people only - the Jewish people - and no other people" ?

Or is a Jewish country one which acts in accordance with moral principles of justice and lovingkindness rooted in Jewish tradition?

We're about to find out.

It's begun to rain here. In most of the Holy Land, there are few greater blessings. And then there's Gaza.

Even before the devastation of the summer war, Gaza was ill-equipped to deal with the flooding and sewage disruption which can accompany storms. Last December, heavy rains forced some 40,000 residents from their homes, and flood waters reached a height of 2 meters (6 1/2 feet) in some areas.

And that was before. During the 50 days of the war in July and August, Israeli air strikes and shelling left tens of thousands of homes destroyed or significantly damaged the length of the Strip. The availability of water for home use was curtailed in many areas. Sewage and drainage infrastructure were hard hit as well.

And now it's begun to rain.It's time for Israel to put aside blame, long-term strategic goals, long-held and counter-productive tactics of embargo and siege. It's time for a truly Jewish state to step up and help Gaza.

It's time for a country which sent medical teams and aid to earthquake victims in Haiti in 2010, and emergency housing to a temblor-ravaged, diplomatically estranged Turkey in 2011, to find ways to help our immediate neighbors in Gaza rebuild now. It's a matter of Tikkun Olam, of helping repair a broken world.

The need is particularly pressing, as the siege on Gaza is worsening by the day. Egypt, responding to the recent killing of 33 of its soldiers, has clamped its Rafah entry point closed, and is bulldozing hundreds of houses along a wide newly declared buffer zone to further choke the flow of goods into Gaza.

If Israel is true to its word - if, as the prime minister told the UN in September, "We deeply regret every single civilian casualty," if Israel truly has nothing against the residents of Gaza - this is the time to step up, to rescind the blockade, to allow and enable reconstruction to go forward.

And not only because, as veteran Israeli defense analyst Ron Ben-Yishai reported last month, the siege of Gaza has in many ways done Israel more harm than good ("The security establishment now admits that Israel's airtight closure of the Gaza Strip has worked against [Israel's] general interests."). The siege only enriched and entrenched Hamas, and, in so doing, helped it rearm itself, again and again.

A truly Jewish country would now actively help rebuild Gaza, if only because of how a Jew is commanded to treat a neighbor.

Two thousand years ago, the Talmudic sage Rabbi Akiva taught that the overriding principle of the Torah was the commandment in Leviticus 19:18 to "Love your neighbor as yourself."

The 19th Century German Rabbi Samson Raphael Hirsch, a forerunner of modern Orthodox Judaism, cited an earlier biblical passage, "Don't put a stumbling block before the blind" (Leviticus 19:14), interpreting it to mean that "the whole great sphere of the material and spiritual happiness of our neighbor is entrusted to our care. Our care and consideration must be exercised for the benefit of our neighbor," he wrote, "to prevent his coming into any material or moral harm through our means."

There will be those who will argue, and rightly, that Tikkun Olam begins at home. There is no question that the moral challenges within Israel are enormous and immediate.

A truly Jewish state would not condemn Holocaust survivors to poverty. A truly Jewish state would not allow education and health systems to corrode and crumble.

Certainly, a truly Jewish state would protect the Israeli Jews living within mortar and tunnel range of Gaza. It would listen to their pleas for a negotiated agreement to forestall renewed fighting, rather than withdrawing troops from the area, avoiding talks, and preserving the siege of the Strip, thus encouraging a new conflagration.

It's true – Tikkun Olam begins at home. Whether we like it or not, though, the neighbors are a part of any home. And our neighbors have no plans to move.

They need our help now. It's starting to rain again.

PART THREE:
THE ENEMIES LIST

First he came for the asylum seekers.

Nothing personal. Just politics. Barring entry to Syrian war-orphans and deporting many Africans who sought refuge from genocide netted Bibi a fresh and growing reservoir of voters – Kahanists and other young Jewish supremacists, whom the prime minister courted with hellish visions of millions of black refugees flooding over the border and delivering a death blow to the concept of a Jewish state.

He had found the magic bullet, the wonder drug which would polarize the population of Israel just enough to keep him in office indefinitely.

The fact that he was also destabilizing key support columns of Israel, that he was gradually fostering a brushfire civil war that, by 2023, would roil the military, derail the economy and cause a close-knit society to implode, only seemed to energize his electoral base.

The disintegration of Israel, which would be a key factor in the Hamas decision to launch its atrocity offensive on October 7, had begun.

Netanyah's Enemies List would grow longer by the year – Arab citizens, the news media, all leftists, Reform Jews, LGBTQ+ people, war-bereaved families, and finally, anyone who did not vote for his rule.

He would never look back.

WHEN THE MESSIAH COMES, ISRAEL WILL DEPORT HIM

JANUARY 6, 2011

When the Messiah comes, he will be without papers.

When the Messiah comes, he will be taken into a small room, off-white and chilled, with one gray metal chair at each side of a gray metal desk. When the Messiah comes, he will be questioned by a junior officer of the Shin Bet, and by an official of the Interior Ministry, who got his job through his cousin, who is an inspector of ritual dietary observance at a cookie bakery and who got his job through his sister's father-in-law, third assistant to the deputy chair of the Shas party branch in Ramle.

When the Messiah comes, no one will know.

His donkey will be impounded in a leaky underground police lot near the Lod railroad station. There will be no paperwork. By nightfall the animal will have disappeared, spirited into a closed truck by the lot's watchman, who after his shift will drive the donkey to a moshav. Money will change hands, and the donkey as well, four times, until it is sold by settlers to Palestinians, some of whose ancestral land now lies inside the settlement fence.

When the Messiah comes, the first sign will be a gag order. A coded report on a high-profile news website will be made to disappear. It will reappear on a blog in Seattle, and then in the *Guardian*. The government will delay response, finally issuing a statement ascribed to sources in Jerusalem, reading "We have no knowledge of this." The IDF, quoting an unnamed senior military official, will state that there is no evidence that a Messiah of any kind has come. It will later soften the denial, saying it is checking the report and directing reporters to the Defense Ministry, which turfs them to the Prime Minister's Office, which cannot be reached for comment.

When the Messiah comes, rabbis will treat him like Jesus. They will brand him disloyal, diseased, Reform. In wall posters, Sabbath sermons, ritual decrees and signed petitions, careful not to use his title, chief rabbis of cities and towns will warn of an existential threat to the essential Jewish character of the state. Under no circumstances are Jews to sell or rent homes or lots to someone like this. The rabbis' wives will vilify him as a carnal threat to Jewish girls.

The rabbis' declarations will divide the Jewish people and bring wrath and dishonor upon Israel. The rabbis will continue to draw large civil service salaries, as well as generous tips, in cash, goods and services, under the table and off the books.

When the Messiah comes, the Right will crucify him. Im Tirzu will roll out ads and billboards showing him with a tail to go along with his horns. A blogger from *Commentary* will call him a whiny, petulant boob. In *Maariv* and the *Jerusalem Post*, seven columnists will all have at him in the same three-day period. NGO Monitor will ask for donations to expose his sources of funding.

When the Messiah comes, the Occupation will end.

But before it does, a global social network led by the Republican Jewish Coalition, Fox News, The Zionist Organization of America and Daniel Pipes, will launch a campaign aimed at exposing the Messiah as a Muslim.

When the Messiah is crucified, the army will deny that he was even present at the time. When the Messiah comes, an Israeli political party whose voters are routinely denigrated by native-born Israelis as whores and non-Jews will propose legislation declaring him a de-legitimizer of Israel and of the army (over the crucifixion accusation), a blasphemer of Zionism (for suggesting that the Palestinians were not the sole obstacles to peace), and rendering him ineligible for citizenship unless he signs a loyalty oath stating that even if Israel did practice crucifixion, it did so in a democratic and Jewish manner. Aides to [Kahanist] Knesset Member Michael Ben-Ari, along with Beitar Jerusalem soccer fans, will take out a Facebook page headed *"Mavet L' Mashiach"* – Death to Messiahs.

When the Messiah comes, he will be granted refugee status by the United Nations as a legitimate seeker of asylum, but will be held at a detention camp in Israel's Area 51, near the perimeter of the Dimona nuclear reactor facility, where a judge will trick him into signing an illegible document, which will force his deportation to Chad.

By the time the Messiah leaves, he'll be thrilled to go.

THE ONLY HOME THEY'VE EVER KNOWN

OCTOBER 9, 2012

There are things no one wants to discover. Starting with the deaths of children. In this case, children who used to live among us, who were born here and called this place home. Children who loved this place, and whom we sent away - some, it now turns out, to their deaths.

For six weeks in June and July, Israel pushed the repatriation-in many cases, the forced deportation – of some 900 refugees to their South Sudan homeland, among them families with small children. Requests to delay the process so that the transition could be more orderly were denied. Many had to leave without much of their personal property, which was only returned to them after two months.

This week, journalist Dimi Reider reported in +972 *Magazine* that at least seven of the children forced to move to Sudan this summer have since died of disease.

The summer expulsions came at the initiative and the order

of [then-leader of Sephardi Ultra-Orthodox Shas party] Interior Minister Eli Yishai, who has now vowed to resume mass deportations of asylum seekers beginning as soon as this coming Monday, October 15.

"We will make the lives of infiltrators bitter until they leave," Yishai said in late August. Two weeks earlier, Yishai asserted that Africans migrants posed no less severe a threat to Israel than the Iranian nuclear program.

Despite, or perhaps because of, his position as strongman of Israel's largest religious party, Yishai has staked his reputation on policies, plans and declarations that have at times bordered on the sadistic.

Accusing asylum seekers of bearing a wide range of infectious diseases and of having committed dozens of unreported rapes in Israel, Yishai has lobbied the government to build and expand detention centers in the south. His spokesman has said that literally all the tens of thousands of African asylum seekers currently in Israel could be locked up, pending eventual deportation.

Yishai's ministry has also sponsored a bill which would force refugees to leave the country before being allowed to appeal the government's decision to deport them.

"Whoever wants to act, in order to ensure a Jewish and Zionist state for our children, should act," Yishai told Israel's Channel 2. "I choose action."

So should we all.

If you do only one thing for Israel this year, let it be this: Send a message. Write a letter.

Message Prime Minister Netanyahu. Write Barack Obama and Mitt Romney both.

If you live abroad, contact Israel's ambassador in your area. Write your member of congress, senators, or members of parliament.

Tell them that the deportations must be put on hold. Tell them that the influx of refugees into Israel has largely ceased, and that the refugees - and certainly their children - pose no threat to Israel.

That special consideration should be given families with children, as in the past.

Tell them that human rights organizations have said that rounding up and jailing survivors of genocide from Darfur and north Sudan violates the UN Refugee Convention.

Tell them that creating what amounts to a concentration camp for refugees would be a moral catastrophe for Israel.

Israeli officials have acknowledged that up to 35,000 of the estimated 60,000 Africans in Israel are from Eritrea, north Sudan and Somalia, and cannot be repatriated in any event because their lives would be at risk.

But Yishai is determined to continue to expel asylum seekers from South Sudan at once, despite indications that more preparations must be made for an orderly return to a difficult new country.

At the same time, Yishai has maintained a tacit but across-the-board ministry policy of refusing to process Africans' requests for refugee status and asylum.

Israel has every right to jail and deport undocumented migrants who have been tried and convicted of crimes in an Israeli court. But that is not at all the focus of Yishai's policy.

Send a message. The asylum seekers want nothing more than to live productive lives and contribute to this society. It makes much better economic sense to integrate asylum seekers into workplaces and schools, than it does to waste millions on building, maintaining, and operating centers for endless detention of non-criminals and their children.

Their children are as Israeli as anyone. Write a letter before we force one more of these children into detention cells, or abroad, to face malaria or war. They belong here. They belong in the only home they have ever known.

Amid strong international and domestic pressure, a succession of anti-migrant and pro-deportation Netanyahu governments failed in plans to expel the refugees. But tens of thousands of African migrants still live in Israel in a fearful state of limbo, the threat of expulsion a constant in their lives.

Amnesty International noted that in the mid-2010s, while EU nations recognized 92.5 percent of Eritrean nationals who applied for refugee status, in Israel the figure was 0.1 percent. Of 15,200 Sudanese and Eritrean asylum seekers who applied for refugee status in Israel, only 12 were recognized as refugees.

In 2015, with horrific reports of unchecked genocide unfolding just north in Syria, the leader of the Knesset opposition, Isaac Herzog, urged the Netanyahu government to allow Syrian refugees into Israel. "Jews cannot be indifferent while hundreds of thousands of refugees are looking for safe haven," Herzog argued.

Netanyahu responded with scorn. "Israel is a small country, and we do not have the geographic and demographic depth" to absorb Syrian refugees, nor African asylum seekers, the prime minister told his cabinet.

"Therefore, we must control our borders and block migrant infiltrators and generators of terrorism." Israel will continue to send humanitarian aid, he continued, quickly adding that work would begin at once on a fence to bar entry from Eilat in the south to the border with Syria in the north. "We will surround Israel with a security and barrier fence," he declared. "Israel must not be flooded with infiltrators, migrant workers, and terrorists."

Herzog replied with unusual fervor. Alluding to the Holocaust, Herzog responded to Netanyahu: "You've forgotten what it means to be Jews. Refugees. Persecuted. The 'Prime Minister of the Jewish People' does not shut his heart and the gate when people are fleeing for their lives from persecution, with their babies in their arms."

Netanyahu would not be moved. Not then. Not ever.

HOLOCAUST REMEMBRANCE DAY AS A DISGRACE WE'VE COME TO LIVE WITH

APRIL 19, 2017

This Sunday night and Monday, the Israeli calendar will mark Holocaust Remembrance Day, Yom HaShoah.

The Israel of Benjamin Netanyahu will not. Not in any real sense. True, there will be ceremonies and speeches. There will be air-raid sirens calling an entire citizenry to stop in place and stand at attention. There will be mournful cello solos and a paratroop honor guard and soul-lacerating documentaries filling the airwaves.

But Netanyahu, true to form, will go on his way.

Part of it you probably already know, because it's been going on for years. It's the part that goes like this:

If the Israel of Benjamin Netanyahu were to relate to Yom HaShoah in any real sense – other than the prime minister's televised annual campaign-style speech at the central commemoration - there is no way that tens of thousands of Holocaust survivors living here would have been abandoned to eke out the last years of their lives in abject poverty, forced to choose between buying medications and buying food, forced to decide between adequate heating and adequate clothing.

It's a disgrace. It's certainly a disgrace to the memory of the Holocaust. It's a particular disgrace because the funds to help these survivors always existed, but were siphoned off to pay the inflated salaries of bureaucrats paid to see to their welfare, in at least one major case, fraudulently. Government funds, meanwhile, were in many cases lost to waste, or diverted to other purposes, more politically expedient.

It's a disgrace we've come to know. And, perhaps because of that, it's a disgrace which, horribly, we've come to be able to live with.

But what about the Holocaust occurring just to the north of us? What about Syria?

To their great credit, the army and Israeli hospitals have evacuated and treated some 2,800 Syrians wounded in the conflict. The wounded are then returned to Syria.

Still, there remains the question of whether we are doing enough, and how we could do more.

A recent proposal by Interior Minister Arye Dery and Jewish Agency Chair Natan Sharansky to permanently accept 100 Syrian war orphans has run aground.

Netanyahu and other ministers have reportedly shelved the proposal, because it would entail providing permanent residency status to the refugee orphans.

It's time to ask the prime minister who cites the Holocaust with such frequency and fluency: What has it taught you?

A clue may perhaps be found in the words of one of Netanyahu's prominent explainers, commentator Caroline Glick.

Appearing on Israel Channel Two's morning talk show earlier this month, Glick was asked by anchor Avri Gilad, son of a concentration camp survivor, about Israel's relative non-involvement as the Syrian genocide proceeded.

AVRI GILAD: "Can a people which has survived the Holocaust simply stand by and watch while children of another people, and innocent adults as well, are being annihilated by being gassed? That is the question."

CAROLINE GLICK: "Of course we can. After all, for us in Israel, the lesson of the Holocaust is not that we have to save everyone from all sorts of terrible things happening to them, rather that we have to take care of ourselves.

"For us, the lesson of the Holocaust is that we must never return to a situation where we need to pray that the righteous of other nations will come to save us. We can't live in that situation."

I'm not arguing that Israel militarily intervene in Syria. I am asking why, apparently in the name of avoiding a demographic precedent, the Netanyahu government can hold up a decision on allowing just 100 Syrian orphans to stay here. Do we really need to think twice?

This is what I'm really asking: What kind of man does this? What kind of people are we, that we let him?

We even honor him in the name of the Jewish people he presumes to speak for, in whose name he presumes to act. As if he knows something, anything, about the concept of *HaLev HaYehudi* - what it means to see and feel and act with a compassionate Jewish heart.

Netanyahu knows where he can make a start. By coming to the aid of 100 Syrian orphans, and of thousands of needy Holocaust survivors. By coming to their aid, that is, before it's too late.

No refugees would be allowed to enter from Syria. Netanyahu buried the proposal. Underlying the ban was Israel's decades-long refusal to formulate policy regarding Palestinians who fled or were driven from their homes in wars and other military and administrative actions from Israel's 1948 wartime founding and still today.

Meanwhile, year by year, group after group, the enemies list continued to grow: All Muslims everywhere. All non-Jewish citizens of Israel. All Jewish citizens of Israel who were not Orthodox. Liberal Jews in the Diaspora. Barack Obama and his then-vice president Joe Biden. All leftist Jews anywhere. Nearly all Ashkenazim – with the exception of Netanyahu voters and their settler and ultra-Orthodox allies.

He would have no red lines, as bereaved families would learn.

TO HONOR ISRAEL'S MEMORIAL DAY, THEY ATTACKED MY FAMILY

MAY 2, 2017

First you felt the hate.

You've never felt anything like it. Even in this country, in this place of heirloom hatreds, when you think you've felt it all, felt it singe your eyes raw and clench off your blood and sear through your skin to where you can suddenly feel bone, this was something new. It wasn't supposed to be like this. On the outskirts of the city,

On the memorial day for the fallen of Israel's wars and for victims of terrorism, thousands of people, many of them bereaved of loved ones, had come together to grieve in their own way, to remember in their own way; somber, quiet, respectful. Inspiring.

For two hours, you could feel the future. The pain involved in a change of heart. The hope in it. The humanity in it. The beauty in it. The healing in it.

The annual memorial, organized by the Bereaved Parents Circle and Combatants for Peace, joint Israeli-Palestinian groups actively working for reconciliation and peace, has resonated so deeply within this society that after a dozen years, even the Tel Aviv-area basketball arena in which it was held this year, proved too small to contain all those who wanted to take part.

And this was even after Israel denied entry permits to hundreds of West Bank Palestinians who wanted deeply to attend.

But for those people who did take part, to come together to recognize nightmares they had experienced in their lives, a whole new nightmare awaited.

The worst of the worst of Israel, the very ugliest of us, an organized, street gang of Kahane-worshippers wrapped in Israeli flags and personal heat waves of rage, waited near the entrance to terrorize anyone who tried to go in.

They shouted sexually charged misogynistic curses, and hailed their heroes, Jewish terrorist murderers of Palestinians.

And when the participants came out, the level of curses only intensified. They got personal. Bereaved parents of Israeli soldiers were branded traitors. As our family walked through the parking lot, a young woman wished cancer on us. Young men yelled "Amalek" at us, branding us members of a tribe the Bible identifies as arch-enemies of the Jews, to be hunted down and killed, down to the last infant. They called us terrorists and sluts. They screamed at our family that our mothers were whores.

My wife, a daughter of Holocaust survivors who as a nurse had saved lives both Jewish and Arab, guided us out of the lot with a sharp U-turn that avoided the youths trying to advance on our car.

After that it got worse.

Social media exploded, led by one of Israel's princes of racist incitement, rapper Yoav Eliasi, known as *HaTsel,* the Shadow. "Believe it or not," he posted on Facebook, "even soldiers in uniform came as guests to the extreme left's ceremony desecrating Memorial Day."

"With God's help, may a suicide terrorist blow himself up among them," one of Eliasi's followers responded.

Others wrote of the joy they would reap at the violent deaths of traitors - soldiers who attended the memorial - including a woman soldier, whom one called "whore daughter of a thousand whores."

Why was it so important to these self-appointed saviors of the Jewish race - and these self-appointed defenders of the honor of fallen soldiers and of Memorial Day - to spend their Memorial Day going out of their way to abuse bereaved families?

Because in the furious blindness of their hatred, they saw the people in front of them as a danger.

And, in a sense, they were right.

They saw the 4,000 people in that arena, and the 400 more taking part in a companion Beit Jala ceremony for those denied entry from the West Bank, and the some 15,000 who watched online, as a threat to the reality in which all of the Holy Land is enslaved, a reality in which only they - Kahanist supremacists - can do anything they damn well please. To anyone.

Underneath their foul language, the Kahanists are scared to death.

The groups who organized the memorial, and the people who attended, did what the extremists fear most: They created a safe space for both Israelis and Palestinians. For two hours, Palestinians and Israelis both felt free to tell the stories of the depths of their loss, without sugarcoating. Without ideology. Without lying.

The Kahanists outside needed to lie. The next day they needed to tell the press that the memorial had glorified terrorists. An absolute lie. They needed to tell the press that the memorial had compared soldiers to suicide bombers. An absolute lie.

They – the Kahanists – they are the nightmare.

In their land, in their minds, there's no place for Arabs at all. And in this country, in their minds, there's no place for Jews like us, either.

They wanted to hurt people. They wanted to hurt Jews. Most of all though, they wanted to stop people from coming.

And they failed.

Try to imagine what it was like. I was there, and I still can't quite imagine it. First you felt the hate, then you felt the future.

In a place where nothing seems to change - in one night, in one small place, for two hours - everything seemed different.

If things are ever going to change, we can now be sure that things will get a lot uglier before they get at all better.

But there's a light down the road. We saw it. You just have to make the U-turn.

PART FOUR:
DOWN THE LONG DEAD END

As early as 2010, a new generation of hard rightists began a broad campaign to anchor authoritarianism in law, and to excise any legal expression of the principle of equality. At first, Netanyahu kept the legislation at bay, perhaps anticipating the breeder reaction which would eventually result in the norm-shattering "judicial overhaul," whose impact on the nation's social cohesion, would leave Israel vulnerable to attack as never before in early October, 2023.

If there were a single point of no return for the stepwise erosion of the elements of democracy in Israel, however, it came late on the night of March 17, 2015.

Something profound and permanent came over Benjamin Netanyahu when polls closed on that election night. The prime minister had pulled out an upset, come-from-behind landslide victory. Desperate for re-election, clearly behind in opinion polls, Netanyahu had turned his campaign over to a coterie of young, right-wing, social media-savvy advisors led by his loose-cannon elder son Yair. Their election day goal: re-motivating thousands of Likud-voting families who had cooled on the long-serving Netanyahu and had decided to sit out the election. Their solution: racism.

"Rightist rule is in danger!" Netanyahu announced on Facebook, backed by a map of Muslim nations hostile to Israel. "Arab voters are advancing on the polling places in enormous droves! Leftist organizations are transporting them there!" - pause for dramatic effect – "In buses!"

The victory transformed him. Hubris took him over, to an extent that would shock longtime colleagues for years to come. Neither Netanyahu nor the country would ever be the same.

I AM ASHAMED THAT MY PRIME MINISTER IS A RACIST

MARCH 18, 2015

This week, push came to shove.

This week, we saw how things really work. How our prime minister really thinks. What he's willing to do, how far he's willing to go, how many of us he's willing to sell out, slander, abuse, for the sake of hanging on to the thing that matters to him more than anything: his job.

After this week, we can never again say that we didn't quite know who Benjamin Netanyahu is.

As an Israeli, I am ashamed that my prime minister is a racist.

On Election Day, knowing that the whole country would see it or hear about it, he warned in social media videos, in texts and in tweets, that the rule of the Right was imperiled, that Arab voters were moving in huge numbers toward the polling places, and "the NGOs of the Left" were busing them in (to God knows where).

How should Jews respond to the threat of Arab hordes advancing on ballot boxes? The posts were explicit: Rush to the polling places, grab your loved ones and get them there as well, to vote Likud. Against the implied threat of these the Arab voters, he pleaded, "We have only you."

"With your help, and with God's help, we will put up a nationalist government which will safeguard the state of Israel," my prime minister wrote.

Lest there be any question of how we should view this, when he took the stage for his victory speech late Tuesday night, Netanyahu invited singer Amir Benayoun to come up and join him. The prime minister's message was clear: If you are religious and write a racist song ("Ahmed Loves Israel," which refers to Arabs as scum and murderers) - a song so incendiary that President Reuven Rivlin felt he was duty-bound to revoke Benayoun's invitation to the President's Residence - well sir, your place is right here, right now, by my side.

I am ashamed to know that the prime minister of Israel is either a racist, which is a horrible thought, or that he incites racism in others for the sake of votes, which is arguably worse.

I am ashamed that my prime minister is a cheat. I am angry that in order to win, on the eve of the election, his campaign defied a judge's ruling and knowingly defrauded thousands of Israelis into thinking that rival Kulanu party leader Moshe Kahlon was messaging them to switch their vote to Netanyahu.

I am ashamed that my prime minister can humiliate and exploit Moshe Kahlon, an earnest and honorable man, and get away with it.

As an Israeli, I am ashamed that my prime minister is a liar, a huckster, a calculating, desperate coward, a schmaltz merchant.

Now we finally know what he meant, just last October, when he told President Obama that he remained "committed to the vision of peace of two states for two peoples."

He explained it all on Monday night, when, standing behind bulletproof glass in the square where Yitzhak Rabin was assassinated— the choice of venue, in itself, an obscene act by a politician whose incitement eased the way for the murder - Netanyahu addressed a rally of thousands of right-wing Jews, many of them – yes - bused in from the West Bank at the expense of the Israeli taxpayer.

Just after telling the crowd that they should avoid incitement, that he was prime minister even of Israelis who don't agree with him, and that "We pride ourselves on upholding the unity of Israel," he made it all clear:

There are already two states for two peoples. There are the People of Us - that is Zionists, which is to say Jews who are right-wing, who prize settlements above all else, and who resist all compromise, forswear any concession, oppose all negotiation, and who will vote for Benjamin Netanyahu when he declares that there will be not one settler uprooted, even from outposts which Israel itself has declared illegal.

And then there are the People of Them. All the rest of us. People he calls anti-Zionist. People whom he describes as haters of Israel. Dark forces, treacherous, in league with foreigners.

"Yes," the uber-secular prime minister told the crowd, suddenly putting himself forward as the pious, commandment-keeping, mezuzah-kissing SuperJew, explaining who "We" are: "We keep the traditions of Israel."

Then the man who is bought and paid for by an American gambling billionaire took it up a notch. "They have V15 [a grass-roots anti-Netanyahu funding drive], but we have the People." They have the money, but we have something more important, he concluded. "It won't be money that decides this. Rather, it will be heart, soul, belief."

We're all going to need it.

I am ashamed that my prime minister believes - and is quietly pleased - that many young people who love their country, have served their country, have endangered their lives for our sake, but who are not part of Us - not settlers, not ultra-Orthodox, not right- wing, and in many cases, not Jewish - will solve their own problems of housing and providing for a new family, by leaving Israel.

I am ashamed that my prime minister perceives, and accepts, that many people who are indigent, elderly, chronically ill, disabled, will meet the challenges of a neglected and failing health care system, by dying.

I am ashamed that my prime minister is declaring that millions of Palestinians are unentitled to rights, beginning with the right to have a say as to the kind of government and country they want to live in.

Most of all, I am ashamed that what my prime minister does, works. I am ashamed that racism works here, with my people. As a Jew, I believe that if all we are left with is bigotry and fear, it will be the end of us.

All this week, Benjamin Netanyahu made us one consistent promise: In his coming term as prime minister, there will be no hope.

It is one promise that we have all come to believe he can keep.

"A prime minister up to his neck in (corruption) investigations has no moral or public mandate to make fateful decisions for the state of Israel."

"There is a fear, I must say, and it is real and not unfounded, that he will make his decisions based on his own personal interest for political survival, rather than the national interest."

The speaker of these words was Benjamin Netanyahu. The year, 2008. Netanyahu had just led his Likud Party to the worst defeat in its history, barely eking out a fourth-place finish with only 12 Knesset seats. Undeterred, refusing to accept responsibility, Netanyahu then launched an intensive, ultimately successful campaign to force then-prime minister Ehud Olmert to resign over suspicions of graft.

The next year, Netanyahu would wheel and deal his way back into the premiership. Over the next decade, he would prove, if nothing else, that with great power comes great corruptibility.

By the summer of 2018, it was clear that Netanyahu was to face indictments in at least three major scandals, the charges likely to include bribery, breach of trust, and fraud. Floundering yet again, he actively courted extremists on the right, even politicians with criminal records, militants whom he had once ruled out as unfit for high office.

For years, hardliners had lobbied for passage of the Nation-State bill, a law which could rewrite Israel's most basic contract with its citizens, underpinning cross-the-board legal favoritism for Jewish citizens over non-Jewish Israelis. Legislation so intentionally supremacist that Likud elder statesman Moshe Arens denounced it as an injustice and a "slap in the face" to all of Israel's Arab citizens, whom, he wrote, the measure had "thrown under the bus".

A sinkhole had opened, never to close. From here on, Bibi would need every last far-right ally to salvage his rule, and he would need to salvage his rule to stay out of jail.

THE ISRAEL YOU KNOW JUST ENDED

July 22, 2018

Look around. The country looks the same. But it doesn't feel the same. Not even close. The Jewish mourning day of Tisha B'Av came early this year.

The date marks two tragic occasions in the past during which the Jewish people effectively lost the Holy Land. Sages taught that the ancient Temples were destroyed on that date because of *Sinat Hinam* on the part of Jews - gratuitous hatred, hatred without just cause, hatred which does nothing but take a place of conflict, despair, bigotry, violence, and make it worse.

Why is this Tisha B'Av different from all the others? Because this year, in an explosion of legalized, governmentally weaponized *Sinat Hinam*, it marks the week that this country, as we have known it, ended as well.

In the dead of night early Thursday, Netanyahu led the government in passing the Nation-State Bill, a law which effectively repealed and superseded the equality and democracy provisions of Israel's Declaration of Independence as a guide for the future of the country. Gone is any mention of equality. In its place, directives that veer Israel as a whole toward genuine apartheid, including downgrading the official status of the Arabic language and therefore of Arab citizens of Israel.

The wording of the law, though manicured to avoid an outright endorsement of Jim Crow-type housing segregation, retains an element of implied support for what are commonly Jews-only communities.

Sinat Hinam.

But there was more. Soon after on Thursday, in a pre-dawn raid, police rousted out of bed and detained a Conservative rabbi under a law forbidding officiating at weddings outside the government's Orthodox Rabbinate. The law carries a maximum sentence of two years in prison.

Sinat Hinam.

Still later on Thursday, in a direct slap in the face of Hungarian-born Israeli survivors of the Holocaust and of the anti-Semitism-besieged Jewish community of Hungary, Netanyahu hosted a love-fest welcome for Hungarian Prime Minister Viktor Orban, who based his recent re-election campaign on dog-whistle encouragement of Jew-hatred.

Tisha B'Av doesn't even start until Saturday night. Beginning this year, it may go on indefinitely.

Earlier this week, Benjamin Netanyahu publicly promised Israel's LGBTQ community—among them his own voters and a Likud lawmaker—that he supports surrogacy rights to same-sex couples. Two days later, knuckling under to rightist and Orthodox politicians, Netanyahu led his coalition in voting to kill the bill.

Sinat Hinam.

Then security services at Tel Aviv's Ben-Gurion Airport's departures area took aside and interrogated at length and with pronounced incredulity a prominent Jewish-American philanthropist who chairs Brandeis University's Board of Trustees, is Orthodox, and has close family in the settlement city of Maaleh Adumim. The reason? His suitcase had been searched, and guards had found an ostensibly pro-Palestinian pamphlet in his luggage, left over from coexistence meetings the philanthropist had attended between Jewish-American community leaders and Palestinians.

Sinat Hinam.

This is what Netanyahu's new Israel feels like.

Thursday morning, Israelis woke up to a country in which Netanyahu's goon squad of legislator-enforcers feted like drunk yahoos the passage of the single most gratuitously hateful legislation in the nation's history.

Turning the Knesset floor into their home locker room, Bibi's all-stars - politicians who mock and shout down bereaved parents, politicians who insult and mimic disabled colleagues – posed grinning with Netanyahu for a victory selfie minutes after their Nation-State Law had disposed of Israel's Declaration of Independence,

This, then, is Netanyahu's legacy: He has transformed Israel from the Start Up Nation into the Shithole Nation-State.

Call it irony or call it inevitability, it turns out that this man who has spent every waking minute of the last decade warning Israelis about the dangers of the Iran of the ayatollahs and the Revolutionary Guard, spent that same period turning Israel into the Iran of the Rabbinate and the rogue settler.

Back when he was called King Bibi, back when he was lip-servicing peace, back when he had an overwhelming Knesset majority and American backing for far-reaching diplomacy and for enhancing democracy and equality in Israel, he could have done anything he damn well chose to do. His legacy was his to create.

His legacy could have been coexistence, flexibility, humanity, respect, diplomacy, 21st Century education for everyone, a good life for all people who share this land.

After all these years, though, Benjamin Netanyahu's legacy is finally clear, clear enough to be summed up in two words:

Sinat Hinam.

I wasn't expecting it at the time. But there was something personal, painful even, about my last reporting assignment as a journalist in Israel. It had nothing to do with journalism. It had everything to do with Israel.

I didn't truly understand this story, this interview, until the war forced us to see what our leaders, what all of us, were made of.

War doesn't tell you everything about people. But it may tell you the most important thing.

Even before the war, we knew that militant settlers with a stranglehold on the government had left virtually unprotected the Israelis living alongside the Gaza Strip – by one account, as many as 32 IDF battalions deployed in the settlers' West Bank, just two in the Otef Aza region.

What we did not yet know, was how settler extremists would exploit the war for their own ends, hoarding funds which could have been directed toward aid for the war-ravaged needy, proposing a mass expulsion of Gazans ("a Second Nakba") to make room for Jewish settlers, attacking West Bank Palestinians and their agricultural livelihoods, fighting against already-earmarked financial support for Israeli Arabs and the Palestinian Authority, some even suggesting that the religious right could resettle kibbutzim which were invaded, massacred, and demolished by Hamas.

God in heaven.

ON A CLEAR DAY, YOU CAN SEE THE ISRAEL YOU LOST FOREVER

MARCH 24, 2019

HAVAT GILAD, West Bank

It took me a long time, many visits to the West Bank, before I realized that this is the exact place where dreams come to die.

Dreams of a democratic Israel, one which respects and values minorities. Dreams of a free and independent Palestine. Dreams of peace.

Many of my friends had dreams like that when we moved from North America to Israel as young people in the 1970s. But we watched those dreams get crushed, one after another, cut down and trampled and intentionally, systematically, rendered impossible by the settlement movement, its allies, and the extremists on both sides who play into their hands.

At the same time, in this, the eternal capital of the zero-sum, there are settlers aplenty who will tell you, without the merest ounce of cynicism, that they are living the dream.

A few weeks ago, I paid a visit to one of them: Daniella Weiss, prophetess, politician, fanatic, great-grandmother.

I came to her home in the settlement of Kedumim to ask her, a person whose long-ago predictions for the future have already largely come to pass, what she believes lies in store for Israel in the long term.

More than forty years ago, when my friends and I were struggling to found a kibbutz in central Israel, Weiss saw something which we did not. It was something in the occupied territories, a settlement project, then non-existent, which would in time effectively come to run the state of Israel as a whole.

"I came to Shomron with the idea of it becoming an inseparable part of the state of Israel," Weiss says, using the Hebrew term for the northern West Bank, the biblical Samaria.

Weiss, her husband, and their two small children were part of the group of 10 families who in 1975 became the first settlers in the region.

It was clear to her from the very beginning – even before the beginning – the goal, the way things were going to take place, the way they would eventually look here. "Just as I saw the small state of Israel with millions of people, I was going up the hills [of the West Bank] to see the state of Israel getting broader and bigger, with millions of Jews settling the hills. That was the picture."

From the very beginning, Weiss had a sense that this was an undertaking which would utterly transform Israel. From the very beginning, Weiss's creed never changed.

She wanted then, and wants today, to bring the country to a standstill, to set it on its ear, to convert it to her way of thinking, "because my revolution affects not my life, but the life of every single person there, even if he doesn't know it."

At that very time, in the mid-1970s, as Weiss and her group were squatting on land which had in part been confiscated from neighboring Palestinian villages, my friends and I were establishing a lost colony of Woodstock in Israel, near the ancient site of Gezer—young North Americans whose dreams were shaped by what they sensed had gone wrong in America, and what might just go right in Israel.

We dreamed that Israel could progress on a path toward a true social democracy, living at peace with an independent Palestine, expanding existing government safety nets for the disadvantaged, building on pioneering models of health care, education, collective ownership, affordable housing, agriculture, and industry.

To prepare me for this new reality, the kibbutz movement trained me to be a shepherd.

What we failed to recognize, what we did not want to acknowledge, was something that Weiss already sensed. The revolution of the labor movement, which had founded Israel and run it for decades, was fast dying of old age. In time, the revolution of the settlers would take its place.

Just as members of kibbutz and moshav collectives had once wielded disproportionate influence across many spheres of life in Israel, particularly in government and the military, they would be supplanted by true believers of settlement, among them settlers themselves – like Weiss's neighbor, the openly bigoted firebrand politician Bezalel Smotrich.

In her suburban-style home in Kedumim—whose population has now grown from those 10 tent-squatter families to nearly 10,000 residents – Weiss cordially welcomes us, a film crew from *Haaretz*, a news outlet widely viewed by settlers as an institution so left-wing as to constitute a treasonous arch-enemy.

She and I realize that we have often been at the same place at the same time: She as a settler, I as an occupying soldier; she as a settler, I as an anti-settlement protester; she as a settler, I as a journalist from a hated media outlet.

She expresses sympathy for my political distress and my

obsolete dreams, agreeing that the settlement movement has been instrumental in shaping the reality I so abhor. And yet, she continues, for her, the overriding feeling is one of satisfaction, "that my philosophy has had the upper hand, and indeed, it blocked the two-state solution."

How do you react, I ask her, when someone says those words, Two-State Solution?

"First of all, I know that it will not happen. Practically, we see here hundreds of thousands of Jews. We see even in the eastern neighborhoods of Jerusalem 300,000 Jews in the areas which were liberated in the Six Day war, so where will there be a [Palestinian] state? Even Netanyahu understands that [the most] he can afford to do here for the Arabs is no more than autonomy."

Weiss takes us on a tour of the nearby unauthorized settlement outpost of Havat Gilad, "Gilad's Farm," long a flashpoint of violence. She was instrumental in founding the outpost, built as a memorial to the murder of a settler, a murder which led to acts of settler vengeance against Palestinians, then spirals of bloodshed, concentric vicious circles which have yet to be broken.

There is a stretch of soil here, rocky, pale as death, which, when you add water, sticks to your shoes and will not let go.

Weiss, who knows these things, tells me to avoid stepping in a certain unremarkable, shallow-looking puddle.

"It's like quicksand," she says. I look down, thinking of the Hebrew homonym – botz tova'ni – in a play on words, "mud that makes demands."

The ridges surrounding us are dotted with settlements. One of them, Har Bracha ("Mountain of Blessing"), now boasts high-rise apartments. We were both there when she helped launch it, on Independence Day 1983. I was on leave from military duty in Lebanon, my pregnant wife and I among a group of Peace Now protesters hoping to stop the settlers. I ask Weiss to look again into the future.

"Would you like Israel to expand further, beyond Gaza, beyond the Jordan River?"

"Yes, I want to have for the Jewish nation the promised land from the Bible, the land that was promised to Abraham, Isaac and Jacob, from the Euphrates to the Nile. And I'm sure it will be. Of course, I cannot know how many years it will take, because it wasn't specified by our prophets."

"What about southern Lebanon?"

"It is part of it. All of it. Even parts of Syria. Part of Iraq. Part of Iran. It's huge! This is the promised land. The only question I have is, 'Why does it take so much time?' But I also learn from the prophets that the plan of God is not a human plan."

"Do you think you have any way of convincing people that this would be a good idea?"

"I've convinced many. All the people that are connected with a movement that I run, and many, many, many religious people are sure that this will be the future. Many people believe in it."

"When the Likud party was Herut," she says, referring to the Likud's staunchly right-wing precursor, founded in 1948 by Menachem Begin, then beginning the transition from terror militia chieftain to politician and, decades later, prime minister, "when it was [Begin's mentor Ze'ev] Jabotinsky, the right-wing parties and movements believed in the Promised Land in biblical terms. So I don't see anything extreme in my approach.

"This is the basic Jewish approach. The clearer we make this point, the better it will be for all of us – for Jews and Arabs alike. That this is going to be a state just for Jews."

What will life be like in that future Israel?

"I believe that the future of the state of Israel is a religious country run by religious laws. Yes. So I believe," she says.

Moreover, "Only when you take the bible completely, all of it, on the personal and national and human, universal level, only then do you feel free."

I change the subject. Or so I think.

"Let's say that under a certain administration in Washington and a certain coalition in Israel, the government decides that it's time to move some settlers elsewhere. How do you feel about that idea?"

"We will not let it happen. I know it happened there – I know it happened in [2005, in then-prime minister Ariel Sharon's mass withdrawal from settlements and army bases in] Gaza. I'm fully aware of these things. But thank God, we have passed here the line where things like that can happen again. Because in the communities around here there are 500,000 Jews – half a million Jews. And this is power. To evacuate here means five times the evacuation of Jews from [Inquisition-era] Spain."

"Do you oppose the evacuation of even one?"

"Even one settler."

"From anywhere, even from settlements which Israel considers completely illegal?"

"No doubt," she says, adding, "The settlement movement is very strong, and affects all fields of Israeli society, atmosphere and politics."

She notes that there are now 250 settlements in the West Bank, nearly the total number of kibbutzim that existed when we founded Gezer in the 1970s.

In the end, our small kibbutz, a moribund labor movement, and the weaknesses and inconsistencies of Israeli democracy were no match for the single-minded crusade of the settlers, with their Old Testament vision, scope, and antipathy to compromise.

"I could spend my life as a great-grandmother. No, but I'm dedicated to the covenant between God and the Jewish nation, in Sinai, where we got orders," she says. "What I see is the direct blessing of God. Now we are in a time of redemption. And in a time of redemption, the blessing of God is immediate."

I'd come to the West Bank to see how they did it. How they won. How they ruined any chance that the extraordinary Israel we moved here hoping for, could become reality.

What I learned was that the settlers are nowhere near done yet. These days, when I talk with young North American Jews, by far the strongest elements in their alienation from Israel are the settlement movement, the entrenchment of Israel's military occupation of the West Bank, and what the occupation represents in the abject denial of rights to millions of Palestinian people.

"It is very clear to me why the young Jewish generation in the United States in North America are very much aggravated by what people like me do here," says Weiss. "It's very clear."

"People say to me," she continues, 'Why don't you explain to the Jews of the United States what it is exactly behind your thinking?'

"I [do] explain," she laughs. "'You have to brainwash all the time. You have to say it, to explain it, to live it, to cope with it.'"

"You know, we have a family confrontation," she says, a bit more quietly. "My husband says to me every week, 'Why do you speak to your children all the time about Zionism, pioneers in Judea and Samaria, settling and settling?' And all my family are settlers here. Because this is the only way to continue Zionism. If there is no enthusiasm, there is no sex. If there is no sex, there is no pregnancy. If there is no pregnancy, there are no babies. This is the problem in the United States today."

Moreover, she continues, with respect to young U.S. and Canadian Jews, "When they come here, if they come here, and they live [here] a few months, and they encounter difficulties, and they cope with the things we cope [with], not just in the settlements but in the state of Israel, they gradually change their mind."

Now she turns back to me. "You live here, and you know the things that I've said, and [yet, still] you do not change your mind," she says. She imagines my next question, which she says out loud. "'Okay,'" she begins, taking on my persona. "Why didn't the brainwashing work on me?'"

Her own answer is at the ready. "Because I didn't do it on you.

Two hours of a meeting is not brainwashing. I do it to my children a few hours every day. My husband says to me, 'What do you do all the time?' I brainwash."

I then suggest why the brainwashing didn't work on me. In an Israeli army uniform I got plenty of brainwashing from many people in several languages. In the context of that uniform I occupied northern Sinai, southern Lebanon, this West Bank, Gaza, East Jerusalem. I occupied everything that it was possible for an Israeli to occupy. And all that I have come away with is: It's occupied. The West Bank, still. Not "liberated," not "administered," not "disputed." Not Israel. Just occupied. That's all I've managed to come away with.

She is undeterred. "This brings me to the very primitive analysis of mine. About the left-wing mind."

Earlier in our conversation, when I'd told Weiss that I would not buy wine made in her settlement, nor in any West Bank settlement, she'd told me that this did not upset her at all. She said, "There is a right-wing mind and a left-wing mind. These are two different creations. You have a left-wing mind."

"Let's say your victory is final," I begin again. "The West Bank stays in Israeli hands. Why shouldn't the Palestinians here have full rights, in particular the right to vote?"

"The reason that the Arabs of Judea and Samaria cannot have the right to vote for the Knesset is because if the Arabs should have a right to vote, it's dangerous to the future of the Jewish nation in the land of Israel."

In the future, she continues, "It will all become a Jewish state. The Arabs can be here [in the West Bank], not as citizens with full rights, but just human rights. But not the right to vote for the Knesset."

There is no point in changing what Israel's first prime minister David Ben-Gurion did in granting citizenship to Arabs within the pre-1967 borders, she goes on, "but by no means [can we] enlarge the right of Arabs to vote for the Knesset, God forbid, to Arabs who live here."

Why should the Palestinians agree to this?

"If we utter these words clearly, and we are self-confident that this is the truth - and it's not anti-democratic, and it's not against human pride – then the Arabs will be affected by it. They will know that the Jews have come here to stay. For good. Forever."

I mention that [then-president] Reuven Rivlin of the former right-wing Herut party and the founding generation of the Likud has suggested that the Palestinians of the West Bank be granted the right to vote in Israeli elections.

"Rivlin," she laughs, "has become a leftist since he became a president."

"Some on the far right think the solution is expelling the Palestinians from here—'transfer.'"

"I am very much not for the idea of transfer. I believe that the right thing for us to do – us, the Jews – is to establish more and more [West Bank] communities and encourage more and more Jews to come to Israel. Immigration from the United States from England, from France."

This, after all these years, is what I know, and what Daniella Weiss does not:

They won't come. Those millions of Jews from America. They're not coming now. They won't come specifically because of what the settlement movement has done to Israel. And this is how I leave her: "I am worried," I say. "I am worried that this is the place that will result in the end of Israel."

"Oh no," she says, with the broadest of smiles. But not at all in a cruel way. She is absolutely sincere. And matter-of-fact.

"This is the future of Israel."

Less than three years after our conversation, Daniella Weiss's neighbor, a self-described proud homophobe, the unapologetic racist and onetime terrorism suspect Bezalel Smotrich, was named by Prime Minister Benjamin Netanyahu to one of the two most senior positions in Israel's cabinet, that of finance minister.

Soon after he took office, Smotrich announced a principal mission for the state: a million Jews living in the West Bank.

Israel, now subject to the far-reaching governmental demands of militant settlers, the hard right of Netanyahu's Likud, and an exponentially expanding, monolithically right-voting community of ultra-Orthodox Jews, has turned all but unrecognizable. Smotrich's partner, the convicted accessory to terrorism Itamar Ben-Gvir, has been given control of the police. Ben-Gvir demands, in addition, a militia under his direct command.

Horrified by the proposed changes, hundreds of thousands of protesters fill Israel's streets week after week. The highest echelons of the military and intelligence services, denounced by cabinet ministers as little more than spoiled, over-honored, over-privileged Ashkenazi anarchists and slime, hint at mutiny if the government's revolutionary authoritarian "reforms" are implemented.

Ominously in retrospect, the government allows publication of reports of it having withdrawn thousands of troops from areas like the Gaza border region, the Otef, in order to beef up security at a host of illegal settlements in the West Bank.

Nothing remotely like this has ever taken place here. Abruptly, in a country whose watchword is often "What has been is what will be," not one person now knows what will be. Netanyahu included.

NOTHING HERE WILL CHANGE
UNTIL EVERYTHING DOES

MARCH 19, 2023. Less than seven months to the war.

What would it take to radicalize a critical mass of a deeply conservative, hope-deprived Jewish community?

For my Grandma Ashi, it was a pogrom. Trained as a little girl to hide in the dark of a woodshed at the approach of rioters, she experienced the smells and hoofbeats and terrified screams of three separate pogroms in a village on the outskirts of Pinsk, then Czarist Russia, now Belarus.

To the end of her days, she never healed.

It was that rotting empire which gave the world the word *pogrom,* literally wanton destruction, but a term which came to describe violent rampages and massacres targeting Jews, mainly in Eastern Europe in the 19th and 20th centuries. That empire, and those pogroms, made her who she was. A lifelong anarchist. Though a tiny woman, Ashi was tough as spikes. If she ever smiled, it wasn't around me. I knew, though, that she came by her unflinching radicalism honestly. A pogrom can do that to a person. And to a country.

Consider the brutal onslaught by 400 settler zealots one night this month in the West Bank village of Hawara. For decades, Israelis turned a collective blind eye to innumerable settler pogroms targeting Palestinians. The violence had been smaller in scope, but pogroms had been going on for years, and usually with neither consequences nor notice. Until Hawara.

For the first time, the reaction of many Israelis was profound shock, anger, shame, and, for some, even the radical realization that the Hawara pogrom embodied the very meaning of occupation – a vulnerable Palestinian population deprived of the most basic rights and protections, oppressed and under direct attack by state-supported and state-shielded Israeli settlers.

"I'm done doing reserve duty in the territories," a reserve soldier in his 30s serving among the charred ruins and the traumatized villagers, said out loud this week. "What happened that night to me and my friends is something that will stay with us the rest of our lives. It was Kristallnacht."

For the first time, there was broad sympathy for the Palestinian victims. There was disgust and disgrace over the enormity of the onslaught, the savagery of the destruction, the wholesale failure of Israeli security forces, and, no less, the sight of pogromists taking a break to gather and say their evening prayers, silhouetted against the background of burning buildings, only to resume incinerating homes and assaulting scores of innocent people.

"Since the Sunday attack on Hawara, I'm having a tough time sleeping," Etgar Keret, one of Israel's best-known authors, wrote in the mass-circulation *Yedioth Ahronoth* newspaper several days later. "This time, something feels different. More threatening. As if all the ground under my feet is shuddering."

Then, on the festival of Purim, zealots launched another attack on Hawara. Mainstream media, which in the past had rarely covered settler assaults on villagers, now focused on the violence. We all saw how, after settlers had injured several villagers, one a two-year-old girl, soldiers joined the pogromists in a ghoulish circle of holiday dance and song.

The assailants grinned and howled, safe in the correct belief that there would be no arrests, no punishments, no consequences. After all, the prime minister had put their man, Itamar Ben-Gvir - tried and convicted in the past on charges relating to incitement, racism, and terrorism - in charge of the police.

Moreover, during the recent election campaign, Ben-Gvir and the other extremists who have since taken over the government, had already hinted at their long-range solution for a one-state solution and the millions of non-Jewish residents of the West Bank: *Girush*. Expulsion. The ultimate trigger word for both Jews and Arabs.

Unaccustomed to the etiquette of elected government, the extremist leaders made the mistake of speaking honestly about the Hawara pogrom. And, by implication, expulsion. Far-right lawmakers voiced understanding and sympathy and high praise for the pogromists. And in a direct hint at expulsion, the extremist Finance Minister Betzalel Smotrich declared that Hawara needed to be wiped out altogether. "The State of Israel needs to do that," he added, "not, God forbid, private individuals."

Smotrich later tried to walk back the comment. But on Sunday, soon after the second Palestinian terror attack against Jews in Hawara in three weeks, a spokesman for far-right MK Limor Son Har-Melech amplified the call, tweeting "Hawara needs to be wiped out—Now!" In Grandma Ashi's day, pogroms spurred the emigration of millions of Jews from the Russian Empire. If it worked for czars who wanted to solve what they saw as their "Jewish problem," why shouldn't it work for Jewish settlers seeking to scare off Palestinians?

Meanwhile, the process of radicalization has gained momentum, driven in part by outrage over profane demonization of such opponents of the judicial overhaul as former heads of the Mossad, the Shin Bet, army chiefs, air force and El Al pilots, and the reservists without whom the military cannot function. Rightists have also attacked peaceable protesters with pepper spray, eggs, metal cans, spit and fists and curses, kicks to the gut and face, side-swipes from motorcycles, and head-on blows from cars.

The protests have kept pace with the outrage, growing by the week. When Ben-Gvir ordered his police to storm protesters in Tel Aviv with charging horses and stun grenades - one of which ripped a protester's ear from his head - Netanyahu, infuriating a broad sector of the public, then equated the demonstrators with the pogromists who had devastated Hawara.

As a young girl growing up in a village near Pinsk, my Grandma Ashi came to fear holidays and loathe religion. She lived in a place where holidays were often spent in hiding from pogroms. A place where arrogance and corruption went hand in hand with oppression. Where state religion and state bigotry, divine right, and hatred went hand in hand with hopelessness.

A place where nothing would change until everything did. A place, shockingly, not unlike this one.

Something has, in fact, shattered here. Still, one thing remains true. To a great degree, everyone in Israel is on their own to make and act on moral decisions. To defend human rights or trample them. To fight for democracy or to countenance dictatorship.

After Hawara, we are seeing, at long, long last, the beginning of signs of a reckoning. Demonstrators took police aback by chanting "Where Were You in Hawara?" Rooted in our genes are the memories and the wounds of pogroms against Jews, and of police and soldiers who stood by and let homes burn to ashes and the blood of innocents run in the streets.

After Hawara, we are beginning to see the occupation for what it is. To see the settlement enterprise for what it is – fundamentally, philosophically undemocratic and authoritarian, hardline Orthodox-dictated, racist and macho in tone, bullying and uncompromising in practice, and, at its worst, willing to take advantage even of the assassination of a prime minister if that could mean permanent dominion over the West Bank.

That enterprise which could always have curbed the zealots in its midst but chose not to. Which could have fostered chances for peace, but instead exterminated them.

We're finally seeing the occupation's leaders and their agenda in a horrible and accurate light. Because they're now *our* leaders. They have begun to bring the occupation here, to our doors. They are beginning to rule over us the way they lord over the Palestinians, with contempt, violence, supremacism, and denial of rights. And we hate it.

Those hundreds of thousands of everyday people in the streets are beginning to sing *"Demokratia O Mered"* (Democracy Or Revolt). Grandma Ashi would not have smiled at this. But she would have sung those words as loud as anyone.

PART FIVE:
IT DIDN'T NEED TO BE
LIKE THIS

"You may not like the word, but what is happening is an occupation – to hold 3.5 million Palestinians under occupation. I believe that is a terrible thing for Israel and for the Palestinians."

"It cannot continue endlessly. Do you want to stay forever in Jenin, in Nablus, in Ramallah, in Bethlehem? I don't think that's right."

Ariel Sharon to Likud leaders, May 27, 2003

You forget. Lost in the smoke and mirrors is the memory of a time when it all could have turned out differently. A time when there were actual glimmers of hope for positive change, hints of willingness for a livable future in place of what we have come to accept as war eternal.

We saw it again and again: It all comes down to that one chair. It all comes down to that one exceptional figure willing to renounce the direction of their entire life, willing to risk everything, literally life itself, to try to take an entire country of wounded skeptics on a perilous, wholly unanticipated, never-travelled path with no guarantee of success, a leader compelled as if by prophecy to seek a better future for their people, a workable peace with their neighbors, a better life for their children, and theirs.

For all their militarism and rigidity and deep resistance to compromise, for all the pain and death they had caused over their long lives, David Ben-Gurion, Menachem Begin, Yitzhak Rabin, Ariel Sharon and in Egypt, Anwar Sadat, each had grown in their later years to take on that role.

Netanyahu, given opportunity after opportunity, never had it in him. The guts.

THE ARABS WILL NEVER FORGIVE US

MAY 7, 2007. Sixteen years before the war.

Response from a reader in Germany:

"My biggest sadness is that very few people learnt from our terrible past and I am very angry at Israel for repeating so many of our mistakes. For years I polished your (Israel's) halo - but you lost it quite a while ago.

"You should ask yourself one question - will the Palestinians ever forgive you?

"Linda, Frankfurt"

Columnist's Reply:

The Palestinians will never forgive us. Not only those who are alive today, but many of their children will despise us until their dying day, and theirs, and theirs. They will revile us for having occupied them, exploited them, shelled them, and bombed them, and for having robbed them of their dignity and their land.

The hatred is such that, for some, it will continue even if we do what we must, and end the occupation. There will be those who will hate us for having robbed them for generations of their ability to govern themselves, for undermining their efforts to persuade others of the morality of their cause, for creating the conditions for rule by gangs, fragmentation of the family, loss of national purpose and memory. Unto the 10th generation and beyond, for some we will serve the Palestinian national imagination as have, for us, Pharoah and Amalek, Hitler and Khmelnitsky, Titus and Tomas de Torquemada.

Neither will the Lebanese ever forgive us. Not for the refugees our Christian allies murdered a quarter century ago in the Sabra and Shatila camps in West Beirut, and not for the civilians our fighter bombers and artillerymen killed last summer in apartment houses in the south of the city.

The Syrians, too, bear their scars and their permanent grudges. Even many those with whom we have made peace, in Egypt and Jordan, still hate us and are not about to stop.

The Arabs will never forgive us. Nor we them.

There is no forgiving the killing of a child. There is no forgiving the firing of the rocket that kills a pregnant woman, a loving great-grandfather, a toddler in her crib. There is no forgiving the stupidity of this endless, fruitless war.

On the face of it, the future is a lock: No peace, no hope, no way out. And yet, if you look deeper, there are signs pointing to a quiet trend that may save us all: We are losing our belief in war.

Not our belief in the inevitability of war. Perhaps the only thing that can save us from a new Lebanon war this summer is the universal belief that such a war is unavoidable.

Neither have we lost our will to fight. The peoples of the Middle East have been feisty and feud-happy since well before the time of their Father Abraham, and there are no signs that is about to change. What has changed is our belief in war as a solution to issues which we as a society are accustomed to avoid addressing candidly by other means. We want war to do our bidding. We want war to set borders, to teach foes lessons, to teach youth civics, to free captives, to right historic wrongs - to fix, that is, what we ourselves hate about our lives and cannot fathom how to remedy nor how to forgive.

Perhaps, though, we are beginning to recognize that war has other plans.

Even before it was clear that the Lebanon conflict was going irrevocably badly, there was something pathetic in [then-prime minister] Ehud Olmert's description of why he made the decision to go to war.

"I'll surprise you," the prime minister told AP in early August. "I genuinely believe that the outcome of the present (conflict) and the emergence of a new order that will provide more stability and will defeat the forces of terror, will help create the necessary environment that will allow me ... to create a new momentum between us and the Palestinians."

The surprise, of course, was on Olmert.

But it was on Sheikh Hassan Nasrallah as well. There is something no less pathetic, something quietly desperate about the Hezbollah leader's need to quote from the Zionist entity's Winograd war probe report in order to prove to his fellow Lebanese that the war was a victory for Lebanon and not - as an increasing number of Lebanese observers are concluding - a calamity.

"It is regretful that we, the Arab world and Lebanon, are waiting for an Israeli commission to settle this dispute for us and to tell us 'Seriously, you have won and we [Israelis] were defeated,'" Nasrallah said this week.

Edmond Saab, editor-in-chief of the Lebanese An-Nahar daily, reached a different conclusion. He urged a state inquiry into Hezbollah's accountability for the war and the devastation the conflict caused in Lebanon. "An investigation of a military and legal nature is an appropriate measure," Saab wrote. "We must investigate whether Hezbollah erred in miscalculating the Israeli retaliation."

There is something pathetic, as well, in the shuck and jive of the Hamas organization, once the most disciplined and single-minded of all Palestinian groups pursuing the armed struggle.

Acutely tuned to Palestinian public opinion, faced with a war-jaded public, Hamas has found itself unable to return to full-scale conflict as a means to an end. Even the end has become muddled.

Once the goal was clear-cut – zero tolerance for a Jewish state, and wholehearted endorsement of its elimination by force. Now Hamas leaders including Damascus-based Khaled Meshal take turns trooping before Western and Arab cameras to announce that a Palestinian state in the West Bank and Gaza could co-exist with a Jewish state in pre-1967 Israel, for an indeterminate amount of time, perhaps exceeding 60 years.

So milquetoast has the message become, and so close to a tacit recognition of Israel, that Al Qaida has called to complain. "Where is revenge, where are the bombs, where is the fire?" Abu Yahya al-Libi, an Al Qaida leader, said in a recent Internet statement addressed to Hamas, accusing the movement of "betraying its own martyrs and God."

"Hamas has abandoned jihad for politics. It has betrayed its youths. Its main activity is politics. Since its decision to go down the path of politics, Hamas has begun to descend on a downhill slope. They betrayed the dreams of their young fighters, and they stabbed them in the back," al-Libi said.

After seven years of disastrous, inconclusive war in the territories and a disastrous, inconclusive summer in Lebanon, what we have learned, Arab and Jew, is this: Both sides cannot win a war, but both sides can lose one.

We are very slow, Arab and Jew, but we are learning, all of us, disenchanted Olmert voter, disenfranchised [Labor Party leader Amir] Peretz voter, disgruntled Haniyeh voter, dismayed and disadvantaged Nasrallah voter. The voters were promised that war would do the trick, turn the tide, eliminate the enemy, pave the path to a golden tomorrow.

Now we clearly have our doubts. Thank God. Doubt is the great enemy of war. That is why, when going to war, we prefer that the decision, the determination, be unequivocal, fully beyond the shadow of a self-doubt. As T.S. Eliot wrote in 1925, seven years after the worst war the world had ever seen, "Between the idea and the reality, between the motion and the act, falls the shadow."

Doubt, the quality we most fervently hate, the trait that scares us to death, the weakness we cannot forgive, may turn out to be our salvation.

This is the way the war ends, not with a bang but a shadow.

After a humiliating defeat in the 2006 election, when Netanyahu led his Likud to an all-time low 12 seats in the 120 -seat Knesset, he returned to the premiership in 2009. The newly elected Obama administration was keen to salvage an Israeli-Palestinian peace process, as settlement expansion had already begun slamming down the window of opportunity for a Two State Solution.

Pressured by wide social unrest and growing protests across the country, and commanding an astounding parliamentary majority coalition which eventually reached 94 seats, Netanyahu could now make game-changing strides toward peace.

If he so chose.

A number of fresh proposals for a workable peace emerged, as in the following example.

A PALESTINIAN PEACE PLAN
ISRAELIS COULD LIVE WITH

NOVEMBER 30, 2009

Palestinian-American journalist Ray Hanania recently presented an outline for a future Mideast accord. The following is an advance look at the radical heart of the proposal, the Settler-Refugee Exchange Program.

The plan targets the conflict's Gordian Knot, braided of the wrongs done the two peoples, and the rights both claim to the same land.

It recognizes how the dimensions of the issue have expanded and grown more complex over time, with the direct parties to a solution now including half a million settlers living in the territories and nearly five million Palestinian refugees the world over.

"We need to be imaginative as well as to be ready to speak the truths that we have avoided in the past," Hanania writes. His plan includes a land swap in which Israel cedes pre-1967 territory to the Palestinians, equal to the area of the settlements it seeks to annex

- an element of many current peace proposals - but it breaks new ground in the solutions it offers for settlers and refugees.

Under the proposal, for every settler living in settlements annexed to Israel, a Palestinian refugee would be allowed to return to Israel. They would also be eligible for dual Israeli-Palestinian citizenship. "They would be treated the same way as Jews who return to Israel, and be given the same benefits and compensation and support from the Israeli government," the proposal states, adding, pointedly:

"If Israel seeks to retain all of the settlements, then Israel must be prepared to allow 462,000 Palestinian refugees to return to live in Israel, should they chose to do so, as Israeli citizens."

"Israel can reduce the number of refugees it accepts by returning settlers and disbanding existing settlements. The final number is up to them."

The remaining Palestinian refugees would be resettled in the Palestinian state, or elsewhere, with the Arab world "required to provide a home and land in their countries for every Palestinian seeking resettlement in this plan."

At the same time, settlers living within the borders of the Palestinian state would be given the choice of accepting compensation and moving back to Israel, or remaining in their homes and becoming dual citizens of Israel and Palestine.

"Their rights would be fully respected and safeguarded. Settlers would have to apply to the State of Palestine for citizenship in the same way that Palestinian Refugees would be required to meet Israeli immigration standards."

In part, the proposal may be read as an appeal to Jews to pause for a moment before condemning the Palestinian Right of Return as nothing more than a thinly disguised call for the extermination of Israel.

It asks Palestinians, as well, to accept that statehood and peace, in the context of a two state solution, can be achieved through simultaneous recognition of, and compromise over, the Right of Return, an accommodation based on "an exchange of land, an exchange of people, and an exchange of apologies."

The plan for settler-refugee exchange is predicated on the creation of funds for resettlement of Palestinian refugees, and for compensation for Jews who lost land or other property when they fled or were forced to leave Arab countries.

It is also based on an explicit Israeli acknowledgment and apology for its role in the creation of the Palestinian refugee problem.

"Israel's Government must be prepared to assert the highest level of Jewishness if, in fact, Israel is truly a Jewish State, to seek atonement and offer a genuine apology to the Palestinian Refugees. "

In parallel, "It is essential that the Arab World also offer its apology in the same context to the Jews who now reside in Israel for losing their lands and homes," the proposal declares.

"As a Palestinian," Hanania writes in a preamble, "I believe the Palestinian refugees and their descendants have an absolute right to return to their original homes and lands that were vacated by them either by military force or as a result of fear or coercion based on the International Rule of Law, on principle, on morality and on human dignity."

However, Hanania continues, the truth as it exists must be spoken to the refugees and to the Palestinian people as a whole.

"I recognize the sacrifices the Palestinian refugees have made over the years by remaining in the refugee camps as a reminder to a world that refused to recognize the existence of Palestinians as a people and that the Palestinian people do exist.

"We are a people. We are Palestinian. To have had them assimilate into the Arab World and societies around the world would have conveniently erased the need for justice and resolution of this situation.

"But today is not 1948. Lives have come and gone. Events have occurred and circumstances on the landscape of the conflict have changed dramatically. Their homes and villages simply no longer exist.

"There are millions of Jews who have immigrated to Israel from other countries who now live in homes once occupied by Palestinians either voluntarily or fleeing persecution. Both have seen new generations arrive and old pass. Lives have been built and we cannot simply tear them down."

"I and the majority of the Palestinian people are ready for a historic agreement based on international decisions that will allow a Palestinian and Israeli state to coexist, side by side, in peace and stability."
—Jailed Fatah leader Marwan Barghouti, in letter to be read at a ceremony marking the 30th anniversary of Israel's Peace Now movement, 2008.

FREE BARGHOUTI NOW

JANUARY 4, 2010

I t's a spellbinding opal of a Saturday afternoon in winter. A number
of family members and close friends are tackling the *Haaretz*
weekend trivia quiz, the Hebrew edition of 20 maddeningly arcane
questions.

They manage to get 16 right. No small feat. The talk then turns to
Israeli politics. At last, the question is a simple one. If there were an
election now, who would get your vote? There are 10 people present.
Not one of them manages to come up with a single answer.

Moral: If Benjamin Netanyahu plays his cards right, he could be
prime minister indefinitely. Not because he's done so well. Rather,
because there's no one at all to vote for, and thus, no reason for
Israelis to vote.

Corollary: This may, in fact, be Netanyahu's big chance. In
vacuum there is opportunity. In this context, the time may never
be more auspicious for a move that, in its boldness, changes the
Mideast subject overnight.

It's time, in short, for Netanyahu to let the Palestinians have someone to vote for. Marwan Barghouti.

The Palestinians are at least as deeply disenchanted with their current leadership as Israelis are. Polls show Hamas' popularity continuing to decline. Even in its power base of Gaza, Hamas is no longer viewed by Palestinians as the disciplined, fearless, corruption-free organization which valiantly and efficiently sees to their social welfare and to their personal defense. In an era of shut-down futures, it appears that hatred of Israel's policies can no longer be reliably equated with love of Hamas.

Hamas' blood rival Fatah, meanwhile, has political problems which run even deeper. It is dogged by an aging, graft-tainted, calcified hierarchy, woefully unable to heal the disunity which has crippled the Palestinian drive for statehood.

The decline and death of Yasser Arafat in 2004 left Palestinians with only one unifying figure, Barghouti. His credibility with his people was established in his role both as a central architect of both Palestinian uprisings, and in his spearheading of drives within Fatah to combat corruption and human rights violations on the part of Arafat's own people. Now, more than ever, Palestinians need Barghouti.

But Israel needs Barghouti as well. He is the key to the future of the two-state solution, and therefore, to an Israel which is democratic without qualification, peaceable without biennial war, demographically Jewish without apartheid, a true neighbor to its neighbors - for once, a full member of the community of nations, economically, diplomatically, and, on the level of one-on-one human interaction.

Israeli leaders who have worked with Barghouti - even some who had him arrested and, before that, nearly assassinated - know the potential value to a future peace of his political skills, his standing and charisma among Palestinians, his work on behalf of Israeli-Palestinian negotiations in the past. [Barghouti was convicted in 2004 of having authorized deadly terror attacks, and sentenced to five cumulative life sentences plus 40 years].

The Israeli security and government officials who have lobbied for Barghouti's release include former senior Shin Bet official and ex-public security minister Gideon Ezra, and cabinet minister Benjamin Ben-Eliezer, who served as defense minister under Ariel Sharon during the second intifada.

Although known as a relative hawk - as an IDF brigadier general he was once Israel policy chief for the territories - the Iraqi-born Ben-Eliezer has often demonstrated a unique understanding of Israel's Arab negotiating partners. In August, Israel's Channel 10 television quoted Ben-Eliezer as saying that Barghouti "is the only one" capable of bringing the Palestinians to a final-status peace deal with Israel.

There will, of course, be those who will who dismiss and disqualify Barghouti as a terrorist. Most Israelis, however, need look no farther than Menachem Begin, Yitzhak Shamir, and, in fact, Ariel Sharon, to recognize that a tough neighborhood tends to yield statesmen with dark, not to say murderous, passages in their resume.

Should Barghouti be freed now, and not under the terms of a prisoner exchange for [Israeli soldier held hostage by Hamas] Gilad Shalit, Israel will have deprived Hamas of a central victory in bragging-rights over the release of the Fatah leader. A stand- alone Israeli decision to free Barghouti is a sign of strength, in stark contrast to caving, hands wrung, to Hamas demands.

Moreover, the Palestinian center of political gravity and diplomatic momentum would shift overnight back to Fatah and its administration of the West Bank. The release of Barghouti would be an incentive to progress in peace negotiations, and Hamas would find itself hard-pressed to openly oppose, or continue to snipe at and boycott, a Barghouti-led Fatah.

This is a decision which could dramatically alter the Mideast equation. It is one of the few which, under the current political constellation, Netanyahu can carry out. It is one of the first that he should.

When Netanyahu finally made a decision, it had the effect of bolstering Hamas. He agreed to a prisoner exchange in which more than a thousand Palestinians held in Israeli prisons would be returned to win the release of one Israeli soldier, who had been kidnapped to Gaza and held captive by Hamas for more than five years. One of the many senior Hamas leaders freed was Yahya Sinwar, now leader of Hamas and, as such, an architect of the October 7 massacres.

It took courage to agree to the deal. All the courage that Netanyahu had. Because, as soon as he did, he was put on notice by his hard right allies that, were he interested in their support, he was never to do anything like this again.

In other hands, the deal could have led to further negotiations toward an eventual agreement with the Palestinians. But Netanyahu was nothing if not lechitz, pressure-able.

The fierce pushback from the right forged his future choice of allies, hardline Israeli Jews who felt overlooked, underrepresented, betrayed: settlers, whose world had imploded in the 2005 withdrawal from Gaza: a substantial proportion of the Mizrachi community, who had suffered for generations from broad discrimination and bigotry; and the ultra-Orthodox, objects of much secular scorn, whose burgeoning growth and autonomy would come to depend on massive support from the state.

For foreign consumption, Netanyahu would now need to pay lip-service to a Two-State Solution while his government did everything in its power to assist West Bank settlers in gutting any possibility of it ever succeeding. At the same time, Netanyahu effectively strengthened Hamas as a counterweight to the Palestinian Authority, which had come into being specifically for a Two-State Solution.

From the standpoint of a search for peace, the deal with Hamas would be neither an overture, nor an opportunity, nor any sort of beginning. This would be nothing but an end.

BRAVO FOR THESE PEOPLE, THESE ISRAELIS

OCTOBER 18, 2011

Keeping a promise can entail a terrible choice. Which is why Israelis' outpouring of support for a prisoner exchange for Gilad Shalit deserves profound admiration, even wonder.

In pushing their leaders to accept the deal, in supporting Benjamin Netanyahu for having assented to it, Israelis by the millions are gambling their very lives, and those of their loved ones. And all just to keep a promise.

On the face of it, the exchange is preposterous, in some ways, borderline suicidal. On the face of it, agreeing with Hamas to the release of more than a thousand Palestinian prisoners, many of them to this day proud of having committed heinous murders of innocent people in premeditated acts of terrorism, makes little sense.

Israelis know that the exchange will bolster the recently flagging popularity of Hamas, in particular its more militant figures. It could seriously undermine Palestinian moderates, foster a return of large- scale terrorism, and deal a telling blow to the Palestinian Authority, in the process eroding the security of Israelis on both sides of the Green Line.

The deal to bring Gilad Shalit back to his family is painful to Israelis bereaved by terror. It is, by any measure, chillingly dangerous.

And it was the right thing to do.

The deal is a remnant of an Israel which is fast disappearing. It is a remnant of a particular brand of quiet, exceptional courage. It is an expression of a national character that goes generally ignored in a media environment which prizes the extreme over the honorable. It is evidence of a people true to values which time and sectarian agendas may appear to have diluted and erased.

The deal for Gilad Shalit is a remnant of a promised land that – to those everyday people who donate their very youth, their very lives, to defend it – still believes it important to keep its promises.

The first of those promises is a simple one. In the military, when they draft you and process you and inoculate you and arm you and begin to use you, they spell it out, to you and your family both. They make you this one promise: If you are lost on the field of battle, we will get you back. Whatever it takes.

Whatever it takes. Even if it takes much too much.

The list of the terrorists being released is unendurable. The numbers are beyond understanding. Until you consider that this is how it's always been.

In Israel's nine prisoner exchanges with Arab enemies, dating back to the first, 54 years ago, Israel has freed 13,509 prisoners in order to win the release of a total of 16 soldiers. An average of well over 800 for each one. This is the price.

It is said that the people on the list for the current deal have been directly responsible for the deaths of 599 Israelis. Had Israelis waited longer for a deal, however, Gilad Shalit might well have made it 600. On Tuesday morning, Israelis by the millions heard a sentence that allowed them, at long last, to begin to breathe again: Gilad Shalit is no longer in Hamas hands.

There is something still extraordinary about the core of these people, the Israelis. In the summer, when hundreds of thousands marched in the streets for social justice, they roared their endorsement of a deal such as this to free Gilad Shalit.

In perhaps the most exceptional expressions of backing, even some of those most personally and deeply wounded by the terrorists to be freed, have come out in support.

"From the standpoint of a mother, I'm in favor of the price that's been paid in order to bring Gilad Shalit home," Sarit Golumbek, who lost her son Zvi 10 years ago in the bombing of the Sbarro restaurant in Jerusalem, said last week. "My heart is with the Shalit family."

There is no understanding what Sarit Golumbek has been through. There is no understanding what Israelis as a people have just done, in keeping that kind of promise, displaying this depth of compassion, taking this kind of risk, to bring home one of their own. Someone they never knew until it was too late.

But Israel being what it is, many, many of them came to know the Shalit family personally, on their walks the length and breadth of Israel, or in the tent by the prime minister's residence in Jerusalem, the protest tent that was their home until the news came that their son was finally to be freed.

Bravo for the people who brought Gilad home. Bravo for these people, these Israelis, who held a part of their breath for five years and four months, waiting for news of someone they did not know, but who could just as easily have been their own.

Bravo, as well, for Benjamin Netanyahu. He did what the people of Israel wanted. That is his job. He did not do the bidding of a raucous, threatening minority. He took courage in a courageous people. That is why he is there.

He did the right thing.

AN ISRAELI IN AWE OF A
PALESTINIAN ACT OF NON-VIOLENCE

JANUARY 15, 2013

An act of non-violence is a fuse playing the role of a bomb. If the act of non-violence is creative enough, appropriate and resonant and shocking, and, therefore, dangerous enough, it will do what no bomb can: Change things for the better. Persuade. Put the lie to the liar. And cause a man like Benjamin Netanyahu to panic.

On Friday, nearly a hundred men women and children pitched tents on a Palestinian-owned plot of land in the patch of the West Bank called E-1, a political and diplomatic minefield which Netanyahu has vowed to build on, and Washington has warned him not to. The place was given a new name - Bab al-Shams, the Gate of the Sun.

The Palestinians who staked down the tents were explicit in calling their rocky hilltop encampment a village. But the manner of its founding made it all too clear to Israelis what it was as well - a *ma'ahaz*, a settlement outpost, no less and no more illegal than the scores and scores of rogue farms, tent camps, rude shacks and proto-suburbs which Israeli settlers have staked across the West Bank and East Jerusalem.

We know it in our bones, Israelis and Palestinians as one. This is how the settlement movement began. This is how it grows. This is the very engine of occupation. This is the heart and the hand of the beast.

The founding of Bab al-Shams was genius. And no one knew that better than Benjamin Netanyahu. The encampment sent a message that was clear, piercing, and entirely non-violent. The proof: Netanyahu said it had to be destroyed at once.

It needed to be destroyed despite a High Court order that appeared to give the new villagers six days to remain on the site. But in a peculiarly contemporary reinterpretation of the Nakba, the police announced that the injunction only applied to the tents. The people could be taken out. In the dead of night.

So desperate was the need to destroy it quickly, that the head of the Justice Ministry's High Court division was pressed into service at midnight Saturday, to sign a statement to the court declaring "there is an urgent security need to evacuate the area of the people and tents."

The government also sent a sealed note to the court, containing further "security information" – classified Secret, as was the reason for its being kept from the public – as to why it was necessary to give the order immediately for 500 police to move in.

But everyone here already knew the secret.

Bab al-Shams needed to be destroyed because it was fighting facts on the ground with facts on the ground.

It needed to be destroyed for the same reason that a hundred similar, patently illegal Israeli West Bank outposts are coddled, honored by visits from cabinet ministers, and rendered permanent with state-supplied electricity, water, access roads, security protection, and retrofit permits.

Bab al-Shams did not simply touch a nerve. Bab al-Shams had to be destroyed because, where the occupation is concerned, it touched the central nervous system.

On Election Day next week, when I enter the voting booth, I will be taking a small piece of Bab al-Shams with me - my respect and admiration for people who cannot vote in this election, but who each cast an extraordinarily forceful absentee ballot in booths they set up themselves in E-1.

They are fighting the Netanyahu government with the one weapon against which this government has no defense - hope. Hope is this government's worst enemy, more threatening by far than Iran.

For years and years we've been taught to believe that the occupation is irreversible, unassailable, so permanent that there is no occupation, there is just this Israel of ours – like its prime minister, sour, anxious, bloated, contradictory ... but Ours. We are told what to believe by settlers and their champions in places like Ra'anana. That there cannot be two states, one for Israelis and one for Palestinians. That we, the Jews, have been here forever and will stay in East Jerusalem in the West Bank forever and ever.

It turns out, though, that other people, on other hilltops, Palestinian people, have something else to teach us. May they succeed.

IT'S WOMEN WHO WILL MAKE
AN ARAB-JEWISH PEACE

OCTOBER 10, 2017

It will happen. Women will make peace in Israel and Palestine.

It will be women – like the members of Women Wage Peace, the pioneering grass-roots group that organized the Journey to Peace, a 17-day series of marches, rallies and other events that brought together women from across deep divides of identity, religion, nationality, age and politics.

These and other extraordinary women activists working in other groups and as individuals will one day do what women do every day – the impossible. And around here, nothing at all feels more impossible than peace. But women will do anything, go to any length, cross any divide, make any sacrifice to keep their children safe.

It's going to happen. But it won't be soon. You, reading this, may not live to see it. It may well take what feels like forever. Tragedy and ruined lives, warfare and murder will go unprevented. Not because thousands of extraordinary women didn't work hard enough. They work plenty hard. They work with astounding imagination and good humor, and they keep at it no matter what. It's not that.

It's going to take an obscene amount of time because of the rest of us. It's because of men. It's because of what we have inside.

Here it is: Peace scares men.

Not war. War excites us. We can pretend otherwise. But something about war quickens our blood. It's built in. It's as much a part of us as the need to take sides, to do what we believe protects our own side at the expense of another. It's as much a part of us as our weakness for weaponry and our urge to possess, to avenge, to vanquish. To rescue but also to conquer. To repair but also to wreck. To focus on certain truths, but to hide or hide from others.

It's how we're built.

Peace scares us because to us, deep down, something about it smells like what we fear the most: betrayal. Loss. Loss of control. Loss of position. Loss of dominance. Loss of what we most firmly believe.

No matter which side we're on here, we men say of the other side – the only thing they understand is force. And, for once, maybe the men on both sides are right.

Because we cannot trust what we do not understand. And force, we understand. Not peace. In force we trust. Peace we see as so fragile that one single man with a handgun could fire three shots at the back of a prime minister and kill peace for 21 years. And counting.

We treat peace the way we treat women. With that thin, knowing smile of disdain. And little wonder. Because, when all is said and done, women scare men.

We know that we do not understand women in the slightest. And that's just the day-to-day. The process of bringing life into the world is, to us, a mystery beyond all imagination. The stamina and physical resources, the sheer fact of the ability to do what it takes to grow an entire new life, to contain and sustain and survive the cataclysm necessary to give birth, is so far beyond our experience as to occupy a constellation all its own, distant and untouchable as a night sky.

In the very essence of what they are capable of accomplishing, women threaten us men. Deep down, we know that they are the stronger sex.

Why else would we need to interrupt them, bully them, belittle and silence them, mansplain, underpay, overwork and underappreciate them, brand them naive and unrealistic, bury them under glass ceilings and guilt trips and gaslighting.

And yet.

There is clear momentum building within Women Wage Peace and other movements and communities in which women, especially young women, are taking the lead.

Their journey to peace is likely to be maddeningly frustrating, all but impossible. But they will get there.

We men can't hold them back forever. We're not built for it.

Postscript: Please take a moment to honor the memory of Vivian Silver, a founder of Women Wage Peace. Vivian was a one-of-a-kind visionary, a hands-on driving force in projects to heal the rifts and address the injustices of the Holy Land. She was also a beloved mother and grandmother, and, for so many of us, a cherished friend who was family.

Vivian was in her home at Kibbutz Be'eri, minutes from the border from Gaza, when she was murdered by Hamas on the morning of October 7, 2023. She was 74 years old.

The Holy Land she imagined and strove so tirelessly to bring into being is tragically in ruins. May the memory of the countless hearts she touched be a blessing to all those whom she inspired to carry on her work.

PART SIX:
MOVING PICTURES

'WALTZ WITH BASHIR,' GAZA, AND THE POST-MORAL WORLD

JANUARY 1, 2009

I went to see "Waltz with Bashir" this week, not suspecting for a moment that the story it told would have anything to do with me.

That, it turns out, is precisely what the film is about. It has to do with everyone who has been in a war here, which is everyone here. It has to do with all those who have succeeded in getting on with their lives by turning a blind eye to, blaming away, repressing, or somehow ideologically reprocessing genuine, tangible horror. It has to do with the fear of memory here, the reluctance to look inward, the quiet terror over what one might actually uncover. And because it has to do with the moral failings of bitter enemies, we are, every one of us, in the movie.

I knew, going in, that the film had to do with the filmmaker, Ari Folman, and his inability to remember his experiences as a 19-year-old soldier during Israel's 1982 invasion of Lebanon, and, in particular, at the time of the Sabra and Shatilla refugee camp massacre.

What I did not know was that, scene by scene, the film was about to invade me, rumble over me and through me, corner me and take me over. I went to see "Waltz with Bashir," but it wasn't really seeing that I did. It wasn't long before the film turned visceral. I saw armored personnel carriers and knew how to operate and load and clean the machine guns at their turrets, and I began to feel a fist inside rise from my gut upward until it took my windpipe, still from the inside, and strangled the air out of me, long ago, in a green uniform gone black with sweat, in what I would only later and only for that one instance recognize as claustrophobia.

The Christian Phalangists began emptying their AK-47s into the air, and I could smell the cordite as if they were in the next row.

For the time of war, adrenaline can seem good for whatever ails: claustrophobia, moral qualms, mortal fears, sleeplessness, free-floating anger, free-floating anxiety, depression. When it wears off, there are other palliatives for those of us who get off lucky, alive, limbs intact, minds formally whole. There is survivor guilt, which can manifest itself in self-delusion and/or self-hate and/or political activism and/or political extremism. There is denial. Then there is my personal favorite, a certain silence born of superstition, the sense that if you don't talk about a fortunate near miss, or those killed and crippled in a place you might have been, then it won't happen to you or your loved ones in the cumulative balance sheet of grief.

On January 11, when "Waltz with Bashir" won the Golden Globe for Best Foreign Language Film, the war in Gaza had been raging for more than two weeks. Without commenting directly on the fighting in the Strip, Folman told *The New York Times* that the film, which he has called apolitical but anti-war, "will always be up-to-date because something will always happen again."

In a modern climate of diminished reality and computer-generated truth, the honesty of "Waltz with Bashir" comes as an astonishment. The *Times* interviewer, somewhat taken aback, responds: "You mean the prospect for peace seems so remote? That's sad."

"But it's true," Folman answers.

Folman's comment, and no less, his film, suggest that we now live in a post-moral world, a world in which, if nothing else, we can discern that both sides to this conflict commit grievous crimes, to little if any lasting effect, other than the injury done the victims on both sides.

If there is to be peace, and this is one of the world's faster growing of all "ifs," perhaps it will be just this post-moral outlook which will save us. For far too long, the attitude of pro- and anti-Israel sides to the wrangling over the Holy Land, has revolved over sophisticated versions of an "I was right all along" approach better confined to a kindergartener's arguments in schoolyard fights.

Perhaps it's time we surrendered to what we know to be true, Arab and Jew both: The leaders on both sides lie. That is their job. They resort to war to protect the lies. Lies like We Will Never Recognize the Enemy. Our Efforts Will Bend Their Will. Only If We Demand Our Full Rights Will We Prevail.

We try to look beyond our leaders, to see someone better, but we can see little down the road.

There will be an election here in a week, but there will be no one to vote for. If the Palestinians were going to the polls on Tuesday to decide between Fatah and Hamas, they'd probably feel exactly the same.

The problem goes far beyond elected officials. We have learned from weary experience, that the apologists and apparatchiks on both sides lie. That is their job. We try to look beyond them, but there are too many of them to see beyond.

As Jews, we have come to see the post-moral world as caving in on us. On the eve of International Holocaust Day, the Vatican rehabilitated the post-moral British Catholic Bishop Richard Williamson, who had flatly denied both that 6 million Jews died in the Nazi Holocaust, and that any had been gassed.

Classically anti-Semitic incidents have multiplied, with daily reports of hate crimes from Caracas to Turkey.

Meanwhile, Palestinians every reason to echo the cries of a woman seen at the end of "Waltz with Bashir," who calls, in her distress, "Where are the Arabs? They should be rushing here [to help us]!" For all of the concern and identification expressed across the Muslim world, the misery of Gaza remains a tragic constant.

Every night of the three weeks of hell in Gaza and the south, I had a different dream about the war. This is the one that, in retrospect, made sense:

As Ahmadinejad's campaign for June elections stalls, he orders the Hail Mary, ostensibly to avenge deaths in Gaza: a proportional military strike against Israel. He miscalculates, however, and annihilates everything in the Holy Land, Israeli and Palestinian alike, except for the three things that even nuclear holocaust cannot eradicate - cockroaches, Qassams, and settlement outposts.

Years from now, we may well look back on "Waltz with Bashir" as a work of rare maturity, a signpost toward a future less enamored of military means to political ends.

Years from now, we may look back on the film not only as anti-war, but, perhaps even more usefully for our purposes and future, a message that our humanity is better left open to the air, than locked away for safekeeping.

HOW HOLLYWOOD LIKES ITS JEWS

FEBRUARY 23, 2009

Hollywood is about message. It is not, strictly speaking, about subtlety, nor idle fretting over obvious irony.

So when Israelis woke up before dawn on Monday to watch the 81st running of the Oscars, the message was clear enough. Hollywood knows exactly how it likes its Jews: Victims. Civilian victims. Targets of genocide. None of this Goliath stuff. None of these pre-emptive, disproportionate, morally amorphous behaviors.

My wife, the daughter of Auschwitz survivors, saw it right off, even in the dark. Even before they announced the winner of the Best Actress award.

Against a well-deserved paean to eventual winner Kate Winslet, a giant screen showed hunted, gaunt, clearly doomed figures. "This is how Hollywood likes its Jews," my wife said. "Hunched over and dressed in rags."

Minutes before, as if to underscore the Hollywood principle that Jewish history ended in the Holocaust, and Israeli history ended with

"Exodus," the Oscar ceremony enlisted Liam Neeson - star of the ultimate Hollywood version of the Good Christian-Bad Holocaust epic, Schindler's List - to deny the Oscar to a film showing Jews not as they may have been, but as they, in fact are.

The narrative of Israel has become increasingly uncomfortable for the limousine left of Hollywood. Not necessarily because of the specifics of occupation and overkill. No, there are wider problems with these Israelis. Their story arc doesn't work.

They are neither cutesy, comedic Yiddishers nor noble, chiseled, ascetically moral kibbutzniks. They bear as much resemblance to Zohan as Adam Sandler does to Tzipi Livni. Israelis are often complicated, angry, unhappy, family-oriented, insular, flawed human-beings. Perhaps, in the Hollywood context, the problem with these Israelis, is that they are not identifiable as Jews at all.

Last year, "Beaufort," an exceptional Israeli film about IDF soldiers at war in Lebanon was one of the five nominees, but lost to the Austrian entry, in which a Jewish concentration camp prisoner forges currency for the Nazis.

This year, "Waltz with Bashir," an extraordinary, soul-shattering Israeli film about IDF soldiers at war in Lebanon, was one of the five nominees. Its only connection to the Holocaust, however, is an uncomfortably authentic one. As Neeson's announcement suggested, with his small but ringing note of incredulity, a nominee it will forever stay.

There were at least eight films classed as Holocaust-based, released in 2008. "Waltz with Bashir" was not one of them. But in dealing with searing honesty about war, memory, the violent death of innocents, as well as about the complex darkness at Israel's heart, it has fundamentally more to do with the Holocaust than any of the eight.

Ari Folman, the director of "Waltz with Bashir," is also the son of Holocaust survivors. The Holocaust informs the film in ways that Hollywood is literally incapable of imagining. Because this is the real thing.

"Waltz with Bashir" was not made for Hollywood, it was made for human beings. It was made for the people who went through the horror it shows, and who are still going through new horrors which feel exactly as unbearable.

The story of how Hollywood likes its Jews has been told before, of course, never more succinctly - or with a heavier cargo of irony - than when Kate Winslet played a satirized version of herself in a 2005 episode of the U.K. series "Extras."

Winslet, then winless in four trips to the Oscar nomination altar, explains to series star Ricky Gervais, why she's decided to act in a Holocaust film.

> **Gervais: You doing this, it's so commendable, using your profile to keep the message alive about the Holocaust.**
>
> **Winslet: God, I'm not doing it for that. We definitely don't need another film about the Holocaust, do we? It's like, how many have there been? You know, we get it. It was grim. Move on.**
>
> **I'm doing it because I noticed that if you do a film about the Holocaust, you're guaranteed an Oscar. I've been nominated four times. Never won. The whole world is going, 'Why hasn't Winslet won one?' ... That's why I'm doing it. Schindler's bloody List. The Pianist. Oscars coming outta their ass ...**
>
> **Gervais: It's a good plan.**

This year, despite general agreement that her performance as a 1950s-era Connecticut housewife in "Revolutionary Road" was far better than her role as a former SS guard in "The Reader," life imitated Gervais, and the Oscar was finally Winslet's.

Back in Israel, meanwhile, the debriefing of the Academy Awards had begun. On an early morning television news show, Meital Zvieli, the lead researcher for "Waltz with Bashir," said that despite their disappointment, the crew members watching in Israel felt that, in any case, "The film won." It had been seen by people who needed to see it, people who in many cases began to speak to their families about their own experiences only after having experienced the film.

That may be the only point that really matters.

In the end, the cultural distance from the Jews of Hollywood to the Jews of Israel may be impassible.

The oldest and most basic need of the Jews who invented the film industry, the compulsion to reinvent themselves, early on developed into the need to reinvent the Jewish people. There, after all these years, the industry remains.

Perhaps, after all these years, it's time for Hollywood, at long last, to take seriously and with intelligence another piece of Gervais' scripted advice.

Move on.

GO SEE 'FOXTROT,' IF ONLY BECAUSE ISRAEL IS WARNING YOU NOT TO

OCTOBER 17, 2017

RECOMMENDATION 1: Go see "Foxtrot." Go see this magnificent film, if only because Israel's spite-right minister of culture - the former IDF chief censor who refuses to see the award-winning new Israeli film herself – has told you not to.

Warned you not to. Without having seen it. And the film is Israel's nominee for the 2018 Best Foreign Language Film. Culture Minister Miri Regev condemned it as viciously anti-Israel, "disgraceful," in sum a "defamation" and a mendacious "incitement of the younger generation against the most moral army in the world."

Or, go see "Foxtrot" because a leading voice of the Israeli hard left, totally rejecting Regev's caustic denunciations, also warned you against it.

"A lie is a lie, no matter what direction it takes," my Haaretz colleague Gideon Levy wrote earlier this month. The film, while beautiful, "poetic, symbolic and metaphorical," is deceptive and misleading, he continued, a hallucinatory embellishment of the brutal realities of occupation and the soldiers who enforce it - in sum, "propaganda, not cinema."

RECOMMENDATION 2: Go see "Foxtrot" if you believe that one side is saintly and righteous and wholly victimized, and the other composed of bloodthirsty villainous genocidal beasts.

Whichever side you happen to pick.

Go see it, but be warned that the human beings in it - frightened, repressed, explosive, suffocating, furious, smiling with apparent inappropriateness, intentionally harming themselves, tragically harming others – are severely, congenitally damaged goods, whose heritage, whose very lives, are an unending cycle of trauma and post-trauma.

Both sides.

Pause for the inevitable "Yes, but – the other side is to blame because ..."

Go see "Foxtrot" if you sincerely believe that there's no such thing as an Israeli occupation. You're taking the easy way out, and you're dead wrong.

Or go see "Foxtrot" because you sincerely believe that Israel's is the only occupation in the world, or because you believe that the Syrian genocide pales before Israel's treatment of the Palestinians, or because you see Israeli occupiers as the Nazi SS, only wearing green rather than gray.

You're lying to yourself and to everyone in your echo chamber. Take it from a moviegoer who's been there again and again: the occupation is as alive and unwell, as destructive to Palestinians - and also to Israel and Israelis - as ever. The allegory that is "Foxtrot" is what trauma – and occupation - feel like from the inside. The pacing, for both sides, walks the edge of unbearable. The moral failings, like the blindness, are unavoidable. The rage, like the past, irreparable.

Go see it, because Samuel Maoz, who wrote and directed "Foxtrot," is the kind of person who both loves Israel and hates occupation, and both for good reason. Go see it, because Maoz, someone who is both heir and ancestor of generations of trauma, is willing to open his soul and tell you about it as no one else has.

Go see "Foxtrot" if you're one of those people who tells us we must get over the Holocaust

Or see "Foxtrot" because you're one of those people who sees the Holocaust in everything that happens here. Everything that is done to us, that threatens us. Or in everything we ourselves do.

When you see it, you'll understand. And you may yourself feel a particular kind of trauma, a spiked club to the core, a claustrophobia which spreads in reverse, from the inside of your body out.

Go see it because the people here, in this movie and in this land, are human beings, goddamn it. Not just pawns. Not just an axe to grind. Not just proof that our side alone is right. Human beings, as the film shows with humor and also searing pain, human beings sinking into mud.

All of us occupied. None of us survivors.

RECOMMENDATION 3: Go see it for one other reason as well. There's war in the air. Make the effort to see "Foxtrot" if only because, whether your leader is Trump or Netanyahu, they may one day, much too soon, get us all killed in a war, and you need to hold your loved ones today, now.

ABOLITION AND OCCUPATION: WATCHING 'LINCOLN,' SEEING ISRAEL RIP ITSELF APART

FEBRUARY 26, 2013

I've been hearing people say lately, that if they hear one more negative thing about Israel, it will drive them nuts.

I've heard this from people who hate Israel to death, from people who adore Israel all but uncritically, and from the group I belong to, people who love this place and find it maddening in every sense of the term, painful to love, painful to leave, terrifying in prospect, an indelible, at times miraculous shadow sewn to the soul.

In theory, a movie house ought to offer a certain escape from this. No such luck. When my wife and I took the bus to see "Lincoln" this week, the driver let us off at the stop closest to the theater: Rabin Square, site of the 1995 assassination and, although we didn't know it yet, a lens through which to understand the darkness of Abraham Lincoln, an America torn to catastrophe by slavery, and, most of all, ourselves.

I know something of American history. I know much about the Civil War. But for my wife and I, the two and a half hours we watched "Lincoln" were spent watching our Israel tear itself to death over how we relate to, or manage not to relate to, Palestinians as people.

Over and over, in the film's debates over slavery, an endless, unbearable war, and their interconnections, it was impossible not to see the parallels to Israeli society, politics, warfare, and daily life.

It was impossible not to see, in this theater across the street from Rabin Square, what one determined, inspiring, all-too-human leader, in cooperation with the vast majority of a nation, could accomplish for the sake of fundamental human justice - and the price that one fuming, armed extremist might make that leader pay for any success in moving forward.

Sometimes you have to look away from what you're over-used to, in order to see it at all. Sometimes you need to be in some faraway dark place, for there to be light shed on your own.

I realize now why "apartheid" is too easy, too slick, too Madison Avenue a term, for what occupation truly is and does.

Occupation is slavery.

In the name of occupation, generation after generation of Palestinians have been treated as property. They can be moved at will, shackled at will, tortured at will, have their families separated at will, lose their children at will. They can be denied the right to vote, to own property, to meet or speak to family and friends. They can be hounded or even shot dead by their masters, who claim their position by biblical right, and also use them to build and work on the plantations the toilers cannot themselves ever hope to own.

The masters dehumanize them, call them by the names of beasts.

The clergy of this Old South in the new West Bank, claiming God and the Bible, preach that it is permissible to rebel against the government, against the army, in order to protect the plantations and the sanctity of the institution of occupation.

The spokesman of this Old South, speaking to us across the

secession lines, trade in fear of those under oppression, warning that they will take us over and kill us, if they are allowed to be free.

The day we went to see "Lincoln," headlines spoke of 15 Jewish youths nearly killing an Arab Israeli in Jaffa, bloodying his head and one eye with bottles and glass shards, sending him to hospital in serious condition. The victim was attacked as he re-filled his vehicle with water, in order to continue to clean their streets. His wife quoted the attackers as saying as they beat him, that Arabs were "trying to take over the country."

I realize now that I am an abolitionist. I realize how many, many people I know, people in that unnamed, largely unorganized group I belong to, are abolitionists as well, people for whom the central, the crucial, the overriding issue facing Israel and Israelis – and Jews the world over – is how to bring the occupation of the West Bank and East Jerusalem to an end.

I realize now that I need to pay more attention to Abraham Lincoln, in his ability to remind us all – in our natural desire not to hear one more bad thing – of the wisdom hidden in the obvious.

"Those who deny freedom to others," he once said, "deserve it not for themselves."

And this: "Whenever I hear anyone arguing for slavery, I feel a strong impulse to see it tried on him personally."

PART SEVEN:
SINS, MINE AND OURS:
APARTHEID,
OCCUPATION, NAKBA

FOR THE UNFORGIVABLE: AN APOLOGY TO PALESTINIANS

JULY 7, 2014

I owe you an apology. I owe you many, in fact. Many more than I have space for here. But a person has to begin somewhere. So I'll begin with what's right in front of me, right now.

I want to apologize for the unforgivable.

For the boy whose face in the photograph I can see even with my eyes closed. The face of the boy before he was wrestled into a car by people on my side, who charred him to death.

I close my eyes on purpose, to see his sweet face. And to try to keep from beginning to imagine what people on my side did to him. How he looked. After.

I want to apologize to the loved ones of 16-year-old Mohammed Abu Khdeir, his family in Shoafat. And to his cousins in Sacramento, who remember him as a kid who loved to tell jokes and riddles, and who was never serious.

You can't tell how old he is in the pictures. It's something about the eyes and the taut smile, the wariness just under the humor.

I want to apologize for the unfathomable.

For Mohammed's 15-year-old cousin Tariq, the one whose straight-A grades in his Tampa, Florida high school earned him a summer vacation to visit family in the Holy Land – where Border Police troops from my side punched him and dragged him on hard ground and soccer-kicked him until they fractured his jaw and his nose.

I want to apologize for the unconscionable.

For the people on my side who, the night before Mohammed's murder, attacked and tried to kidnap Musa Zalum, only nine, but were forced to flee when his mother and others fought them off.

I want to apologize for the people on my side who will never do so, who believe that it is wrong to do so. Weak to do so. A betrayal of my side, my people, to do so.

I want to apologize for what's in the air.

I want to apologize for those on my side who can speak with appropriate condemnation about brutal kidnap-murders - but who feel they must add, as Prime Minister Netanyahu did this week, that the moral high ground is my side's alone:

"This is what differentiates us from our neighbors. There the murderers are welcomed as heroes, and squares are named for them." He went on to say that my side jails and puts on trial those who incite, while your side makes incitement part of the work of officialdom and educators.

I want to apologize for those on my side who are guilty of incitement, and whom we neither jail nor try, but rather furnish salaries as cabinet ministers, heads of youth movements, civil servant chief rabbis, and commentators. And, yes, the prime minister.

I want to apologize for *Israel Hayom* columnist Haim Shine who, without relating at all to the horrific murder that sparked demonstrations and rioting in Arab towns and centers – and without relating at all to the people on my side who rioted immediately after learning that three of our teens had been murdered – wrote this:

"The hypocrisy of the Arabs of Israel is unchecked and disgusting. Unfortunately, they do not realize that their actions keep them walking a tightrope that could collapse if their traitorous conduct persists."

I want to apologize to good people who are being driven out of this place by the actions and words of bad people.

One of the good people is a colleague, Sayed Kashua. Last week, he published some of the most painful and powerful words ever to appear on these pages. "I was silent," he wrote, "knowing that my attempt at living together with others in this country was over. That the lie I'd told my children about a future in which Arabs and Jews share the country equally was over."

I want to apologize for the people on my side who never will. I want to apologize for those on my side who suggest that you imbibe murderous vengeance with your mother's milk. I want to apologize for the tens of thousands of people on my side who, in anger over your side's murder of our three teens, are promoting revenge as a value for Israeli Jews.

Some of these same people will demand that only you have something to apologize for. That only my side is owed an apology. If you do offer an apology, though, expect these same people to dismiss it as nothing more than empty words, servants of a darker agenda.

It may be, in the end, that the only message we've really needed to hear over the past unbearable weeks, my side and yours, was a simple one, nothing more than one headline which appeared on Sunday: Sane People On Both Sides – Unite.

And one last apology, perhaps the one which should have come before all the others: For sometimes forgetting that, where actual people are concerned - actual children, mothers, fathers, daughters, sons - my side and your side are the same.

IT'S TIME TO ADMIT IT.
ISRAELI POLICY IS WHAT IT IS: APARTHEID

AUGUST 17, 2015

What I'm about to write will not come easily for me.

I used to be one of those people who took issue with the label of apartheid as applied to Israel. I was one of those people who could be counted on to argue that, while the country's settlement and occupation policies were anti-democratic and brutal and slow-dose suicidal, the word apartheid did not apply.

I'm not one of those people anymore. Not after the last few weeks.

Not after Jewish terrorists firebombed a West Bank Palestinian home, annihilating a family, murdering an 18-month-old boy and his father, burning his mother over 90 percent of her body - only to have Israel's government rule the family ineligible for the financial support and compensation automatically granted Israeli victims of terrorism, settlers included.

I can't pretend anymore. Not after Israel's Justice Minister Ayelet

Shaked, explicitly declaring stone-throwing to be terrorism, drove the passage of a bill holding stone-throwers liable to up to 20 years in prison.

The law did not specify that it applied only to Palestinian stone-throwers. It didn't have to.

Just one week later, pro-settlement Jews hurled rocks, furniture, and bottles of urine at Israeli soldiers and police at a West Bank settlement, and in response, Benjamin Netanyahu immediately rewarded the Jewish stone-throwers with a pledge to build hundreds of new settlement homes.

This is what has become of the rule of law. Two sets of books.

One for Us, and one to throw at Them. Apartheid.

We are what we have created. We are what we do, and the injury we do in a thousand ways to millions of others. We are what we turn a blind eye to. Our Israel is what it has become: Apartheid.

There was a time when I drew a distinction between Benjamin Netanyahu's policies and this country I have loved so long.

No more. Every single day we wake to yet another outrage.

I used to be a person who wanted to believe that there were moral and democratic limits – or, failing that, pragmatic constraints- to how low the prime minister was willing to go, how far he was willing to bend to the proud proponents of apartheid, in order to bolster his power.

Not any more. Not after Danny Danon.

Not when the prime minister's choice to represent all of us, all of Israel at the United Nations, is a man who proposed legislation to annex the West Bank, effectively creating Bantustans for Palestinians who would live there stateless, deprived of basic human rights.

The man who will represent all of us at the United Nations, the man who will speak to the Third World on our behalf, is the same man who called African asylum seekers in Israel "a national plague."

The man who will represent all of us at the United Nations is the same politician who proposed legislation aimed at crippling left-leaning NGOs which come to the aid of Palestinian civilians and oppose the institution of occupation - at the same time giving the government a green light to keep financially supporting right-wing NGOs suspected of channeling funds to support violence by pro-settlement Jews.

What does apartheid mean, in Israeli terms?

Apartheid means fundamentalist clergy spearheading the deepening of segregation, inequality, supremacism, and subjugation. Apartheid means Likud lawmaker and former Shin Bet chief Avi Dichter calling Sunday for separate, segregated roads and highways for Israelis and Palestinians in the West Bank.

Apartheid means hundreds of attacks by settlers targeting Palestinian property, livelihoods, and lives, without convictions, charges, or even suspects. Apartheid means uncounted Palestinians jailed without trial, shot dead without trial, shot dead in the back while fleeing and without just cause.

Apartheid means Israeli officials using the army, police, military courts, and draconian administrative detentions, not only to head off terrorism, but to curtail nearly every avenue of non-violent protest available to Palestinians.

Late last month, over the explicit protest of the head of the Israeli Medical Association and human rights groups combating torture, Israel enacted the government's "Law to Prevent Harm Caused by Hunger Strikes." The law allows force-feeding of prisoners, even if the prisoner refuses, if the striker's life is deemed in danger.

Netanyahu's Public Security Minister Gilad Erdan, who pushed hard for passage of the bill, has called hunger strikes by Palestinian security prisoners jailed for months without charge or trial "a new type of suicide terrorist attack through which they will threaten the State of Israel".

Only under a system as warped as apartheid, does a government need to label and treat non-violence as terrorism.

Years ago, in apartheid South Africa, Jews who loved their

country and hated its policies, took courageous roles in defeating with non-violence a regime of racism and denial of human rights.

May we in Israel follow their example.

I HELPED DESTROY THE ISRAEL I LOVE.
APARTHEID WILL DO THE REST

FEBRUARY 9, 2017
AMONA, West Bank

The first place I ever occupied was called the House of God.

I was new here. In the army. I was young and in love with a still young, still hopeful country, its democracy still a work in progress. There were only a handful of settlements anywhere in the West Bank. Beit El, Hebrew for House of God, was new, too. Desolate.

A few shacks, a few trailers, and one huge, handsome, glass and limestone house of worship.

When the army issued me a submachine gun and taught me to use it, the first thing they did was to send me to the gleaming synagogue, to keep it safe. There was only one person there at the time, a yeshiva kid from Chicago. He showed me the plaque that said the building was funded through the kindness of the Ministry of Agriculture.

I'd come to Israel to be a farmer, so I had to ask. "What, exactly, do you guys grow here?" His answer came without hesitation.

"Rocks."

I thought about that conversation a few days ago, when I watched young pro-settlement Jews not far away from Beit El at the Amona outpost, throwing rocks at Israeli troops and police officers ordered to expel them from the outpost, which even Israel acknowledges was built illegally.

Not only rocks. Heavy, sharp-tipped iron fence posts, bleach, a fire extinguisher, bricks, car tires, a kitchen table.

From past experience, the settlement activists at Amona knew what the government would do in response to their attacking Israeli forces. They knew how the cabinet ministers would react when the Hilltop Youth called the soldiers Nazis, when they broke the windows of police vehicles and buses, and defaced the outpost's synagogue, putting up a fake Israel Police shield bearing a large swastika where a Star of David is supposed to go. They knew exactly what the prime minister would do:

Shower them with rewards.

They were right. And they only had to wait a day or two. Late Monday night, the Knesset awarded settlers defying the government their most spectacular prize yet.

The bill the Knesset passed late on Monday sounds pretty much like any other law. They gave it the blandest name they could. *Hok HaHasdara*, which means the Law to Make Things Alright.

But this is not just another law. This is one small step for settlers, and one giant leap for Apartheid.

The law says Israel can expropriate land which Israel itself confirms is Palestinian-owned, and on which thousands of settler homes have already been illegally built.

Nowhere but in the West Bank – not within Israel's 1967 borders and nowhere else – can a government do this. Take land from private individuals – denied basic rights for 50 years under military occupation – and grant it to other private individuals, who are citizens of the government.

The Knesset passed a law saying that the proper response to decades of settlers stealing land, threatening the government, abusing and intimidating and defrauding law-abiding Palestinians, is to grant them the grand prize.

But that's not all it says. It says that Israel is now officially ruled by the worst fanatics of the right. They no longer need to listen to the prime minister. Benjamin Netanyahu now takes his orders from them.

To begin to get a proper grasp on this, you have to go back a whole century before George Orwell. You have to go back to the heyday of colonialism, when the French anarchist Pierre-Joseph Proudhon asked "What is property?' and answered "Property is Theft."

Monday night, with Netanyahu ducking responsibility by leaving the country, the Knesset officially asked the question "What is Theft?" and by a vote of 60-52, the answer is now "Theft is Property."

Think what you like, but be honest about this. Don't ever let anyone tell you that settlements are not an obstacle to a peace process. Because that is exactly, literally, what settlements are there for. To seize land permanently.

What's the problem? The right has a sophisticated strategy for taking over the West Bank, but no workable plan for sharing it with the millions of Palestinians who live there, denied basic human rights to movement, assembly, immigration, property, speech, exercise of religion, the vote.

Entirely separate sets of laws for Israelis and Palestinians living in the same place? Literal Apartheid? No problem. What are laws, anyway? And what about that democracy which was once a work in progress? That country I love.

I helped destroy it. I see it now. I was too cooperative, too long. I was not crazed enough, not aware enough of my own power. I wasn't fierce enough early enough. I wasn't loud enough soon enough.

I should have learned the lesson of the rocks of Beit El, where in Genesis 28, a fugitive and crafty Jacob uses a stone for a pillow, dreams a dream in which God gives the land to him and his descendants, and Jacob pledges in return that the stone will mark God's House – provided that God keeps him safe and fed and clothed.

I should have known that over time, when people come to imbue particular stones with holiness, they may begin to have a certain contempt for people who don't see things their way.

Twice I was almost shot to death at the entrance of a settlement. By people living there. Both times, I was told, it was because I looked too much like an Arab. I truly believe that Israelis will keep outside enemies from destroying their country. But with every new law, with every unimpeded mass contempt of court, the march of Apartheid is annihilating Israel from within.

In just the past few weeks, as a sop to the hard right and the settlement movement, we've seen unusually large numbers of abrupt demolitions of houses of Palestinians in the West Bank and within Israel. Many of the structures belonged to families who had tried but were unable to receive construction permits from Israeli authorities. In the worst example, during one demolition operation, police shot dead a Bedouin Israeli under circumstances which seem entirely unjustified. In the meantime, Israel spent years of time and an estimated $58 million to evacuate a few dozen houses at Amona, promising the evacuees every incentive under the sun as compensation.

On Friday, veteran settlement leader Daniella Weiss refused to condemn the rock-throwing, Nazi epithets, and, in an unusually obscene protest, synagogue defacement on the part of pro-settler activists [militant protesters, before being ousted from the synagogue, painted a swastika on one wall, and above it, the words "Israel Police"].

"The one who defiled a synagogue and destroyed a synagogue was Netanyahu, and even more serious, [pro-settler Bayit Hayehudi party leader Naftali] Bennet.

"I saw everything, and I believe that the defective one is anyone who does not protest against the destruction of a synagogue."

No problem, says the right. It's on a roll. The Geneva Convention, the Hague, the army, the police, Israel's own attorney general and Supreme Court be damned.

The right's next step is to try to annex land in the West Bank, without extending rights to Palestinians. This is their replacement for the two-state solution.

A new step, but one which already has a familiar name: Apartheid. I haven't given up. I'm more crazed now. I accept that I helped destroy the Israel I love. I'm going to try like hell to save anything I can. Before Apartheid does the rest.

SCROLL TO THE FIRST NAKBA

SEPTEMBER 5, 2021

Judaism has gone through radical evolutions in its thousands of years of history. But if there is one constant, a single spine to its convoluted DNA, it is the gravity, the trauma, the memory, the omnipresent threat of exile.

From its very founding by the restless migrant who takes the name Abraham, exile drives our common narratives, our greatest tragedies, and - as we are commanded to remind ourselves every year on Rosh Hashanah - our original sin.

We begin our year by turning the Torah scroll to the story of the first Nakba.

We begin our year with our ancestors Abraham and Sarah, their house slave Hagar, and Ishmael, the beloved young teenaged son of Hagar and Abraham. The four live together. Until, that is, Sarah gives birth to Isaac, takes offense at what she perceives as Ishmael mocking her, and tells Abraham, "Throw out that slave woman and her son, for that woman's son will never share in the inheritance with my son Isaac."

And there it is. Our real-time 21st century failings foretold, lived out in a story about the 21st century B.C.

Abraham and Sarah can't deal with their guilt, can't deal with their inability and/or unwillingness to share the land, can't deal with their horrible treatment of the people who live under their control. So they don't. Abraham casts out Hagar and her child to wander in the harsh wilderness of Beer Sheva, with little water and food. When the water runs out, Hagar puts the boy under a bush, and walks several paces away from him, sobbing, saying "I cannot watch the boy die."

God hears her, and comforts her, and saves them from death. This is the Lord which Hagar has given the name *Elro'i*, the God Who Sees Me.

Abraham, the story tells us, is greatly distressed by it all, but he goes ahead and carries out what he sees as his duty. *Ein Mah La'asot*, we can hear him say to himself. What can you do?

Today we know him in Israel by a different name. The center-right. Sarah, the hard rightist in our Hebrew political present, seems much less troubled. But she's a mess as well. And in the blink of an eye, in the public reading on the second day of Rosh Hashanah, fast-forward to the possibility that Abraham will face the unbearable, the threat of sacrificing Ishmael's younger brother Isaac. And for what?

Exile, the story tells us, is a life sentence for some, and a death sentence for others. Today, we call the consequence of Nakba by a different name. Some dislike the term. Many hate it. But if there's one Hebrew word that Jews everywhere should learn this time of year, and study at this time of reflection and repentance, this is it: *Kibush. Ki* is pronounced as "key," as in a device which can keep all of us in some sense locked up and locked in. And which can keep peace, acceptance, recognition, reconciliation, cooperation, and living together as equals, firmly, permanently, locked out.

It means conquest by force, and also military occupation. It means sacrificing children, whether they are under Kibush or enforcing it.

We have grown far too used to glossing over yet another year of making the Kibush ever more permanent, ever more invasive, ever more hidden from our consciousness, ever more poisonous. We have grown far too used to denying away the knowledge, somewhere in the back of our minds, that every Palestinian mother and child deprived of their home, their freedom, their future, is a new Nakba of its own.

Yes, Kibush is an ugly word. A repulsive concept. And therein lies its power. We should all get used to using it. Just as we should get used to using the word Nakba, studying the enormous suffering it has caused and continues to cause. We need to mark the Nakba, give it its name, in order to begin to seek ways back to healing the rift at the heart of the family of Abraham.

Like the word Nakba, many of us treat Kibush as a curse word, and never utter it. And a curse word it literally is, a word which describes a curse that afflicts all the children of Abraham, Arab and Jew, Israel and Palestinian, whether here or in exile.

There are those, many of them Jews and even evangelical Christians, who will tell you never to use the word. That it doesn't apply. That you can't occupy your own land, granted to you by God.

Take it from someone who, in the uniform of the Israel Defense Forces, armed with a heavily loaded assault rifle, spent – lost - large blocks of time away from home and family, often on the High Holidays, occupying territory after territory after territory after territory: Kibush is Kibush. The disaster of occupation. As Nakba is Nakba. The catastrophe of exile.

As Jews, we begin every year commanded to look inward, to redress our wrongdoing. This year, we can begin by giving it its proper names. As a people and as individuals, until we learn to live with our family, the descendants of Abraham, Hagar, and Ishmael, and share with them our inheritance, we will never truly be able to live with ourselves.

PART EIGHT:
AMERICAN JEWS
WITHOUT ISRAEL,
ISRAEL WITHOUT U .S . JEWS

I WANT TO TALK WITH YOU AS IF YOU WERE HERE

JULY 19, 2010

For David Twersky, my long-lost older brother
      It is the worst week of the worst month of the entire Jewish calendar, and my friend is dead.

It is the month of Av, the anniversary of the gamut of calamity of the Jewish people. It is the birthday of the idea of Diaspora, and of the creativity and aching and poetry, the episodes of soaring and soul disease by which we have come to know it, here and gone, for 3,000 years.

My friend is dead, thousands of miles from where I last saw him happy. It was here in Jerusalem, this year. He was already ill beyond doctors' reach. But in the way of life at curtain, he rallied for one last visit to this place that he loved.

In his one lingering smile, there was every ounce of the seer in him, the shrink in him, the ringleader in him, the Jon Stewart, the Myron Cohen, the Perry White in him, the Toots Schor, the Allen Ginsberg, the inveterate political animal in him, the ballplayer in him, the rock star, the rebbe.

Half a lifetime ago, young and dumb in the fire of the years in which the future is of no consequence, my friend and I left the United States for an idea, a shared and, by all accounts, attainable, dream. By heritage and accidents of history, we, the offspring of revolutions past, had become the disciples of revolutions future.

He was my neighbor once, on what was in those days a working farm and a collective. One day years later, he then a magazine editor and I a novice reporter, he invited me to his office in the city, to tell me that he and his family would be moving back to the States. His phone rang a few minutes later. It was the Labor Party, telling him that the party had completed its list of candidates for the Knesset elections, and his name was on it.

This is what, trying to be fair, trying not to be cruel, I could not tell him while he was still with us:

We needed you here. We need you now.

I believe absolutely that America's Jews needed you just as much. Certainly your family did, your children, your father. You chose well.

But we've needed you here for a long time.

I never met anyone who loved Israel more than you. I never met anyone who saw through Israelis like you did. You were built in the mold of the old guys, the realists who succeeded because they were under the mistaken impression that they were dreamers.

Maybe it's just as well you were spared some of today's Israel and its leaders, the pipe dreamers who fail because they are under the mistaken impression that they are realists.

This is what I want you to know. This place is a vastly better place for your having been here, for the lives you touched and the minds you opened.

When you left, I wanted to believe that our worlds, that of Israel and the American Jewish community, were halves of the same heart. On this awful day, when it seems that most of what is between these two communities is sea water, I want to talk with you as if you were here.

Since you left, the country has gotten better at building walls than bridges. You knew how bridges worked. You knew how to build them.

You had the secret talent, the double-edged gift of the minority artist: the capacity to see the majority when the majority can't begin to clearly see itself. You saw Israel's curse for what it was.

After centuries of the 9th of Av, after temple demolitions and expulsion and incineration and oppression and rootlessness and dread, you met the generations of Jews who had at last been born a majority. And you met their native-born children, on their way to power. After centuries of acute Jewish sensitivity to the feelings, the hopes, the pain of minorities, too many of these sabra leaders, couldn't – and still can't - seem to fathom minorities at all.

Worse, it doesn't seem to bother them that they can't.

Not just the Palestinians are a mystery to them, nor just the Israeli Arabs, nor asylum seekers from Darfur, nor the very sabra children of foreign workers. This generation of sabra leaders, and some of their partners, whom you helped leave the Soviet Union, seem to have even lost the sense of what it means to be part of a Jewish minority.

Now the cabinet is marking the 9th of Av by discussing a conversion bill that many U.S. Jews find terrifying and repellent. You would have loved the interview that the bill's author, David Rotem gave JTA, knowing he was speaking to American Jews. "It is only an Israeli matter," he said. "This law has got nothing to do with American Judaism or anyone in the Diaspora."

Once, long ago, weeding endless cotton fields, we bandied the concept of what American Jews and American Judaism would be like if there were no Israel, and what Israel would be like if there were no American Jews.

This week, incredulous at having to say goodbye to you, trying to imagine your burial in a cemetery overseas, I have a sense that I am beginning to find out.

We once took a walk past the cemetery on the kibbutz. I said that this was where I figured I would end up. You gave out with that throaty snarl of a laugh and nothing more. Maybe you knew that we both were bound for other lives, other places. Looking back, this much I know:

It matters, what you did here. You helped write Jewish history. You fought for a more human, more humanist Israel. You hoped against hope. It was not this Israel, this *bulvahn*, that you dreamed of. But you are still at the heart of what is good here.

Part of you never left this place where the terrible month of Av brings out the worst and the best in the people who make a difference. You made a difference, my friend. Your life gave others life. The Talmudist in your veins, the prophet in your eyes, the poet in your lungs. We needed you. We need you now.

IF A MILLION AMERICAN JEWS MOVED TO ISRAEL

JULY 12, 2012

There are things we never write about here. Sometimes it's because doing so may betray a certain prejudice or bear the dangers and fictions of generalization. It may be hurtful. The subject may be painful to the writer, or prick a certain shame.

Sometimes it's because the topic seems unserious, petty, beneath the dignity and gravity of questions of Middle East import.

In the case of the following paragraph, it's a little of all of them. It's a quotation from a Moscow-born soldier I once served with in the army.

"If a million American Jews had moved to Israel," he said in heavily accented Hebrew, "there would be peace."

A friend of his, also Russian-Israeli, was quick to respond, his tone midway between derision and a certain sense of triumph. "No danger of that happening."

The subject changed before I could ask the second man which he thought was impossible - a million immigrants from North America, or peace. It was fairly clear, however, that he meant both.

Without really giving it serious thought, I could sense that it was one of those observations that, once repeated, manages to offend a large number of people at once. I let it rest.

That conversation came to mind this week for two reasons. One was what my colleague Carlo Strenger called his counterfactual dream: that graft allegations had not unseated Ehud Olmert as prime minister, and by last year he would have forged a workable peace with the Palestinians.

The other was a speech I heard over the weekend, when tens of thousands demonstrated against, among other related issues, the practice of granting the ultra-Orthodox blanket exemptions from national service of any kind.

Toward the distant end of the rally held in the jungle heat of Tel Aviv, an American who moved to Israel in 2004, rose to speak. It was Rabbi Dov Lipman of Beit Shemesh, himself ultra-Orthodox. For some time, Lipman has been waging a battle of rare courage against harassment and violence by ultra-Orthodox extremists in the town.

It's not every day that I feel proud to be an American immigrant to Israel, but this was one of them. The speech was stirring, unifying, and, shunning the cavernous ruts of Israeli political argument, extraordinarily fresh.

Drawing on traditional sources and rabbinic wisdom to show how church-state political deal-making can warp the spirit of Judaism and cause a society to unravel, Rabbi Lipman was able to bring people from opposite sides together in the best sense. It was a true example of a mitzvah which American Jews are at times accused of over-emphasizing: Tikkun Olam, repairing the world.

I do not for a moment believe that a million American Jews will move to Israel. I believe that they will not. But if I were capable of putting aside my fears of being exposed as essentially uncool and insufficiently right-on, if I were to write about what we do not write about, if I would tell what I see as the truth about my *Eidah*, my congregation of Israel, my ethnic sub-tribe of the Jewish people, this is what I would come out and say:

American Jews who live here make Israel a better place.

Not all of us. Not all the time. But a remarkable percentage of Israel's most invisible minority spends an inordinate amount of its energy, talent, and forbearance on the business of repairing the world, and in particular, this far corner of it.

You won't see them on television. Those the news media do seek out, an unrepresentative but vocal sample, are settlers, and gunslinging militants at that.

If a million North American Jews – if a representative sample of an overwhelmingly left-liberal community - had come to live in Israel 20 years ago, or even five, this would be a different country. And not only because people might drive less aggressively or even make sure that their kids used seat belts.

If there were a million U.S. and Canadian Israelis, lawmakers would not be able to get away with overt racism against Africans. Shas lawmakers would not be able to get away with covert bigotry against American Reform Jews. Rabbinical Orthodoxy, ultra- Orthodoxy, and the settlement movement would lose their status of privileged aristocracy, unbound by the laws of Israel at large. Civil marriage, true recognition of and openness to non-Orthodox Judaism, true separation of religion and state – for the direct benefit of both – would become a reality.

Equal rights and opportunities for Arab citizens would not be a dashed hope. When Arab Americans or Israeli Arabs arrived at Ben-Gurion Airport, they would be far less likely to be humiliated, detained without cause, and treated as terrorists unless proven otherwise.

If a million Americans had moved here, the foreign minister would not be Avigdor Lieberman, and Avigdor Lieberman might well be behind bars.

The concepts of human rights, democracy, and respect for minorities would be more than ammunition to be deflected and redirected at Israel's critics, as in Their Wrongs Make Us Right.

And there would be peace. We would be neighbors to an independent Palestine.

The electoral balance here is so close, that a hundred thousand or less might well have done the trick.

To be fair, not every American immigrant saw Rabbi Lipman's speech the same way. According to Noga Martin, a former editor at the Jerusalem Post, now writing at the Times of Israel site, "tonight's rally in favor of universal draft presented us with a stunning example of another phenomenon – the Anglo Hebrew speaker with an accent that could peel paint off walls.

"Toward the end of the demonstration, an immigrant rabbi took the stage and gave an articulate, impassioned speech in perfectly acceptable Hebrew. Sadly, the power of his words was diminished by his dreadful North American accent."

I want to congratulate Noga Martin on becoming an Israeli. And for demonstrating how easily and on what basis, Israelis can wave away and ignore the few Americans who are here.

It's true. To Israeli ears, the American accent is not easily borne. It is reedy, not an ounce of the bullhorn gravitas in which Israeli ears enjoy being bathed. Where Americans intend openness and polite deference and an urge to give of themselves, Israelis hear the milquetoast and the nerd and the dupe. To Israeli ears, the American accent is as meek and inappropriately innocent as a permanent childhood. To Israeli ears, a voice like that has no business in a place like this.

If I were to write about the things we don't, if I could convince Israelis to listen to a sentence or two in my anemic little accent of a voice, I would put in a word for the North Americans who come here to try to make a life of it:

They lack for neither spine nor guts nor heart. You're lucky to have them.

One other thing, if I may. Personally, I have found that with every passing year here, my Hebrew has gotten a bit better, and my American accent in Hebrew, markedly worse. I have an idea what I sound like to Israelis in their mother tongue, and it is anything but attractive. At some point, I also realized whose problem this is, and it's not mine.

WILL THIS BE THE YEAR
AMERICAN JEWS SECEDE FROM ISRAEL?

JANUARY 1, 2013

One day in the future, when it all comes horribly down, will Israelis finally realize that there were warning signs all along?

More to the point of the ultimate survival of Israel, could it be that when the real alarm sounds, when the genuine danger impends, Israelis won't hear a thing?

The answers may lie in how Israelis react to the canary in the coal mine, their forward recon unit in the world, the American Jewish community.

In fact, as the new year dawns, there are mounting signs that 2013 may be the year in which U.S. Jews – in the main, liberal in outlook, committed to tolerance, pluralism, and a vigorous, sincere pursuit of peace – effectively secede from this state of Israel.

They remain committed to supporting the existence of an Israel which balances Israeli and Jewish culture with respect for minority rights and democratic values. They will stay active in promoting the welfare of Israel's disadvantaged.

But many American Jews are already distancing themselves in word and deed from a government it sees as arrogant and short-sighted, enslaved to a runaway train of settlement, dismissive of the rights of Palestinians and other non-Jews, cold to the concerns of a sinking middle class and the drowning disadvantaged, contemptuous of the concerns of the larger Jewish world.

The catalysts: settlement expansion - especially as it strikes at Israeli-Palestinian peace prospects and mocks Washington – and backhanded insensitivity to the rights and ritual of non-Orthodox Jews.

In recent weeks, some of Israel's most influential defenders in the States have warned of hardline Israeli policies and parties which could lead "to the destruction (the self-destruction) of Israel" (Jeffrey Goldberg), and "national suicide" (Thomas Friedman).

Israeli leaders lent them not so much as a deaf ear. Nothing.

Even when the issue touches directly on the religious concerns of American Jewry, the government's response is as dismissive and condescending as it is dishonest.

Last week, waking, years in arrears, to discover that U.S. Jews are appalled by continuing arrests for violating Orthodox-ordered prohibitions on women praying aloud and wearing prayer shawls by the Western Wall, the prime minister appointed Natan Sharansky to look into the matter.

Within hours, however, the Prime Minister's Office rushed out a message aimed at Israelis, indicating that the appointment was largely a charade.

"There are no changes in prayer arrangements at the Western Wall and no committee has been established," Netanyahu's office was quoted as saying.

There are Israelis who will do anything not to be reminded that American support, anchored by U.S. Jewry, is the strategic asset which makes all other strategic assets possible. The 2012 election, after all, saw prominent members of the ruling Likud-Beiteinu, notably Knesset Deputy Speaker Danny Danon, actively campaigning for the defeat of President Obama.

But that was then.

Now, as Israel's election campaign nears its home stretch, the heavily favored Likud-Beiteinu party, which encompasses the principal authors of nearly all of the anti-democratic legislation of the last four years, offers fresh voices and perilous new avenues for alienating American Jews from Israel.

There is, for example, Moshe Feiglin, who will enter the Knesset following the January 22 election. Something of his political philosophy can be gleaned from a 2004 article on radical settlers, in which Feiglin spoke to Goldberg, then writing in the New Yorker:

"'Why should non-Jews have a say in the policy of a Jewish state?'" Feiglin said to me. 'For two thousand years, Jews dreamed of a Jewish state, not a democratic state. Democracy should serve the values of the state, not destroy them.' In any case, Feiglin said, 'You can't teach a monkey to speak and you can't teach an Arab to be democratic. You're dealing with a culture of thieves and robbers. Muhammad, their prophet, was a robber and a killer and a liar. The Arab destroys everything he touches.'"

Then there is political novice Yair Shamir, catapulted from nowhere to the very upper level of Likud-Beiteinu, thanks in part to his late father's prime ministerial heritage of having warred with then-president George H.W. Bush over the issue of settlement construction.

Last week, an opinion piece by Yair Shamir was headlined, "In Israel-US relations, settlements are entirely beside the point."

Wrong. As his father once inadvertently proved.

But candidate Shamir went further. Taking up where Danon left off, Shamir attacked Obama's nomination of John Kerry as secretary of state - over settlements. In essence, Shamir made acquiescence to settlement construction a condition of Israel-U.S. ties: "Many are liable to feel that his nomination will deter Israel from implementing its decision to build thousands of apartments in Jerusalem, Judea and Samaria, and will be viewed as an obstacle to Israel-U.S. relations."

American Jews want to know what is being done in their name. In the name of Judaism. And if they think that it is self-destructive, oppressive, blockheaded and wrong, it stands to reason they would want it to stop.

American Jews are tiring of being told that opposing Israel's policies puts Israelis in danger. Blackmail is not persuasion. If the hard right is so certain that it can get along without American Jewish support, it may all too soon get the chance to find out.

ISRAELIS WHO HATE AMERICAN JEWS

JULY 4, 2017

Let's imagine that you're a North American Jew. Let's say that for as long as you can remember, Benjamin Netanyahu's Israel has done things to drive you nuts. Break your heart. Act contrary to your most basic principles.

No right to speak out – against any issue. Even last week, when Benjamin Netanyahu drove two quick stakes into the hearts of American Jews. Without a second thought, he agreed to Orthodox political blackmail on non-egalitarian prayer at the Kotel, Jerusalem's ancient Western Wall, and on Orthodox control of conversions to Judaism.

American Jews, for the first time, shocked Israelis by speaking up. When they did, Israelis, led by Netanyahu's interior minister, unleashed torrents of abuse, saying that these people, who aren't really Jews – they're talking about you, now – are bent on annihilation.

"We won't allow all sorts of groups," said Interior Minister Arye Deri, "to come and destroy everything which we have built here in the state of Israel."

The next morning, Rabbi Dov Halbertal, a former senior official of the chief rabbi's office, went on a television talk show to tell American Reform Jews, "We need to throw you out of the state of Israel – not physically, but ideologically."

And ex-Knesset Member Aryeh Eldad, former commander of the army's medical corps, suggested that liberal American Jews would soon get rid of themselves anyway, through low birth rates and intermarriage.

"This is a Jewish community in its death throes," he said. "It's all but dead."

These Israelis are not saying, "Oh, please, come to Israel so we can all live together as soul-mates." They're saying, "We hate you. We don't want your kind here."

The Israeli right wants you to throw up your hands in disgust and just walk away. They want you to abandon the playing field to them.

But why in the world would you want to do what they want? Is there anything – anything – that they want that you want?

More freedom to give Palestinians less freedom? I doubt you see that as a positive goal.

More powers to strip democracy of its powers? Thanks to Trump, you're now seeing what that's like, close up.

More leeway to mistreat and neglect Holocaust survivors, non- Jews, the elderly, asylum seekers, the disabled, the poverty stricken? You don't have to live here to know what's wrong.

Why do these Israelis hate you? For all kinds of reasons. Soft. Spoiled. Left-leaning. Distant. Assimilated. Obama-lovers. And you smile too much.

Oh, and one other thing. You take all the crap we Israelis dish out and you say nothing. You're doormats. *Shmattehs*. Maybe you'll let out a yell about the Kotel, but not about anything else that happens here.

Prove them wrong. They want you disgusted and uninvolved. Put your anger to good use. Show up. Show up here. Raise your voice. Stand up for what you know to be right.

Yell louder where you live. Support the NGOs that promote what you believe in. The Israel that speaks to your values.

Come here more, not less. Put your body where your conscience is.

And about that ironclad right-wing principle of "You don't live here, so you have no right to talk?" The joke is, there are plenty of occupation-lovers like Sheldon Adelson who don't live in Israel. He doesn't have skin in the game. Yet, for all the Israelis who hate American Jews for getting involved, it's just fine for Sheldon to meddle and interfere.

Just like they think it's terrific that Netanyahu intercedes in American electoral politics, attacking Democrats, addressing Congress, licking Trump's upholstery.

In any case, if you speak up, these Israelis may call you names. They may even hate you for it.

But they don't get to decide what you should think. And they don't get to decide how Jewish you are.

They don't get to decide that you hate Israel, just because you care about it enough to try to change it.

The fact is that if you really hated Israel, Netanyahu's is exactly the government you'd want. Destructive. Defensive. Hateful.

The fact is that if you truly hated Israel, you wouldn't want to change a thing.

PART NINE:
SCRAPS OF CLOTH

THE FLAG OF PALESTINE IS BEAUTIFUL

AUGUST 14, 2018

> *"WHEN I GET OLDER, I WILL BE STRONGER*
> *"THEY'LL CALL ME FREEDOM, JUST LIKE A WAVIN' FLAG"*
> *From "Wavin' Flag," by Somali-Canadian artist K'naan.*
> *Originally written for Somalia and its people's aspirations for*
> *freedom. Adopted as a promotional anthem for the 2010 soccer*
> *World Cup hosted by South Africa.*

It took Benjamin Netanyahu to get me to take a long look at the flag of Palestine, and to see the beauty in it.

It took the beauty of families, their smiles as they marched, their pride, their goal. Smiles across a divide that often seems much too wide and deep ever to be bridged. Their signs said it all. The word Equality, the words Arabs and Jews Together, the words Democracy for All, the words Arabs and Jews Refuse to Be Enemies, the words A Different Future for Our Children – all of them in Hebrew and Arabic both.

And there were also flags.

The protest's organizers had asked marchers not to carry flags, in order to strengthen a rare sense of unity among the participants. Thirty-thousand of the marchers complied.

But the people of the Holy Land being, after all, the individuals that they are, a smattering of marchers – at least two of them Jews – carried the black, green, white and red flag of Palestine. A handful of other marchers carried Israeli flags.

And, from the start – taking their cues from a rush-order Netanyahu social-media flurry of incitement – the weight of the mass media, pointedly ignoring the Israeli flags, carried nothing else. "Palestine Flags In The Heart of Tel Aviv," screamed the alarm-bells black-background banner headline fronting the next morning's *Yedioth Ahronoth*.

The headline was illustrated with a large photograph that recalled an iconic image of an October, 2000 incident in which a Palestinian crowd killed and mutilated two Israeli soldiers who had strayed into the West Bank city of Ramallah.

And, if that weren't enough, the photograph was framed with a red-backed, war-worthy headline reading "'In Spirit and Blood We Shall Redeem Palestine,' Cried the Demonstrators in Rabin Square."

With all respect to my colleagues, just this: Fake. F'ing. News.

The few marchers who chanted strident slogans found no resonance with the crowd. The chants that were picked up and reached the level of a roar were entirely different. And, from the personal standpoint of Benjamin Netanyahu, the chants that found resonance were infinitely more dangerous:

Shiv-yon! Equality. *Bi-za-yon*! Disgrace. And then, most dangerous, most thunderous of all:

Bibi habaita! Bibi go home.

LOOK HOW THEY TREAT US,

MAKE US BELIEVERS

With everything they had, Netanyahu and his people drove home the message that the Palestinian flag stands for nothing but terrorism, genocide, annihilation. When you see the flag of Palestine, he made clear with the repetition and rhythm of a hypnotist, what you need to feel is dread – the dread of Arab rising against Jew.

But the real terror that Netanyahu himself feels is in a different photograph, one of the Palestinian flag and the Israeli flag waving one beside the other.

The real terror that Netanyahu feels is the fear that Arab and Jew will rise up together. That Arab and Jew will stand up together against the theocrats and bigots and macho-ists and maximalists who divide them, set one against another, make decisions that result only in suffering and hopelessness and shattered childhoods and violent, senseless, needless death.

Look again at those flags. The Palestinian flag that our leaders have taught us to fear as an emblem of murder and genocide. And the Israeli flag that the Palestinians have learned to loathe as an emblem of conquest, humiliation and, yes, murder.

WE FIGHT THEIR BATTLES,
THEN THEY DECEIVE US
TRY TO CONTROL US.
THEY COULDN'T HOLD US.

No. The flag of Palestine is beautiful. It holds a heritage. It says, "We are our own people." As are you, the Jews. Our cousins. Our neighbors.

It is the flag of the Arab Revolt of more than a century ago.

An uprising that remade its revolutionaries, allowed them, freed them to become themselves. Against an empire, an occupation that denied them the possibility of a national home of their own. A regime that had grown corrupt and brutal, having been in power far too long.

It was a struggle against rulers who did not know them, never appreciated them, underestimated them, colonized them and, in the end, could not continue to colonize them.

It is the flag of past dynasties, of the indelibility of history, the black the ashes of the cruel experience of war, the green the mark of the land worked and loved, the white the sign of aspiration and good deeds, the red an unhealed wound.

I have friends who hate the sight of this flag. I have friends who despise the sight of the flag of Israel, the Shield of David, the stripes of a faith that provided shelter, wisdom and a now-lost unity for thousands of years.

But that picture, the two flags together, is an earthquake in the making. It says that there is a way out of this.

OUT OF THE DARKNESS, I CAME THE FARTHEST
AMONG THE HARDEST – SURVIVAL.
LEARN FROM THESE STREETS. IT CAN BE BLEAK.
ACCEPT NO DEFEAT, SURRENDER, RETREAT

I know what Bibi says. I know what he has done. I listened to him offer the Palestinian flags themselves as proof of the necessity of that same Nation-State Law that, only days before, his loyalists had assured us, does absolutely nothing, changes absolutely nothing.

Now we know. This law, which was meant to suppress and criminalize Palestinian Israeli aspirations, has given them voice. It has amplified them, taken them public, built alliances with thousands of Jewish Israelis.

A law that was meant to sideline and downgrade the Arabic language – and therefore, in an underhanded but potent way, downgrade the citizenship of all non-Jews whose mother tongue is Arabic – has reawakened interest in Arabic on the part of Israeli Jews.

Look again. The flag of Palestine is beautiful.

And the lesson of the Nation-State Law, that gangrenous appendage, is that it's high time to reclaim the beautiful flag of Israel as well.

This is not the flag of land grabs and anti-Arab racism and Islamophobia. This is not the flag of settlement and callous disregard for the vulnerable. This is not the flag of supremacism, xenophobia, apartheid.

This is the flag of exactly the hope and aspiration codified in the Declaration of Independence.

WHEN I GET OLDER
I WILL BE STRONGER.
THEY'LL CALL ME FREEDOM,
JUST LIKE A WAVIN' FLAG.

ISRAEL AS A SLAVE STATE

JUNE 5, 2018

If all of humankind's most overwhelmingly transformative inventions, there has never been anything quite like a flag.

It is an enormously powerful, potentially dangerous machine. It can spearhead the rise of entire empires, or their annihilation. Yet it has no moving parts, no electronics or hydraulics, no fuel source but the human hand and the human mind.

Folded up, you can fit it in your pocket. And, for many of us, no matter how hard you try, you can't get it out of your heart.

Quick, have a look at the flag of Israel. What do you feel?

Generations ago, in its reference to the stripes of the Jewish prayer shawl and the six-pointed shield of David, the flag was material proof that an entire people, thousands of years old and recently hunted down and slaughtered by the millions, had emerged from genocide and had somehow found its way back to its ancient ancestral home.

But that's not what that flag means anymore.

For a while, there was a sense, a hope, that the flag stood for an actual commitment to Jewish values as explicitly expressed in Israel's Declaration of Independence, a commitment to a search for reconciliation after devastating war, a "country for the benefit of all of its inhabitants," a nation "based on freedom, justice and peace as envisaged by the prophets of Israel." An Israel which promised to "ensure complete equality of social and political rights to all its inhabitants irrespective of religion, race or sex," guaranteeing freedom of religion, conscience, language, education and culture."

What's left of all that? A blue and white scrap of cloth.

And now that's been stolen as well, from what we once knew as the Jewish heart.

I feel for the young people who now look at that flag and feel their chests knot up in anguish and fury, for all that this flag has come to mean.

The flag of Israel has been co-opted as the banner of the slave states we call Judea and Samaria, our very own Confederacy, our very own means of keeping millions of people disenfranchised, treated as chattel, exploited as laborers, abused without redress.

And as the masters of the slave states now have become the masters of Israel as a whole – pushing us to reject democracy, dismiss peacemaking, embrace theocracy, take pride in brutality - the flag of Israel itself has come to stand for a slave state.

And yet.

This week in this city, in and around Tel Aviv and Jaffa, in homes, businesses, and even municipal buildings and schools, a different flag is going up. A flag which, I have come to feel in my chest, is vastly more representative of what Israel might have been, should have been, and perhaps, one day in the future, will become: The rainbow stripes of the Pride flag, with the Magen David in its center.

This new flag of Israel stands for inclusion rather than incitement. It stands for respect and reconciliation rather than racism. It stands for welcoming differences of opinion, culture, belief, skin – rather than deporting them.

It seems to me that the message of the Pride flag goes far beyond LGBTQ rights. This flag stands for the freedom of all of us here, all of us shackled by the slave state we serve, the people we oppress, the leaders whose wrong-headed "security considerations" crush us all. This is the new flag of a more human state of Israel. It stands for people created in the image of a God who is neither male nor female, Jew nor non-Jew, a God who is no designated color – a Creator who is all of them, more than them, all of us.

I haven't given up on this place, and what it could be. I'm not ready to cede the flag of Israel. There is still much here to be admired, much that is worth saving, many who manage in a thousand focused ways to work for a semblance of sanity here, a way to a decent future here.

And yet.

There was a time when the flag of the state of Israel was a direct source of inspiration, of welcome, of hope. A power source for a deep stirring in the chest. No more.

Imagine my wonder, then, that this is exactly what I've been feeling this week, in this city, when everywhere you look, the flags stand for pride.

In early June of 2016, just before the abusive, racist, often violent annual Jerusalem Day Flag March by which settlers annually terrorized swaths of the Holy City, a remarkable conference was held in Tel Aviv. The all-day gathering brought together a seemingly impossible mélange of Palestinians, settlers, leftist Jews and the ultra-Orthodox, all to launch a seemingly impossible initiative, an Israel-Palestine confederation under the heading of Two States, One Homeland. Not yet fully formed, the concept reimagines the Holy Land as a place where both peoples could govern themselves, free themselves, remain in the homes, celebrate their own cultures, have an actual future.

It was high time for something entirely new, shockingly so. It was time to begin to come to grips with the fact that after nearly a decade of Netanyahu's rule, Israel was over. Netanyahu was still with us. But Israel was over and gone.

It was time, that is – and with no working compass or road map - to begin to move on.

THIS YEAR, FOR JERUSALEM DAY, WE TOOK DOWN THE ISRAELI FLAG

JUNE 7, 2016

This weekend, as Jerusalem Day approached, our family started a new tradition. We took down the Israeli flag from our roof.

For me, it had much to do with a uniquely Israeli weekend in which I felt, by turns, hope for the future, enormous pride in a certain slice of the present, and, as Jerusalem Day dawned to cap the weekend, deeply rooted shame.

Something changed in me this weekend. And I don't see it changing back any time soon.

The weekend began early, at a Thursday conference of a revolutionary new movement, Two States One Homeland. I will leave the details of the peace plan to others.

For now, though, I want to share a teaching of the late Rabbi Menachem Froman, whose spirit lent both weight and wings to the idea.

In direct contrast to the oft-chanted hardline principle that

"The Land of Israel belongs to Am Israel," that is, only to the Jews, the rabbi taught that we should stop and consider that it is we – Jews and Palestinians both – who belong to this land.

It is the difference, his students learned, between *rechushanut* – possessiveness, a powerful focus on ownership of property - and the concept of *shayechut* – the quality and the feeling of belonging. The next day, the rabbi's teaching come to life in a way I could not have anticipated. Nearly a quarter of a million people took part in Tel Aviv's annual LGBTQ Pride Parade and festival, a perpetual motion blowout in which Israelis and Palestinians, Jews and Muslims and Christians and non-believers of all faiths, tourists from across the region and across the planet, reveled just to be in a certain place in a certain time, with each other, and, for that one day at least, to be free.

I was never more proud of Israel. Period.

There's no denying, though, that as Sunday neared, a shadow began to lengthen over the country, and over our house. We all knew what was coming. It was the March of the (Israeli) Flags, an annual, gender-segregated, extreme-right, pro-occupation religious carnival of hatred, marking the anniversary of Israel's capture of Jerusalem by intentionally humiliating the city's Palestinian Muslims.

We knew what was coming from previous years, in which marchers vandalized shops in Jerusalem's Muslim Quarter, chanted "Death to Arabs" and "The [Ancient Jewish] Temple Will Be Built, the [Al Aqsa] Mosque will be Burned Down," shattered windows and door locks, and poured glue into the locks of shops forced to close for fear of further damage.

This year, with their funding sources – including the Jerusalem city hall and Prime Minister Benjamin Netanyahu's Office – under mounting scrutiny, and a poll showing a majority of Israeli Jews opposing the march through Jerusalem's Muslim Quarter-especially immediately before the observance of the holy Muslim month of Ramadan - organizers sought to keep criminal behavior to a minimum.

Yet the traditional spirit of Jerusalem Day - that giddily bullying fratboy ugliness we have come to know, in stark contrast with the indescribable beauty of the city - still came to the fore.

In a song which the Jewish extreme right has adopted to celebrate the July, 2015 terror incineration of a Palestinian infant and his parents in the West Bank village of Duma, marchers gave voice to a perversion of the blinded Samson's prayer in Judges 16:28: "May I avenge [the loss of] my two eyes with one act of vengeance against the Palestinians – may their name be blotted out!"

The Flag Parade, and with it, Jerusalem Day, has come to symbolize the worst in us. Arrogance, xenophobia, brute dominance, racist hatred.

In our house, ahead of the march, we talked about what to do with the flag on our roof, the flag my wife once saved from being desecrated, the flag which we, by custom, had flown since Holocaust Remembrance Day, to honor long-held hopes and dreams of freedom in a homeland.

It wasn't a simple discussion. On the one hand, you don't want to hand the marchers a victory, and cede the flag to, well, the worst of our worst.

On the other, to fly the flag in sync with the march, is to tell your neighbors, Arabs and Jews alike, that the march has merit.

So this year, for Jerusalem Day, we began a new tradition.

We lower this flag in recognition of the many, many people in the city who worked very hard this year to create "A Different Day in Jerusalem," among them families on both sides bereaved by violence, working for healing and a solution to the conflict.

We lower this flag in recognition of those of the Tag Meir movement, who took it upon themselves to hand out "flowers of peace" to Palestinians in the Old City.

We lower this flag in recognition of those who are working to make us proud of this place. Like the Women Wage Peace movement, which is planning a march and vigil for the fall Sukkot holiday, to urge the prime minister to return to peace negotiations.

Women Wage Peace hopes to have thousands of Israeli and Palestinian women joined by women from Tunisia, Morocco, Egypt and Jordan.

This flag will fly again. But never in sympathy with those who are destroying this land, shattering the Jewish People, and mutilating Judaism itself.

Seven years would pass before we would take our flag out of storage. It was in early 2023, in response to the unprecedented nationwide pro-democracy protests which sought to reclaim the flag – and the nation – from the supremacists who, under Netanyahu's aegis, had taken power in Israel.

Much had changed. Years before, ever since the Nation-State Law was passed, a movement to oppose Netanyahu had taken to the streets outside the prime minister's official Jerusalem residence, with demonstrators carrying black flags as a central symbol. We flew that flag for quite some time.

The black flags, the noise and the creativity of demonstrations, drove Netanyahu – and, crucially his wife – to distraction. Nothing, it seemed, could deter the demonstrators.

Then, just in time, in 2020, the Covid pandemic handed Netanyahu a useful opportunity to choke off mass protests. Just when his power seemed to be slipping away, he had been given a taste of true authoritarian rule. There was a new spark in his eye.

What was it that moved Netanyahu to bet the political farm on the "Judicial Reform," a disastrous drain on his support among Israelis? Part of the answer can be found in his experience as prime minister in the early period of the Covid pandemic. His management of the pandemic afforded him unprecedented elements of authoritarian power.

In any event, for the rest of us, restricted to within a 10-meter radius of our homes (later expanded to 100 meters), there was nothing to keep black flags from flying still, from rooftops and windows.

TYRANNY IN THE TIME OF CORONA

March 19, 2020

There's a black flag outside our front window this morning.

It's nothing but an old towel. All we had. But it's as strong as everything we believe in.

This is about democracy. And how at risk we now know it to be. Until now, until the coronavirus, democracy in Israel was sedated and on a respirator. This week, our tyrant of a prime minister pulled the plug.

We live in a country where his ruling party – which lost the March 2 election by a margin of 62 to 58 seats – has just locked out the nation's parliament, obliterating, in the process, the entire legislative branch of government.

We live in a country where demonstrations are suddenly now illegal – not, God forbid, because freedom of speech is compromised- but because it's unhealthy to have more than 10 people in the same place and at the same time. Unless they're ultra-Orthodox. Or settlers. Who vote for Netanyahu.

Nothing to see here, folks. Move along.

We live in a country where schools nationwide are summarily and abruptly shuttered indefinitely, literally overnight – except for some of the schools tied to an ultra-Orthodox party which the tyrant sorely needs for the fiction of his supposed Majority of the People.

And then, to add insanity to insult, when schoolteachers make herculean, magnificent, instantaneously creative efforts to remotely teach their classes and bring their home-bound students together, the tyrant's people announce that the classes must stop because the government won't pay the teachers.

Nothing to see here folks. Deal with your kids on your own.

The tyrant says nothing about the ultra-Orthodox schools still open and running, business as usual, until footage leaks out, showing not only hundreds of students congregating and potentially spreading the virus – but, to add contagion to contagion – the same holy figures who reply that Torah study is keeping us all alive, are holding weddings where incalculably more potential contagion is taking place, dance by dance, close embrace by close embrace.

And when the tyrant deigns to address this, when pressed to do so, he is careful always, always, to mention Arab citizens of Israel as prime offenders along with some Haredi Jews. And then he defers concrete action against his key political supporters.

In other words, no matter the issue, his defense is racism.

There's a black flag outside our window this morning, in part because, while the tyrant told us on television he was closing down our workplaces, schools, malls, beaches, parks, and all entertainment and leisure venues, he neglected to tell us that hours later, in the dead of night, he had his sock-puppet of a Justice Minister get the tyrant's own trial for grave corruption offenses put off for months.

And, who knows, maybe forever.

For years and years, we wondered when the occupation would come home.

It happened this week.

As the settlers once said in a different context: *Yesha Zeh Kan* – Judea, Samaria and Gaza are here.

One set of laws for the tyrant's allies. Another set of laws for everyone else. Innocent civilians hounded. Their persecutor – never held accountable.

Raise the black flag. Stand up to the tyrant. This is the fitting flag for this new Israel.

Legislative branch, gone. Courts, all but gone. Protests – like the motorists driving cars to the Knesset on Thursday in a black flag pro-democracy demonstration – prohibited. By the Health Ministry.

There's talk of martial law. It's beginning to sound possible. Even inevitable.

Yes, a global plague demands a drastic, life-altering public health response. But to leverage the public's very legitimate fears to achieve wholly illegitimate personal political goals, is obscene, dangerous, and inexcusable.

Yes, part of Netanyahu is surely level-headed and broad-minded. But it's the other part, the tyrant, that must be confronted, even at a time like this.

And the tyrant? He's on television tirelessly now, crowing, gloating, boasting. The whole world is in awe of us, he coos, of me, and how I've managed the crisis. I am the captain of the ship in the midst of a storm! How dare these petty nothings distract me, criticize me, and even attempt to mutiny against my hand on the wheel.

Finally, finally, to protect the People, which is to say, the tyrant, the sweepingly invasive surveillance and metadata resources of the Shin Bet, the Mossad, and, why not, military intelligence, are becoming available to control the once-relatively off-limits, once-privileged, once protected Jewish citizenry of the state of Israel.

And details of the cabinet discussions of all this? Classified. A state secret.

Corona, corona, the tyrant muses to himself, where have you been all my life?

PART TEN:
THE TASTE OF BROKEN GLASS

A PLACE AT THE TABLE

APRIL 11, 1979. Forty-four years before the war

KIBBUTZ GEZER – Passover Eve

It was late, maybe midnight

When we opened the door for Elijah

Fully expecting Aunt Ida, in sable.

But it was Pharaoh that walked in to the wine and the whining and asked for a seat at the little kids table, saying he had a few questions for us.

He said his son would have asked them

Had he been able to attend, that is, had we not killed him.

But that was then, and they, not we, we hastened to mention, and even they, one supposes, were decent of intention

Our mother later insisted he'd been a perfect gentleman.

But for his beard, and the bandages he could have been one of us.

Oh, and except for the dust in the shake of his hand.

It isn't on all other nights, he began, that you toast the anniversary of a slaughter of lambs, the painting of blood on the side of a door.

My son died Erev Pesach. What for? To teach me my place? You didn't seen the look on his face when the embalmers came to powder and pump and wrap him into immortality. They drained him like a crankcase.

You didn't see the look on his face.

But what of the faces whose traces you bear,

As a mirror bears ancestors

As if you were there ?

Sandcrazy, sunblind, crowdcrazy, chainblind, scared of the dark and the blood in the street

Tired of freedom and the nothing to eat but half-baked masonry that tasted like sweat

Aching to remember and afraid to forget what slavery was like.

Admit it. By the waters that parted you sat down and wept when you remembered Goshen.

Once you were slaves to Pharaoh in Egypt and once, for a while, you were free.

But now you are masters with burdens more pressing than dressing a desert in perfect triangles of mud.

You failed your God when he sent a second flood to make of a people, a Noah and more.

What for? Some thanks he got.

A pawnshop in the wilderness.

"Let's see something in a god we can pen up and milk." You needed that calf in its 14 carat clothes. But just who were you fooling with the ring in its nose?

Tonight the celebration of the killing of lambs, their blood dried to doorposts, horseradish jam on the table it took you a week to set. At least a week more, 'fore you get your digestion back right.

You couldn't leave Egypt if you wanted to tonight.

When they came to tell me about my son in that dialect that doctors affect the big words snaking past you like bad handwriting,

"In cases such as yours," they began, "let's speak frankly, in cases of ... amputation, it is not uncommon to encounter the selfsame itches, burns, ticklishness shooting as before from the direction of the ... amputee."

As if nothing had occurred. As if I hadn't heard correctly.

As if he were still a part of me.

In cases such as mine, the good news is the area to which the damage has been confined: To my son, and another in every family in the land.

An extra place-setting at every household tonight, except for the ones with the blood on the door.

What for? A lesson to mothers, drowning slowly in loss? To fathers, who went quicker, strapped to chariots? To horses, perhaps, their eyes bulging back against life, against sea. And all so that you could be free.

Mine is the son unable to ask questions.

His is the blood in the libel of generations.

His, the wineglass untouched at the table.

His, the line that descends from Abel.

He will quietly crash your celebrations. he will spike your festival punch with a vague taste of cracked glass. Why on this night do you so carefully spill his blood onto your best china?

Next year in Jerusalem, or Hebron, or Shechem, don't say I didn't warn you when playing the master has shaken and torn your dreams to small sandy pieces. Your God never did sell his property. He only lets leases.

So shackle that promised land of yours. Take, as your deed, your birth.

But know how much a promise is worth.

For once, you were promised. To me.

THIS YEAR FOR HANUKKAH, ALL I WANT IS A SLIVER OF LIGHT

DECEMBER 11, 2012

This year for Hanukkah, all I want is a sliver of light.

Down the street, the large iron menorah which Chabad set in front of the clock tower in Jaffa, is dark. On this night of Hanukkah, no one came to light it. It stands forlorn, rusting at the base. A tribute to the national mood.

This year, for Hanukkah, I want one person running this country, this Israel, to show me one scrap of light. One move - any move - for freedom, for all the peoples who live here. One step – no matter how slight – in the direction of a better future.

What makes this Hanukkah different from all others? It's the dark. It's the sense that this country – beset by enemies, beset by itself - has locked down every single door against the future, and sealed shut every last window against hope.

Even the prime minister whom everyone says will win the coming election no matter what he does, or doesn't do, even this prime minister is sour of mood on this holiday, rote of speech, out of sorts, short on new challenges, bleak.

This year on Hanukkah, the dark is a trickle-down effect, directly from the top. One lesson of the determined, brave Maccabees, the prime minister told us as he lit the second candle at a former garbage dump, is that in the face of mounting pressure, it takes courage to do nothing, it demonstrates determination to initiate nothing.

Much as the prime minister exploits the dark, it may well be getting to him as well. Paralyzing him. All those years of seeing Iran as Nazi Germany 1938, Ahmadinejad preparing to re-fight the Second World War and annihilate the Jews. All those months of viewing post-Arab Spring Egyptians and Syrians as girding to refight the 1967 war, and push the Jews into the sea. And now Hamas.

"Zionists," a spokesman for Hamas's military wing said this weekend, "you should prepare your passports and get ready to disappear."

For many Israelis, what their own government has been telling them of late, amounts to the same thing. No horizon. Nothing to shoot for. Nothing to expect. Prepare your passports.

Under the circumstances, you'd expect that the fanatics and the sociopaths of Israeli politics would be all too pleased by an epoch of darkness. But no. It's getting to them, too.

On Tuesday night, extreme rightist Knesset members Aryeh Eldad and Michael Ben-Ari invited followers to celebrate Hanukkah by gathering at a Tel Aviv park frequented by African asylum seekers, and demand that Israel boot out the refugees, the sooner the better.

"We've Come To Banish The Dark" was the lawmakers' carefully chosen slogan for the confrontational candle-lighting. It gave a children's sweet Hanukkah song about a holiday of light ("Get out, darkness / Black be gone!") a whole new meaning, sinister and hugely racist.

But the protest was a failure. Barely a dozen people showed up to applaud. They were far outnumbered by journalists, bystanders, and, in the end, Africans. At several points, the crowd, finding the numerous side arguments more compelling, abandoned the orating lawmakers, who often seemed at loose ends.

It's everyone now. This country has begun to feel like a lamp whose body is cracked and whose light seems all but spent. On these long nights, we can make out little but an occupation growing ever more permanent, and a democracy growing ever more temporary.

But there's more. There's still much more in this. That is what the prime minister is telling us, if only by negative example. If only by gagging professors and merchandising fear, mistrust, and despair.

This, by negative example, is what he was telling us at the Tel Aviv garbage dump that was turned into an ecological park, recycling center and green space, as a result of great initiative - by Ariel Sharon, whom the prime minister implicitly denigrated in his speech ("The test of leadership is not in how to concede on vital interests in order to win the applause of the international community" but "in how *not* to concede on vital interests and in withstanding international pressure"):

Hanukkah is a breaking point. The kind that Leonard Cohen wrote about, in what turns out to be worthwhile advice for the people who live here, in the dark:

> "Ring the bells that still can ring.
> "Forget your perfect offering.
> "There is a crack in everything.
> "That's how the light gets in."

There's a reason, after all, that Hanukkah is marked on some of the longest, darkest nights of the year. In the dominion of despair, Hanukkah remains, as it was at first, a rebellion. A reminder that a sliver, a crack, can, with hope against hope, overcome an empire of the dark.

Hanukkah is the victory of the miraculous, the logically

impossible, over the darkness we have come to know and cringe over and suffer from.

In a dark age, Hanukkah tells us that even the lamp that seems broken and empty, rusted and forlorn, can shed great light. It also tells us that no one is going to light it for us. And that, though we have scant resources of faith and political fuel, we have a good idea where the cracks are, and that's a start.

I WANT ISRAEL TO STOP BREAKING MY HEART

APRIL 25, 2017

NATAF, Israel

Today happens to be my birthday. This year, the restlessness of the Hebrew calendar placed the date between Israel's two central days of darkness, the commemoration of the millions of Jews killed in the Holocaust, and of the tens of thousands killed here in wars and terrorism.

This year it also intersected with a period of personal mourning, for a friend who loved this country with the whole of his severely scarred heart.

In a country this small, this awash in wrongful and obscenely untimely death, you learn a great deal, and quickly, about grieving. But it also forces you to focus on what you want from the rest of your life.

This year, for my birthday, I don't want a cake or presents.

This year, for my birthday, I want Israel to stop breaking my heart.

This is not my only wish. But it's the one I feel the need to say out loud.

I want the people who run things here to appeal to the best in us, rather than pander to the worst.

I want to stop waking up to ill will and the cunning codes of hatred.

I want to see people on all sides treated with the respect they deserve as human beings.

We are, every one of us here, permanently scarred. We are scarred by what war does to us. It's the way scars work. They protect and reinforce a wounded place, but they also take away its feeling. They make it less flexible.

Scars have made us what we are.

They armor us in callousness. They steel us to the hurt we cause others. Not only on the level of politics and governmental policy. Face to face. Person to person.

We are deformed. By terrorism. By occupation. They rob of our humanity, our sense of fairness. They kill our souls. They make us into their puppets.

Still, if the reckoning is to be truly honest, there's must be much more to it than just the darkness there. There's also this - a debt of gratitude to be paid.

In the course of the year since my last birthday, I saw something which, entirely unexpectedly, convinced me that my wish for this year could someday actually come true.

It was a terrible fire.

The place our family called home for 20 years was on the point of being destroyed.

The inferno would have taken the whole mountain, every single home, were it not for a war in which Jews and Arabs, Israelis and Palestinians and Egyptians and Jordanians, all fought on the same side. They all fought to save lives and homes, to protect trees and animals. And they won.

To all of you, to the firefighters from Bet Shemesh and across Israel - one of whom is truly family to us – and to the Palestinian

Authority firefighters from Jenin and Tubas and Tul Karm - to the Palestinian firefighters who spoke of their pride in their work alongside the Israelis; to the Israelis, to all of you who helped save the home in which we raised our babies, thank you from the bottom of my heart.

To our neighbors in the Arab village of Abu Ghosh, who were the first to phone us and ask how we were, and to tell us that their home was open to us as if it were our own, and who opened the community center to everyone who had been evacuated, and who brought food in great quantities from restaurants and individuals, and who helped set up activities for the children, gratitude forever.

To our neighbor from Katana, on the next mountain, from the West Bank Palestinian village, who built much of the restaurant that caught fire and was destroyed, and who was instrumental in containing the blaze, words fail me.

I knew that fire obliterates. But I learned then that fire also reveals. Fire burns off our every mask. Fire is a cruel but unbiased mirror. It reveals our character.

I'm not the same person I was a year ago. Some of my most calcified, most unexamined assumptions have been burned out of me.

Something was torn away from my heart in those days.

It might have been scars.

PART ELEVEN:
WAR CRIMES

WHAT DOES 'DEATH TO ISRAEL', MEAN TO YOU?

NOVEMBER 3, 2011

My daughter went to school this morning worried about her civics exam. She came home worried about explosive warheads.

As of this week, she's in range.

Her school is now within reach of rockets that travel farther and with far more deadly payloads than the weapons we knew just a short time ago. With blasts strong enough to shatter apartment windows seven stories in the air.

My daughter is an unarmed noncombatant. That should matter. It should matter, in particular, to progressives who believe, and justly so, that the inalienable rights of human beings, children in particular, take clear precedence over the strategic designs of nation-states and the appetites of nationalism.

It should matter, as well, when progressives turn a blind eye to war crimes committed against Israel - or, for that matter, to war crimes committed by Syria against Syrians. The assumption is that

Israel's crimes are of such Third Reich magnitude, that anti-civilian violence committed by its enemies is either negligible or justified.

I'll grant that it may be easier to see things this way from a distance. Say, the greater Akron, Ohio area, where last week Kent State history professor Julio Pino stormed out of a lecture given by Israeli diplomat Ishmail Khaldi - the first Bedouin Arab to serve in Israel's foreign service - shouting "Death to Israel!"

Prof. Pino did not explain what he meant by death to Israel. Nor did Utah attorney Robert Breeze, when Salt Lake City granted him a municipal permit to stage a 14-hour "Death to Israel" rally in Salt Lake City in 2006.

Closer to home, though, where the Islamic Jihad's calls of "Death to Israel" come wrapped in Iranian steel and 40 pounds of explosives, the message is sharp as shrapnel: a call for genocide.

"Death to Israel" means death to Israelis. It means death to the members of my family. Like many in Israel, a family which has long worked hard and consistently and intensively for the rights of Palestinians, Muslims and Christians alike, to live in safety and sovereignty in a country of their own. What we want for ourselves is no less just. It is, in fact, the very same: freedom to live in safety and sovereignty.

I'll grant also that for some progressives, it may all come down to a question of numbers. I wonder how - or if - Pino relates to the death last weekend of Moshe Ami, the father and grandfather killed by an Islamic Jihad rocket, put to death on the streets of Ashkelon for the crime of Driving While Israeli.

Pino may see disproportionality and injustice in the fact that only one Israeli died in the rocket attacks, while air strikes in Gaza killed at least 10 members of the Islamic Jihad and the Democratic Front for the Liberation of Palestine, several of them while in the act of firing rockets at southern and now central Israel.

It should matter that Israel genuinely took pains to spare Palestinian civilians in these raids. It should matter, just as the wrongheaded, ultimately self-destructive excess and civilian casualties of past Israeli operations have mattered to those who justly condemned them.

It should matter that the Islamic Jihad, Iran's direct foothold in Palestine, knows precisely what Death to Israel means. As does Iran. What is this country that Julio Pino and Robert Breeze believe deserves to die? They may think they know Israel. They may think this is one huge, Arab-loathing, mass-murdering, land-thieving plague of an illegitimate entity.

It is certainly easier on the political conscience to see us this way. But if progressives cannot see Israelis as people, if they - we - cannot summon up the same compassion and concern for unarmed combatants on both sides of a battle front, it's time they checked their ideology for holes.

The country that Pino and Breeze want to see eradicated is far more complex and worthwhile than they want to consider. It is a country in which a clear majority of the population, battered by wars and terrorism and heartbreak and frustration, still wants to see negotiations leading to a Palestinian state alongside Israel, and an end to occupation.

My daughter's civics teacher, who teaches her class about the natural rights of all peoples to liberty and security, gives extra credit to students for going to demonstrations and protests.

You can be sure that each one of those pupils, left, right or center, knows exactly what "Death to Israel" means. Not one of them, left, right or center, will stand for it. Not one of them should.

A WAR CRIME IN JERUSALEM

NOVEMBER 18, 2014

A war crime took place in Jerusalem this morning. In a house of worship. Two men armed with a meat cleaver, a gun and an axe, took it upon themselves to slaughter unarmed noncombatants at prayer.

"I've seen many, many incidents here and abroad, but I don't ever remember the sight of something like this," said Yehuda Meshi Zahav, head of the ZAKA emergency service. "Like pictures we've seen of the Holocaust - seeing Jews wrapped in prayer shawls, phylacteries on their arms and heads, lying in an enormous pool of blood on the floor of a synagogue," he said. In this arena of holiness and obscenity, we have become all too inured to murderers who invoke God's name – as they did this morning – while they massacre God's children.

And, just as ritual guides worshippers at prayer, there is a kind of ritual which informs the actions of those who find ways to explain away, legitimize, or otherwise support their crimes. We first learned this 20 years ago, when a physician named Baruch Goldstein took an assault rifle and executed 29 Muslims kneeling in prayer.

After the attack which took place in a Hebron shrine sacred to both Jews and Muslims, Jewish extremists created a fiction to suit the crime, feting Goldstein as a saint martyred in the act of preventing - the extremists' invention – a planned terror attack. Today, not an hour had passed after the synagogue atrocity, that Hamas and other Palestinian spokesmen had called the attack a "natural response" to the crimes of Israel's occupation. Palestinian extremists cast the killers as defenders of Jerusalem's Al Aqsa Mosque against the evil designs of encroachment by Jews.

This is the war that cannot be brought to an end here, the war between the Jerusalem Syndrome on one side and the Jerusalem Syndrome on the other – between the extremists on the Palestinian side who spread the lie that Israel intends to supplant Muslim worship at Al Aqsa mosque with a Third Temple, and those on the Jewish side whose incendiary actions and words, messianic, apocalyptic, potentially cataclysmic, lend fuel and fire to the lie.

Thanks to the maniacal designs of extremists, none of the rest of us - whether Jew, Muslim or Christian - are civilians any longer. We have become hostages, the pawns, the targets of extremists, demagogues, the exploiters of misfortune and petty politicians who pass for our leaders. On both sides, leaders go along with unconscionable actions by their own side, in order both to curry favor with a young hothead electorate, and to keep more extreme leaders from taking power.

Overseas, meanwhile, another pattern of response obtains. Take this morning's attack, for example. This is what you can expect: On hard leftist and avowedly anti-Israel social media sites, the first response will likely be one of two options. The first is to turn a blind eye to terror atrocities committed by Palestinians until you can report on grass-roots Israeli hotheads calling for the deaths of all Arabs, or until hardline Israeli politicians say something racist or anti-democratic, or until Israel institutes a policy or operation which progressives can easily condemn.

The second option, which you can bet will be a popular one, will be to note that the synagogue's Har Nof neighborhood is built on the site of the former Palestinian village of Deir Yassin, site of a deadly 1948 attack by the pre-state Irgun and Lehi militias.

As if one monstrous act, one massacre of civilians, could ever somehow justify, avenge – or do anything other than make much more likely – yet another.

A PLAGUE OF DARKNESS, AN ACT OF TERRORISM

JUNE 21, 2017

When I was small and the Passover Seder hit the ten plagues, I remember exactly the feeling that came over me. It was throat-fist dread.

I remember thinking about kids in Egypt then. Asking why this night was different from all other nights, because they couldn't drink the water anymore.

And as the plagues got successively worse, as the punishments got serially more terrifying, there was no changing how it would turn out.

It got dark everywhere. And then children began to die.

Last week, discussing what Benjamin Netanyahu called an "internal Palestinian matter" - a request by the Palestinian Authority, part of the PA's campaign to erode Hamas rule in Gaza - the prime minister's security cabinet voted to cut significantly the amount of vital electric power that Israel supplies to the people of the Gaza Strip.

The cabinet did so knowing that the step was liable to

spur escalation toward war with Hamas. It did so knowing that even if escalation did not occur, the Gaza Electricity Authority had warned that reducing the power supply to the Strip any further would likely lead to a humanitarian disaster.

On Monday, Israel hit the kill switch.

On the longest days of the year, in the choking heat of the Gaza summer, with days still to go on the sunrise-to-sundown fast of Ramadan, with the power supply in the Strip already severely compromised, with hospital wards and drinking-water desalination plants already closed down for lack of power, with raw sewage running in the streets and between houses, the cuts on Monday meant that Gazans, who were already somehow making do with only four hours of electricity every 24 hours, would have their power shut down for an additional 45 minutes a day.

It was the worst thing Israel's done all year. Then, on Tuesday, it got worse.

The Israel Electric Corporation cut power even further, Gaza's electricity authority announced. The new cuts left the western part of Gaza City and areas in the northern Strip with just two and a half to three hours of electricity per day.

For its part, Israel throws blame over the cuts onto the Palestinian Authority. The PA says Hamas is responsible.

But everyone knows this: Israel made its own choice. It could have said no to the PA. Israel said yes. The IDF's top generals have noted that the decision could spark escalation (Hamas actually used the term "an explosion"), but a government official contended that the army had recommended against leniency toward Hamas. In any case, senior cabinet minister Yisrael Katz said last week with regard to the power cuts, "First and foremost the Israeli interest should be protected."

So there we are. This is how this government views its own base: people who prize cruelty for its own sake. People who believe that whatever it may be, denying them water, electricity, functioning hospitals – even leaving hundreds children dead in the course of a war - all of the 1.9 million people of Gaza have it coming to them.

This government views its own base as callous, hot-blooded racists. And it acts accordingly. It wants us to know that Israel's finger on the button is the middle one. It sees itself as government of the scum, by the scum, for the scum.

The reduction in electricity has its origins in a fierce political struggle between the Palestinian Authority and Gaza's Hamas rulers. It comes at a time when the PA, which pressed Israel to cut the electricity supply, has also dramatically curtailed vital payments to Gaza's health system.

As a result, according to figures compiled by Physicians for Human Rights-Israel and the Palestinian Health Ministry, shortages in medical equipment and medications, compounded by the power shortages, are gravely affecting a range of Gazans with serious medical conditions.

Among them are 321 cystic fibrosis patients, most of them children, whose ventilators have been shut down by the electricity crisis and whose antibiotics and other medications are in short supply or unavailable.

Lack of medications and other vital goods are also said to be compromising the treatment of hundreds of cancer patients, and also of 240 babies suffering from developmental problems.

If all that were not bad enough, there are strong indications that the serious water pollution resulting from untreated Gaza sewage pouring into the Mediterranean, will soon also foul the water in Ashkelon and other areas of Israel, and could cause outbreaks of disease in Gaza and Israel both.

"The moment that there's a power outage in Gaza, there's no sewage treatment," former Israeli Environmental Protection Ministry director-general Yossi Inbar warned on Tuesday, "and raw sewage which flows into the sea will move northward, because the current goes from south to north."

"Beyond the fact that the water will be polluted and we will not be able to swim, it's also liable to shut down an [Ashkelon-area] desalination plant which is close to the border," Inbar, arguing against the power supply shut-down, told Army Radio. "There may also be pollution of ground water, accumulation of sewage in the streets or 'lakes' of one sort or another are liable to bring about dangers of mosquitoes or other pests, and disease may break out."

The border between Gaza and Israel is virtual and of no significance where the sea is concerned, Inbar continued, and the pollution could reach Ashkelon and then Ashdod-area beaches very soon. He noted that the power outage which was already denying tap water to Gazans could affect Israel's water supply as well. "Beyond the suffering of the residents of the Gaza Strip, diseases and stench will also come to us."

"The fish in the Nile will die," the Book of Exodus says of the first plague, "and the river will stink and the Egyptians will not be able to drink its water."

Across Israel, people are beginning to take action against the government's decision. Last week, the Gisha organization, an NGO which concentrates on Gaza, initiated an urgent letter to Attorney General Avichai Mandelblit, demanding that he advise the cabinet to rescind the decision to cut power.

The letter was co-signed by a large cross-section of human rights groups: Adalah, HaMoked: Center for the Defence of the Individual, The Association for Civil Rights In Israel, Physicians for Human Rights-Israel, Zazim, Bimkom, Yesh Din, Amnesty International Israel, B'Tselem, Breaking the Silence, Haqel, Akevot, Ir Amim, Peace Now, and Rabbis for Human Rights

On Monday on the beach at Ashkelon, dozens of Israeli activists, among them residents of areas adjacent to the Strip, released 150 paper lanterns into the sky to show solidarity with Gazans suffering under the cuts.

On Tuesday, the Women Wage Peace organization stated with

regard to Gaza, "This pressure cooker of millions of people in dire straits, poverty, and now without electricity will explode. Our hearts are with the mothers, children, elderly, and youth - with people who want to live."

As for the Netanyahu government, it can go on blaming the PA for this. Or it can blame Hamas. But we will not be forgiven for this. Nor should we be.

Nor should we forgive ourselves. We have brought down on Gaza the plague of darkness.

This is a punishment which targets huge numbers of people who have committed no crime. This is an act of terrorism.

PART TWELVE:
HOW DO YOU DEFEND ISRAEL?

DON'T ADVOCATE FOR ISRAEL ONE MORE DAY, UNTIL YOU'VE DONE THIS

MAY 5, 2015

You don't know me. I'm just a guy from California who once fell in love with Israel, and stayed. But if you're a person who advocates for Israel in California or anywhere else outside of here, I have a message for you.

It's the same message whether you belong to StandWithUs or J Street, the Republican Jewish Coalition or the New Israel Fund, AIPAC or Americans for Peace Now, the ZOA or Ameinu: Before you advocate for Israel one more day, you owe it to yourself and to Israel to do this: Download and open a report called "This is How We Fought in Gaza: Soldiers' testimonies and photographs from Operation 'Protective Edge' (2014)."

Read it until you can't go on. Then read it some more. Don't go back to advocating for Israel until you've read it to the end. It's not that long. Length is not the problem. Nor is language. It's just people talking. Honesty is the problem. The calmly shocking honesty of scores of brave and deeply scarred soldiers who served in that war last summer. It won't be easy to read this, nor should it be.

Whoever you are, whatever your politics, you need to know what happened in Gaza. You need to be able to begin to explain – first of all to yourself – why at least half, and perhaps many more than half, of the some 2,200 Palestinians killed in the war, were civilians, many of them children.

You need to begin to sense the scope of the devastation in large areas of the Strip, in case after case the direct result of IDF policy and directives from the higher echelons of government.

You need to begin to know what happened. You need answers.

For your own sake.

When you advocate for Israel, you need to make up your own mind. You need to know that the answers you give are honest. Real. Complete.

There will be people – lots of people – who will tell you not to read "This is How We Fought in Gaza." They will tell you that these soldiers are traitors, or defeatist radical activists, or dupes, or made up.

If you hear someone saying this, you're being flat-out lied to. Not only that, the person who tells you this is spitting on Israelis who were willing to give their very lives to defend their country and their loved ones.

There will be people who will slander and denigrate and deceive and misrepresent the organization which gathered the soldiers' stories – Breaking The Silence, itself a project of former and reserve IDF officers and soldiers.

There will be people who make their living suggesting that Breaking the Silence is part of a vast, dark, international conspiracy aimed at destroying Israel.

If you're honest about advocating for Israel, you need to think for yourself.

Whatever your politics, you should know this: These soldiers and the people of Breaking the Silence are Israeli patriots. They are advocating for Israel.

They are not naive. Anything but. They understand, as only veterans of war really can, what profoundly dangerous challenges this country faces.

They are a big part of what enables this country to continue to exist. They are striving, taking personal risks to help create an army, a country, whose actions hew closer to its own stated values and moral principles. They are patriots.

You need to hear these soldiers' stories because the government of Israel has gone silent about what happened there, keeps investigations in-house and under wraps, evades accountability for flawed decision-making, and takes no responsibility for the colossal humanitarian calamity it left when those soldiers pulled out of a Gaza turned, in many areas, to a rubble-strewn, water-deprived, power-gone desert.

You don't know me. I'm just a guy who advocates for Israel in his own way. A guy who once fell in love with Israel, and got drafted in the IDF, and served in Gaza and Lebanon and elsewhere, and who wishes to God that Breaking the Silence had been founded long before it was, in 2004.

HOW DO YOU DEFEND ISRAEL? ABUSE?
A WAR ON WOMEN? FELONY ASSAULT?

APRIL 4, 2017

Maybe it's something in the air. Maybe it's Trump. Or maybe it's the fast-approaching fiftieth anniversary of the Occupation. But something's definitely going on with hardline "defenders of Israel."

Ranks of the loudest, the crudest, the most malevolent of the pro-settlement right, have declared war. On Jews.

They've decided that these days, the best use of their energies in advocating for Zionism, is to focus on a certain sector of proudly progressive young Jews - activists who are opposed to the Occupation but who still harbor strong feelings for Israel.

To focus on them, that is, in order to abuse them, assault them, harass, intimidate, demonize, smear and, in some cases, literally bludgeon them.

All too often, this is how "pro-Israel" activism rolls these days- with a toolbox brimming with malevolence, misogyny, and even physical violence.

Using the wooden poles of Israeli, American, and pro-Kahane flags as clubs, Jewish Defense League extremists swarmed on and severely beat and kicked anti-occupation protesters last week outside the annual convention of the AIPAC pro-Israel lobby. Police later said one of the attackers was charged with felony assault, and another with assault with a deadly weapon.

A Palestinian American college instructor, a 55-year-old father of four, required 18 stitches to close wounds around his right eye. A member of IfNotNow, a movement of young Jews opposed to the occupation, was struck in the head from behind and suffered a concussion.

The JDL people tore up and burned a copy of the Koran. They called the Jewish protesters Nazis and Kapos, and told them they "should burn in an oven." They chanted "Trump, Trump, Trump." Some AIPAC attendees came out and cheered them on with high fives and fist bumps.

Jewish Defense League leader Meir Weinstein summed up the incident in a video to prospective donors: It was an "amazing experience," Weinstein said, adding that his group had "succeeded in a major way."

Three days later, Israel put on a "Stop BDS summit" at the UN. Though one of the ostensible aims of the conference was outreach to left-leaning students, speakers and much of the crowd hissed and cursed the attending members of J Street U, a widespread campus organization which opposes both occupation and BDS.

The J Street U students had come not as protesters but as participants. But this did not stop Republican lawmaker Alan Clemmons from drawing whoops and a standing ovation from the crowd, when he called J Street "anti-Semitic."

Attendees also told the J Street U members that they were pigs, that they would bring about the next Holocaust, that they should become sex slaves, and that they should "try FGM" (Female Genital Mutilation.

In fact, one of the worst facets of this supposed defense of Israel, is a war on women. Many women who care deeply about Israel, have taken leading roles in opposing occupation. And much of the worst hardline venom is reserved for them.

Last month, IfNotNow co-founder Simone Zimmerman was barraged with vicious misogyny after she spoke out against Israel's new travel ban, which would bar entry to supporters of boycotts, even if they are avowed supporters of Israel who are boycotting only the settlements.

Describing Israel as a "place which is so dear to my heart, that has been so important to my life," she noted that while she is not a BDS movement member, she viewed BDS as a legitimate tactic of non-violence in the context of applying pressure against occupation.

"I'm outraged that there's a chance that I might not be allowed to come into this country," she said in a Haaretz.com video. "I want other American Jews to be outraged that there's a chance that because of their political opinions, they might not be allowed in this country. And I want Jewish Americans to be equally outraged that this law is going to most likely disproportionally affect Palestinians and other Arab and Muslim folks."

In one of scores of hateful responses, a man who identified himself as Yaniv Kahane Zohar and a follower of JDL founder Meir Kahane, wrote in poorly spelled Hebrew on Simone Zimmerman's Facebook page:

"You are a slut whore hater of Israel / From our perspective you are not a Jew / Stay abroad there's nothing for you here in Israel / You're a spy for foreign governments / Just so you know, your account is open [we've got our eye on you] both in Israel and with the Jewish Defense League abroad.

"Wishing you infertility from cancer, and that Arabs will rape you, you bitch / Only a slut like you needs so many Facebooks."

Rabbi Jill Jacobs, who heads T'ruah: The Rabbinic Call for Human Rights, has also been a target of obscene hate mail from individuals believing themselves to be protecting and supporting Israel.

After a terror attack, a letter writer wished murder on Rabbi Jacobs' own children. "Where r u tears for the baby girl murdered today by the Palestinians you love, Jill Jacobs Jew traitor murderer whore bitch?

"Blood of this baby is on your head, and your filthy rabbinical 'T'ruah' hands. May God repay you for the suffering of the Israelis murdered and maimed in this latest terror attack by the Palestinians, murderers of Israelis going on since the 1800's. May your baby be their next victim as you dare denounce Israel."

Another wrote that "Ms. Jacobs is a self-hating Jewish cunt who rather than fight anti-Semitism, chooses to attack Jews. Fuck off."

Writer Sarah Tuttle-Singer, an American-Israeli who frequently posts on her affection for the country and its people, but whose left-leaning stances have frequently been met with rafts of online hatred, notes that the responses tend to fall into three main categories.

"There are those along the lines of 'I hope Arabs rape and kill you,' or 'She only says this because all her boyfriends are Palestinians.'"

Then, she told *Haaretz*, there is the hyper-misogyny of some women on the far right, whose attacks against women to the left of them often are armed in heavy use of the b and c words, and in maligning a targeted woman's appearance.

"It's like they have to prove they're one of the guys," she said. "The woman may be doing this to protect her place in the group, to distance herself from woman being targeted. Maybe these women feel afraid that unless they are themselves hyper-misogynistic, they are vulnerable to attack."

Finally, there is the male respondent whose approach is condescension. "This can run the spectrum from mansplaining to full-on infantilization, or trying to 'convert'" a leftist woman, she said.

"Really Sarah, it's time to stop acting out," one commenter wrote. "You're a big girl now."

It's often the case that when Israeli policies draw the criticism of a wide range of progressive commentators, counter-attacks concentrate on singling out and targeting the women among them. Prominent American-Israeli writer Rabbi Daniel Gordis has exemplified this on a number of occasions, most recently in a March 23 response to Simone Zimmerman's video statement. In a *Jerusalem Post* OpEd titled "Enemies come in many forms," Rabbi Gordis – despite having called the travel ban amateurish and a "massive, clumsy blunder" – branded Simone Zimmerman "an enemy of the state." Appearing to sneer at and dismiss her professed love for Israel,

Rabbi Gordis wasn't through yet:

"We can certainly understand why Zimmerman bristles at being called an 'enemy of the state,'" he wrote. "Yet Jews who claim to love Israel but who knowingly endorse organizations that declare that Israel is fundamentally illegitimate are actually much worse than enemies of the state. They are, many Israelis believe, just traitors."

This is the same Rabbi Gordis who suggested in a 2012 essay titled "When balance becomes betrayal," that while he had great admiration for Rabbi Sharon Brous of Los Angeles' IKAR community, she had betrayed and "utterly abandoned" both Israel and his own two sons, then serving in the army.

"What I wanted to hear was that Rabbi Brous cares about my boys (for whom she actually babysat when we were all much younger) more than she cares about the children of terrorists."

Rabbi Brous' response is well worth close study. "It ought not be an act of courage in the American Jewish community to remind us that as Jews we are called to affirm our essential humanity even in the most trying of times," it reads in part, referring to her expression of empathy for lives tragically lost in war, Palestinian victims among them. And in a direct reference to Rabbi Gordis himself, she continues in an essay on the *Times of Israel* site:

"Indeed, many of us see that as a powerful expression of loyalty to Israel, a state built on the promise of freedom, justice and peace as envisaged by the prophets ... If I remember correctly, this is a lesson learned years ago from a former teacher and friend, a rabbi who saw his job as teaching Torah and giving people hope."

And this is the same Rabbi Gordis who wrote in a widely disseminated letter to Rabbi Jacobs in 2003:

"Be honest, Jill: You say it, but you don't mean that you love Israel."

"You might wish you loved Israel, or you might believe that you're supposed to love Israel, or you might love the myth of Israel on which so many of us were raised," he added. "But you don't love the real Israel."

When controversy ensued, Rabbi Gordis later wrote Rabbi Jacobs that "I never intended to embarrass you personally, and if I did, I regret that and I apologize." He also told the Forward, "I definitely believe that she loves Israel."

And this is the same Rabbi Gordis who last year took Simone Zimmerman to task for having used "coarse language, posted by someone with aspirations for public position, [which] illustrated just childish instincts and poor parenting."

Really? Casting Simone Zimmerman as a product of bad parenting, as if she were nothing more than a child? Or "apologizing" to Jill Jacobs in a classic non-apology (if I did this, accent on the IF, then I'm sorta sorry), and then going on to repeat the same behavior, time after time?

In the end, Israel and its dominant right-wing "defenders" spent – and wasted - a fortune on the "Stop BDS" summit and on the AIPAC conference.

In the words of Brooke Davies of J Street U, the summit gave prominence to "voices from the political fringes" that are "virtually guaranteed to alienate anyone with progressive values or real concerns about the Israeli-Palestinian conflict."

"The only result of such an approach will be more and more young people giving up on Israel's future," she wrote.

As for the nastiest, the most black-hearted, the most bent and sadistic and borderline criminal shock troops of the "pro-Israel" fringe, it's time to ask: Why, really, are you doing this?

It's not for the sake of Israel, certainly. It alienates, it repulses, it sickens.

If you think the women you attack will be silenced, you're dead wrong.

If you think that the organizations you attack will roll over and be anything other than strengthened by this, then you don't know the first thing about them.

And if you think any of this will increase sympathy for Israel, you don't know the first thing about anything.

Maybe you do it for your own needs. There, I said it. Maybe you should think again about what those needs really are.

Or let me put this in another form, a tad closer to the oeuvre of condescension I've come to know so well, from you yourself:

You don't need a public. You don't need a following. You might consider professional help.

RACISM AS ZIONISM: NOT A DEFENSE. A CONFESSION

AUGUST 30, 2016

No more.

It's time to stop pretending that racism can ever be good for the Jews. Not in practice, and not in propaganda.

It's time to stop fooling ourselves that there's any reasonable benefit for Israel in practicing racism against Palestinians, whether in flagrantly discriminatory policies in East Jerusalem and the West Bank, or in less obvious but still keenly felt official inequality toward Palestinian citizens of Israel.

It's time, as well, to call out "Pro-Israel" voices who "defend" Israel by demonizing and dehumanizing Palestinians as a people, as a society, as a whole and as individuals. It's time we called racism-as-Zionism what it is: Disgusting.

It's time to stand up and answer the know-it-all social media zealots who, from the comfort and insulation of their armchairs in North American suburbs, post incessantly about how all Palestinians

— people whom they've never ever met nor spoken with — are fanatic, base, primitive, bloodthirsty Jew-hating animals, for whom Jew-murder is the be-all and end-all of their lives, and — incidentally — are also not a real people, so deserve no rights beyond the right to be expelled.

It's time to ask, if this is what "pro-Israel" means, what does this Israel stand for?

Read this:

"There is irrefutable evidence of the barbaric and genocidal nature of Palestinian society. Indeed, the reality is that, despite maintaining a 'moderate' stance to the outside world, internally the Palestinians and the Islamic State group are birds of a feather — although the Palestinians are probably more corrupt."

The author is Isi Leibler, former leader of the Australian Jewish community and ex-chairman of the governing board of the World Jewish Congress, who moved to Israel in the late 1990s and is now a columnist for *Israel Hayom* and the *Jerusalem Post*.

His column, published by both media outlets last week, held out little room for the possibility that Palestinian society is fragmented and diverse, split over a broad range of issues, among them, one state versus two, the role of religion in politics, and the question of an eventual accommodation with Israel.

Two days before the column appeared, a respected poll of Palestinian public opinion showed that 51 percent of Palestinians support a two-state solution.

But for Isi Leibler, the only thing which Palestinians truly support, is slaughtering Jews.

"While Arab hostility to Jews prevailed even during the Mandatory period, it was not comparable to the culture of death and evil that today saturates every aspect of Palestinian life," he writes.

"The Palestinian Authority has become a criminal society and can be compared to prewar Germany when the Nazis transformed their population into genocidal barbarians by depicting Jews as subhuman."

You have to hand it to Isi. A great sense of timing. His statements on Palestinians come just as the school year begins, and students, many for the first time, will be learning about the Israel-Palestine conflict.

According to Leibler, the direction of the debate over Israel is all wrong. In his view, "exposing the barbarity of our neighbors should be made the top priority in our foreign relations efforts, rather than the endless disputes over whether the minuscule 2% of territory comprising settlements (which are not being expanded) is justified."

Let's forget, for the moment, that neither the two percent figure nor the observation regarding non-expansion are, in fact, even remotely representative of the reality of occupation.

The problem is reducing millions of Palestinians, people of all ages and aspirations and backgrounds and temperaments and dreams, to a darkly uniform mass of murderers.

The problem is racism. The problem is using racism against Palestinians as a defense of Israel. Using racism against Palestinians as a substitute for information, for honesty, for any vision at all of a way forward, a way out.

In a reality like ours, a morass of rage, frustration, colossal unfairness and despair, racism has a definite allure. It's the easy way out, the tempting default, the feel-good heat sink.

The problem is not Isi Leibler. For every Isi Leibler, there are countless others, much worse, pumping out hatred against Palestinians on social media as if the hatred itself were somehow helpful, useful, as if it somehow made Israel stronger. Some people even hate Palestinians for a living. Some of them are in the Knesset. One of them now has the biggest office in the Defense Ministry.

There is a prime minister who exhorts Israeli Jews to drop everything and run out and vote for him because Arabs in droves are coming over the hill.

A prime minister who exploits a terrorist attack in Tel Aviv in order to accuse Arab Israelis as a whole of disloyalty to the state.

Is this really the best that Israel's got going for it?

Are there no better arguments from the right supporting Israel — and doing everything possible to fend off any eventuality of a Palestinian state alongside it — than branding Palestinians genocidal, barbaric criminals?

When the right uses racism as a public relations tool, all it's really doing is preaching to its choir. But what does that say about the preacher, and what does that say about the choir?

In the end, in marshaling racist arguments in order to "defend" Israel, what they've shown the rest of us, is only this:

Racism is not a defense. Racism is a confession.

WHO WILL PROTECT THEM?

OCTOBER 25, 2016

At least once a month, I thank God for B'Tselem. For Peace Now as well. Their people seek out, compile and publish facts and figures which nobody wants to hear. On subjects which make everyone uncomfortable. Like the occupation and settlements. I know that I don't want to hear them. But I need to. As Israelis, we all do. I could give you ten reasons why, but let's start with this one:

Sooner or later, what you don't know will hurt you.

That's one reason why NGOs like B'Tselem and Peace Now are so valuable. In working for rights for Palestinians, in revealing what is actually going on behind this wall or that, they are a last defense of what is so valuable and so fragile in Israeli democracy.

That's also why they are so dangerous in the eyes of Benjamin Netanyahu. But he needs to pay better attention.

Ignorance makes you vulnerable. And in a place like this, no one can afford to be vulnerable.

Least of all, Benjamin Netanyahu.

Something's come over Bibi lately. He seems to be threatened by a lack of threats. A lack of external threats, that is, of the kind posed by Iran or lone-wolf terrorists. Which brings us back to Bibi's deepest fear, the threat to end all threats: any challenge, no matter how ephemeral, to the integrity and growth and permanence of the settlement enterprise and to its shield, the occupation.

Nothing else can dislodge him. No one else has the power, the will, the leverage. Only the settlement movement and its pro-occupation supporters, here and abroad.

Which is why, when the prime minister reacted, frothing at the mouth, to the measured, well-reasoned, and informative speeches given earlier this month at a UN Security Council special session on settlements, he failed to respond to a single substantive point raised by B'Tselem's Hagai El-Ad and by Lara Friedman of Americans for Peace Now.

It's not at all clear that Netanyahu read the speeches at all. He may have been too busy bellowing on Facebook about cancelling B'Tselem's National Service worker (they don't actually have one).

He may have been preoccupied offscreen directing his beefy marionette and coalition chair David Bitan to threaten El-Ad with revocation of his Israeli citizenship (the move and subsequent legislative threats had no hope of passage).

Or he may have been too busy misrepresenting what El-Ad and Friedman actually said – condemning it with the familiar malarkey catechism of the Zionism of Our Lady of the Sacrament of Settlement, a dog-whistle to those who repeat and repeat again that "There is no 'occupation'. There is no such thing as 'Palestinians'. The only 'occupation' is that of Arabs occupying Judea and Samaria. All the Arabs want is to kill Jews."

According to Netanyahu, El-Ad and Friedman "recycled the deceitful claim that 'the occupation and the settlements' were the cause of the conflict." A total lie on Netanyahu's part. The speeches were overwhelmingly devoted to human rights, issues of democracy, and the mechanics and human consequences of settlement expansion and fifty years of occupation.

Branding B'Tselem and Peace Now "fly-by-night and delusional" organizations which "subvert democratic principles and which slander the Jewish State and the brave soldiers defending it," Netanyahu then went into an extended Facebook harangue about how "The democratic process is sacred," but that the NGOs having aired their opinions abroad was "anti-democratic."

The prime minister seems to have missed the part of Friedman's speech where she described herself as "someone who proudly and unapologetically cares about Israel and defends its existence."

"It would be unpardonable to allow ourselves to be silenced by the cynicism of some of this body's member states, whose hatred of Israel may blind them to Israel's legitimate needs and fears," she told the UN session. "And it would be inexcusable to allow ourselves to be silenced by the disapproval of some who today equate speaking unpleasant truths about Israeli policies with national betrayal."

The prime minister appears even to have ignored his own Facebook page, on which El-Ad wrote last week that "contrary to the complete overlap the Prime Minister establishes between the occupation and Israel, we insist on saying loud and clear: the occupation is not Israel, and resisting it is not anti-Israel. The opposite is true."

Here, in fact, is the crux of the matter. Netanyahu knows as well as anyone that in just over two months the world will begin to mark 2017 as the Year of the Occupation – the fiftieth anniversary of the 1967 Six Day War.

Netanyahu knows the simple and deadly algebra by which the occupation and the settlements serve as the taproot for delegitimization of Israel:

Israel minus Occupation = Democracy. Israel plus Occupation = Apartheid.

It is nearly the Year of the Occupation and Netanyahu's got nothing to offer. No plan. No hope. No room left to pretend.

All he has left to offer – apart from whipping up one last dish of hatred against Barack Obama and a potential post-election "existential threat" against the settlement enterprise – is incitement against NGOs like B'Tselem, Peace Now, Breaking the Silence, Rabbis for Human Rights, and the Association for Civil Rights in Israel.

All he has left to offer is allies like ultra-nationalist, Temple-crazed, settlement-obsessed Agriculture Minister Uri Ariel, who said that Israel would not become a "suicide state," calling the NGOs "groups that put a knife in our back."

I've lived here a long time. I've yet to meet a single Israeli – not one – who believes that Benjamin Netanyahu will do anything to the occupation except deepen it.

I've learned this much: The truly existential threat to Netanyahu's rule is hope. That's why the worst thing he could think of saying about B'Tselem and Peace Now were that they were transient phenomena. Unlike his settlements, which are eternal. Unlike his occupation, which is permanent. Unlike his rule, which is until the end of time. Too bad, with all his smarts, he seems to have ignored this lesson:

In governance, there is no such thing as forever.

He still has a lot to learn, Bibi does. As journalist Mairav Zonszein noted this week, Netanyahu and the Israeli right "have worked very hard over the years to make sure there is no daylight between Israel and the occupation — to erase any difference between Ariel and Acre, Hebron and Haifa. Ironically, this is the same thing Netanyahu accuses Palestinians of trying to accomplish. But the truth is, any distinction between the Israeli state and the occupation of the Palestinians has long been erased."

While this sounds like the end of hope, it may in fact be the beginning.

What if Netanyahu's wrong that all the Arabs want is to kill Jews all the time? The worst threat to the occupation, of course, is the possibility of extending rights to the Palestinians.

In a remarkable article this week, also in +972 *Magazine*, journalist and film maker Talal Jabari wrote:

"Quite frankly, and although this might make me very unpopular – not because people don't agree with it but because you're not supposed to discuss it publicly – but I'd rather live as a proud Palestinian who happens to be a citizen of Israel than continue the sham that we're living in now under the Palestinian Authority.

"I'd rather fight for equal rights in the courtroom and the ballot boxes, for a balanced immigration policy where Palestinians can apply and have a chance to live in their ancestral homeland which is now called Israel, but which we will continue in our hearts and in our minds call Palestine. It's time to demilitarize, is time to disband the police state, it's time to bring down the wall.

"It's time for us to stop giving Israel the excuse that we're fighting it when the overwhelming majority stopped fighting years ago."

Maybe things are finally starting to change. But we're not nearly there yet. In the meantime, as an Israeli, I've come to know that the work that organizations like B'Tselem and Peace Now do protects me. In working for the rights of Palestinians, they are defending the future of democracy for all Israelis.

But who, now, in this place of incitement, will protect them?

PART THIRTEEN:
HOW DO YOU DEFEND
PALESTINE?

TO THE LEFTIST WHO HAS NO PROBLEM WITH ROCKET FIRE ON ISRAELI CIVILIANS

MARCH 13, 2012

War again. Rockets again. Israel assassinates the commander of a radical Palestinian militia coalition in Gaza. In retaliation, gunners in the Strip fire rockets at cities across southern Israel. Israel launches a series of air strikes targeting the launch crews. More than 20 Palestinians are killed and scores injured. In Israel, questions are raised about the wisdom and the necessity of the assassination.

Sounds all too familiar. Not much new here, from the looks of it. Back pages, even in the Arab world.

In the hard left media, reports on the fighting are often more prominent, but they too have a tone of same-old. Especially when they gloss over or justify rocket attacks targeting civilians in southern Israel.

The attacks of "Israel's latest massacre in Gaza," said a headline post by commentator Ali Abunimah at his Electronic Intifada website, "have followed a typical pattern," with Palestinians responding with rockets of scant consequence, providing Israel a desired pretext for continued bombing of Gazans.

In fact, there has been much about the current fighting that has departed from the typical pattern. In an era of constraints spurred and modulated by the Goldstone Report, the carnage in Syria, Hamas friction with Assad and Iran, a new Egypt, the Iron Dome antimissile system and a host of other factors, both Israel and Hamas have made marked and largely successful efforts to limit civilian casualties on both sides of the border.

One thing that has not changed, however, is the way much of the hard left relates to the moral issues posed by Palestinian rocket attacks on Israelis.

A weekend Mondoweiss.com news account of Israeli air strikes, while acknowledging that most of the Gaza dead were Islamic Jihad fighters, notes as something of an afterthought, "Local resistance in Gaza retaliated and showered nearby Israeli settlements with homemade rockets."

In every account, the rockets are dismissed as little more than toothless, impromptu, life-affirming symbols of Palestinian refusal to surrender.

In recent years, Palestinian rocket fire has become a measure of whether progressives can be compassionate to and respectful of the rights of, civilians on both sides, or whether their attitude is, at root, no more nuanced than Palestine Good, Zionist Entity Unredeemably Evil.

An opinion piece on Tuesday suggested that Israel intentionally brought on the rocket fire in order to give its Iron Dome a trial run. "What better way to test the system," asked Linda Heard in Arab News. "It's hard to believe that a state would put its own people at risk for a test-run, but that's exactly what Israel is doing," she wrote.

In an exchange of reader comments to the Mondoweiss piece, one respondent asks, "Is it relevant that for many months there have been persistent rocket attacks launched from Gaza against Israel?"

A reply comes from another reader. "Yes, why shouldn't they

respond to Israel's violent provocations? That is human nature."

It is also a war crime. In August 2009, Human Rights Watch issued a detailed report condemning rocket strikes by Hamas and other Palestinian groups in Gaza. An HRW official said at the time that "rocket attacks targeting Israeli civilians are unlawful and unjustifiable, and amount to war crimes."

Times like this, with rockets targeting civilian populations, I wonder what it means to call yourself a leftist. I believed, and still do, that to be on the left entails a certain universality of concern for the rights and safety and welfare of people, regardless of nationality, race, religion, culture or political outlook.

There is a current on the left that argues that no one, certainly no Israeli, should tell Palestinians how to respond, how to resist. Moreover, it is unfair and plain wrong to expect Palestinians to refrain from responding to attacks, such as the assassination that set off the current spate of violence.

At the same time, just as anyone - Palestinians certainly included – has the right to tell Israelis what they think is wrong about what they do, anyone – Israelis included - ought to be able to say what they believe about the moral issues involved in targeting non-combatants.

It is wrong to simply grant a moral pass to this response, to rocket fire on civilians, whether you write this off as self-defense – which, in practice, it is not – or as human nature, or as inconsequential relative to Israeli aggression.

In his article, Ali Abunimah waved away Palestinian shelling as little more than a tool for "Israel's tired hasbara [PR] refrain about rockets, rockets, rockets."

"Israeli propaganda insists that the attacks are about preventing 'terrorism' and stopping 'rockets,'" he wrote. Abunimah cited a 2007 HRW study, "Indiscriminate Fire," which showed, accurately, that Israel employs much more powerful weaponry against Palestinians and exacts much higher casualties. What he failed to include, was the report's conclusion that:

"Both sides have shown disregard for civilian loss of life in violation of international humanitarian law (IHL): Palestinian armed groups have directed their rockets at Israeli towns.

"The 10 Israeli civilians killed by Palestinian rocket attacks since mid-2004 range from 2 to 57 in age and include four children. The attacks also have inflicted property damage and created a pervasive climate of fear in affected Israeli communities."

Just one question.

When a leftist places quotation marks around the word rockets, when a leftist terms attacks on civilian populations a matter of human nature, when a leftist dismisses rockets as crude, homemade, and unguided, or blames Israelis for their use, when a leftist notes that rockets have killed "only 28" Israelis, or sniffs or jeers at the fact that one out of seven Israelis, one million in all, are currently in rocket range – it may be time to ask, what it is, exactly, that's supposed to make a person a leftist?

WHAT WE TALK ABOUT, WHEN WE TALK ABOUT ISRAEL AND GENOCIDE

AUGUST 9, 2016

Quick — Don't think, just answer: Of all the hundreds of countries in the world, which, would you say, have no right to exist?

If your answer was "Israel," and only Israel, then this is the week for you.

The darkest day of the Jewish calendar falls this Saturday night. Tisha B'Av, the ninth day of the Hebrew month of Av, is the common anniversary of one monstrous nightmare after another, millions and millions of murders going back as far as 2,600 years, and as close by as the night terrors of living survivors of the Nazi Holocaust — genocide after genocide after genocide, each one threatening the Jews and Judaism with literal extinction.

The first two genocides saw, in each case, not only mass exterminations on the scale of modern genocides, but also the final destruction of a country once known as Israel.

Babylon and Rome, it seems, also came to the conclusion that Israel had no right to exist.

More to the point, and certainly within living memory, so did such leaders as Saddam Hussein, who prior to the first Gulf War threatened to incinerate "half of Israel" with non-conventional weapons, and Iranian Supreme Leader Ayatollah Ali Khamenei, who as recently as 2014 declared that Israel "has no cure but to be annihilated."

Jews, if nothing else, know the meaning of genocide. In their bones. It comes as little surprise, then, that when the authors of the just-published landmark Black Lives Matter movement platform decided to use the word genocide to describe Israel's actions toward the Palestinians, even hard left Jews who support the document in its entirety, recognized that there might be a problem.

Wrote avowedly non-Zionist Rabbi Brant Rosen of Chicago, "The claim that Israel is committing 'genocide' against the Palestinians undeniably pushes all kinds of buttons for many Jews."

But Rabbi Rosen, ducking his own view on the question, immediately went on the defensive. "But there are also Jews and Israelis who feel it is not an inappropriate word to use, particularly in regard to Israel's regular military assaults against Gaza."

One of them is American author Naomi Wolf, who wrote after the 2014 war between Israel and Hamas:

"I mourn genocide in Gaza because I am the granddaughter of a family half wiped out in a holocaust and I know genocide when I see it."

Lest the full Israel-as-the-Nazis connection be unclear, Wolf continues: "I stand with the people of Gaza exactly because things might have turned out differently if more people had stood with the Jews in Germany."

I respect the memory of Naomi Wolf's family. Naomi Wolf is, of course, more than entitled to her feelings and her conclusions. But I would just add this:

I used to live on a farm, and I know when shit is being shoveled at me.

I'm not going to whitewash this. Israel's "Operation Protective

Edge" [the 2014 Gaza War, in which more than 2,100 Palestinians and 73 Israelis were killed] was a horrible war. Massive Israeli firepower and Hamas rockets, mortars, and attack tunnels placed civilians at mortal risk. The IDF fire killed hundreds of children. This was horrific. Unspeakable.

But to call it genocide, you need to stretch the truth far, far beyond the breaking point. In fact, to call it genocide, I believe, you need an ulterior motive.

The motive could be as simple as an effort by strongly pro-Palestinian activists to drive a wedge between Black Lives Matter and progressive Jews. It could also be something else.

Let's cut to the chase. What are we really talking about, when we talk about Israel and genocide?

Why are so many hard leftists so strenuously, tortuously citing legal opinions and ideological formulations to shore up their contention that what Israel is doing to the Palestinians is genocide?

I believe the answer lies in the absolute inability of many hard leftists to give a straight answer to a simple question:

Does Israel have a right to exist?

For all the position papers, declarations and condemnations they issue, many of Israel's severest critics are acrobatically mealymouthed about this crux issue.

One thing we've seen this week, is that it's easier for many of the same people who evade the right-to-exist question, to brand Israel as genocidal.

Do they honestly believe that Israel's treatment of the Palestinians — as oppressive, undemocratic, violent as it much too often is — truly meets the definition of "deliberate and systematic destruction of a racial, political, or cultural group"?

Or is the act of calling Israel a country which practices genocide, a backdoor route to coming out and saying it — that there should be no state of Israel at all?

There is certainly an implicit suggestion that a nation which practices genocide lacks moral legitimacy. For those critics of Israel who take the next step, and compare Israelis to the Nazis, the World War II example implies that Israel is a nation of such singular, implacable evil, that the world must crush it by force, disband it in its entirety, and deprive it of its sovereignty.

It should be stressed that not only the hard left, but also the Jewish far right, are firmly convinced, if in opposite directions, that one side deserves a state and the other one doesn't, one side is a real people and the other one isn't, one side is truly indigenous and the other an invasive, illegitimate implant.

It should also be emphasized that many on the left have shown exemplary courage and heart in endorsing much of the Black Lives Matter platform, while tackling the charge of genocide head on.

This week, we saw activists — many of them rabbis, notably those of the T'ruah human rights organization — as well as J Street and others, standing up both for Black Lives Matter and for themselves. We've seen people who have fought against occupation with words and deeds, standing their ground and raising their voices against the unjust charge of genocide.

Still, the question remains: why should the hard left shy away from coming right out and saying that Israel has no right to exist? Israel, and no other country in the world.

Maybe for the same reason that some on the hard left can never ever bring themselves to utter one single positive word about Israel or Israelis.

Everything — whether it be disaster relief abroad, or openness to LGBTQ concerns at home, or medical treatment for a Palestinian child orphaned and critically burned by Jewish terrorists — must be sniffed away as bogus propaganda.

Maybe it's because there's a name for a belief that there is only one country on this planet which has permanently forfeited the right to exist, only one people which is so abhorrent, so incomparably wicked that it alone has no right to self-determination: Racism.

I'M NO ENEMY OF BDS.
I JUST WANT TO KNOW ONE THING

MAY 26, 2015

I first learned about boycotts when I was small. In California, farm workers with few rights and no apparent power, galvanized an entire state and much of the nation with nothing more than courage and calls for boycotts of table grapes and lettuce.

At first, their cause, winning recognition for a labor union of those who grow and harvest crops, seemed an impossibility. But this is what they had going for them: Clear goals, and straight talk.

These days, as another movement – BDS, the international campaign to boycott, sanction, and divest from Israel – speaks of its success in getting its message across, this might be as good a time as any to ask:

What does BDS really want from Israel?

I'm not asking for much. And I am certainly not asking out of antagonism. I'm just asking for clear goals. And straight talk.

I want to know if BDS wants to encourage two states - for

example, by concentrating on supporting labeling, and therefore boycott of, products from the West Bank and East Jerusalem – or if the goal is a one-state Palestine.

I believe that a boycott can only work if its organizers are clear about what they want to achieve.

I believe that a boycott in which activists describe themselves as "agnostic" about their own goals, is dooming itself to be both perpetual and unconvincing.

In April, a monthly meeting of the members of Brooklyn's Park Slope Food Co-op erupted into unprecedented chaos over Israel, a call for a boycott, and a question that hovered unanswered in the background:

Short of disbanding the country altogether, is there anything that Israel can do that would satisfy the conditions for an end to the boycott campaign?

At issue was a proposal that the food co-op boycott the Israeli-made SodaStream line of at-home carbonated beverage machines.

This is not the first time the co-op, which is one of America's largest such institutions, and one which has been called "a cultural touchstone in Brooklyn," has faced calls to boycott SodaStream. But something significant has changed since the first time.

In 2012, a BDS proposal to hold a general referendum on boycotting Israeli products was defeated in a vote which helped focus international attention on the potential impact of the movement.

At the time, BDS activists targeted SodaStream because one of its factories was located in a West Bank settlement area.

Last October – in a decision understandably hailed as a victory by Palestinian activists - the company announced that by the end of 2015, it would be moving the Mishor Adumim settlement-area plant out of the West Bank, to the northern Negev industrial area of Lehavim.

As someone who would still like to see an eventual solution based on a truly independent Palestine alongside an independent, truly democratic Israel, I saw the SodaStream move to be a positive one, one small but significant step away from occupation.

I guess I was wrong.

In the April Park Slope meeting, BDS activists resumed their campaign to boycott Israeli products, again centering on SodaStream.

"SodaStream is now moving onto land stolen from Palestinian Bedouins, who are also human beings," said Anna Baltzer, national organizer of the U.S. Campaign to End the Israeli Occupation.

Baltzer, a California-born Jewish woman who has said her grandparents narrowly escaped the Holocaust, and who was rather unfortunately described by the far-left Mondoweiss website as "The It-Girl of Anti-Zionism," continued, "We support the rights of indigenous Palestinians inside Israel, including the Bedouins. We can't end our boycott when SodaStream is simply occupying new land of Palestinians."

Is BDS then saying that all of Israel is occupied land? That the events of 1967 are, in fact, irrelevant, and that the events of 1948 are all that matters?

It is certainly their every right to believe that and say so. I just want to hear the answer. Clear. Straight.

Last month in Brooklyn, as the activists made their presentation, several members of the food co-op, their ire aroused, rushed the stage, where projected images showed IDF soldiers intimidating unarmed Palestinians, one of them blindfolded.

The co-op's newsletter later quoted one participant in the meeting as saying "This is starting to become emotionally violent." The meeting became so heated that members of the co-op board noted to the crowd that a threat against another member was grounds for losing one's membership.

Within the co-op, the issue of boycotting SodaStream, and all of Israel, remains unresolved. In a sense, though, within the BDS movement, the issue stands no less unresolved.

Unlike the government of Israel and a huge corps of paid

professionals, I am no enemy of BDS.

I just want to hear what it believes in. This is what I believe: You're either a true activist or a true agnostic. You can't be both.

PART FOURTEEN:
WHAT OBAMA SHOWED US
 ABOUT OURSELVES

IN RABIN'S LONG SHADOW, DIRE FEARS FOR OBAMA

NOVEMBER 4, 2008

JAFFA, Israel

It is a November night in this grizzled patchwork of a market town, but the air is dead. It feels thick to the skin, and much too warm, even at the place where Jaffa ends at the Mediterranean shore. Earthquake weather.

Far across the water, people are voting for president. Here the earthquake has already happened. It is November 4, the 13th anniversary of the assassination of Yitzhak Rabin, three or four miles north of here, in the heart of Tel Aviv.

Asked by a reporter if he fears a Barack Obama presidency, Eyal Barda, a 27-year-old furniture restorer in the adjacent flea market shakes his head. "I'm not afraid of Obama," he says. "I'm afraid for Obama."

"The Americans will never let a black man be president," says produce dealer Abu Yusif S'leiman, 56. "T'fu t'fu t'fu," he adds, shooing away the Evil Eye in an involuntary local reflex.

"It is time to pray for this man Obama," Barda nods. "God, watch over him."

Six thousand miles to the west, Chicago is preparing for a celebration of historic dimension, a sea of jubilation unlike anything the city has ever seen. But here, in the ancient seaport from which the prophet Jonah left for an unknowing and abrupt rendezvous with darkness, it is dread that informs the men talking about Obama.

The dread is not unfounded. Of the 27 presidents of the United States since Abraham Lincoln, more than half have been targets of assassination attempts, including each of the last seven.

The fear has only deepened with the knowledge, gained from stunning and bitter local experience, that the more far-reaching the changes a leader proposes to institute, the more vociferous his enemies are liable to become.

The trepidation is further compounded by a realization that when an assassin takes aim at a leader, the collateral damage deforms the whole of a society.

There was one Israel until shots were fired on the night of November 4, 1995, and a forever-altered Israel from that moment on.

It is that dread that informs this anniversary. This year, it began as early as September, when noted professor and peace activist Ze'ev Sternhell was wounded by a pipe bomb planted in the front walk of his home.

Last month, an extremist settler in the West Bank city of Hebron publicly and explicitly urged terrorism against Israeli soldiers. Another told Army Radio that the troops - who guard the settlers from the Palestinians who surround them - should be kidnapped or killed.

On Sunday, Shin Bet chief Yuval Diskin, whose agency's bodyguard unit is the equivalent of the U.S. Secret Service, warned that settler fanatics could resort to "live weapons - in order to prevent or halt a diplomatic process."

Then, as Americans prepared to set out for the polls on Tuesday, cabinet minister Benjamin Ben-Eliezer told a graveside memorial service for Rabin in Jerusalem that "The writing is once again on the wall, this time in bigger letters. The next political assassination is right around the corner."

Barda is right. It is time to pray for this man Obama. Pray that he will not be targeted for the color of his skin, nor for the content of his character. Pray that he will not be targeted for the height of his aspirations, nor for the inevitability of failing to reach them.

If he has promised to bring succor to infirm and indigent war veterans, to rehabilitate public schools and public works, to rebuild the economy, to make college more attainable and employment more accessible, to better equip armed forces, to launch military action with greater wisdom and pursue it with greater efficacy - and, if elected, he should fail, which, to some degree, he inevitably will - pray for his safety and for his strength to push forward.

Pray that he will not be targeted because a racist has confused the pride of the United States with a shameful past. Pray that he will not be targeted because a rifle-bound paranoid has equated taxation with treason. Pray that obsessions with fame, homebound videogame reality, and a warped sense of grandeur do not find concrete expression.

Pray for the men and women of the Secret Service, who do God's work at great personal risk.

Pray, that is, for the United States of America, and the people for whom it stands.

Take it from two people standing by the black calm sea in Jaffa tonight, an Arab and a Jew who agree on little else. Begin praying for this man Obama. They already are.

IMAGINE ISRAEL ELECTING
AN ARAB PRIME MINISTER

NOVEMBER 14, 2008

I have been trying in the last few days to make clear to Israelis the enormity of the meaning of the presidential election in the United States.

Only one thing works.

"Imagine," I tell them, "that Israel elected an Arab prime minister."

At first there is, without exception, a stunned silence.Then something dawns. Something unformed. And, in general – even with leftists – something deep inside that seems unable to wrap the head around the thought.

I mention, half in explanation, half in something approaching an effort to soothe agitated souls, that it took the United States 232 years before an African-American could be nominated and elected president.

I should have known this would happen. For weeks prior to election day in the United States, countless Israelis, many of them enthusiastic admirers of Barack Obama, told me with conviction that they believed that when Americans saw the actual names on the actual ballots in the privacy of the polling booth, their voting hands would gravitate, Ouija-like, away from Obama-Biden and over to McCain-Palin.

"Obama's great, but they're not going to vote for him," I heard, over and over.

At the time, I chalked it up to a certain historical tunnel-vision vis-a-vis Americans. From this remove, though, I have begun to realize that the Israelis were saying something of significance about themselves.

A case in point: The day after Israelis learned of the Obama victory, Israel Radio aired a discussion of "The Other" in Israeli politics, and why so many groups have remained so long and so completely out of the running for Israel's somewhat shopworn equivalent of the Oval Office.

Panelists, noting that Israel had been led, by and large, by a succession of male politicians of European descent, took turns listing the many kinds of "others" whom major parties had slighted or ruled out in putting forth candidates for the nation's top job.

Although, or perhaps because, Israel has had one woman prime minister and may soon have another, the litany began with women. It then moved on to Mizrachim, Jews who trace their ancestry to the Mediterranean region or the Middle East.

Immigrants from the former Soviet Union were mentioned next, then immigrants from Ethiopia. Settlers then appeared on the list, followed by the ultra-Orthodox, some of whom have yet to recognize the legitimacy of the state of Israel.

Astonishingly, only after foreign workers were cited - that is, non-citizens ineligible to run for the office - did it occur to one of the panelists to add to the list the nation's 1.45 million Arab citizens, more than 20 percent of the total population.

So completely has Israel's majority convinced itself that the Arab population is out of the running for the premiership - either because Israeli Jews see them as an embittered fifth column, or as a group battered into docility - that at this point, politically, Jews here do not, they cannot, see Arabs at all.

When the time comes, and an Arab becomes prime minister of Israel, I want to be a part of the victory celebration. The racists and the far-rightists among us will please pardon me, but something tells me that on that election day, just like the one last week, I won't be able to stop smiling.

MR. OBAMA, SEE THIS BEFORE YOU SEE US

FEBRUARY 7, 2013

When the rumors began about a wholly unexpected decision by U.S. President Barack Obama to visit Israel, I was in a movie theater. My wife and I had gone to see "The Gatekeepers," one of five Academy Award nominees for Best Documentary Feature.

At first, we were going to put this one off. We figured, sooner or later this one will surely be on television. We thought, it's going to be talking heads, and at that, talking heads whom we know, more or less. We thought, we'll save the big-screen outings for the epic likes of "Les Miz" and "Lincoln."

We thought wrong.

What we wound up seeing in that theater in the heart of Tel Aviv, was, among other things, the best travel guide to this Israel that Obama could hope for.

Mr. President, if you haven't already, watch "The Gatekeepers" on the biggest screen you've got.

There's something in the setting of a theater that rams home the

dark words of six men who, for the benefit of the rest of us, spent
most of their lives running an empire of shadow, ferocity, necessity
and tragedy.

In the theater, their eyes are as big as your head. You need every
bit of that kind of resolution – not only to understand, in scale,
the power these men wielded over individuals and institutions,
but also to see clearly the disarmingly complex lessons these men
have learned, and feel an overwhelming urgency to share.

You need this writ large because these men explain Israel. Give
in. Let them rip your skin off for 95 minutes. It'll grow back.

These six men know more about the occupation of the territories
captured in 1967 than any Israeli prime minister, settlement advocate,
diplomat, professor, leftist or rightist. More than anyone. Because
they built it. They made it possible. They kept it going. They know
exactly what it took. They saw what the rest of us did not. They
directed and carried out and stomached what the rest of us were
too pleased – and are still too pleased – not to know about. Not
to ask about. Not to think about.

And as much as anyone else in Israel, these men want to end
the occupation – perhaps more so, and for more good reasons, than
anyone else.

These men are what it means to be an Israeli. We are, all of us, a
part of this. Statistically, many of us in that theater, who were trained
in the military for combat or medical or other support operations,
had found ourselves from time to time working for the Shin Bet
and for the occupation. But these six men were at the crux of it all.
And they are telling us that we need to stop it.

What can a president learn from a film like this, from men like
this? Plenty.

A president can learn that Israeli governments and leaders are
structurally incapable of formulating and implementing strategy.
But the right Israeli leader – if he or she can get past the eminently

reasonable fear of right-wing assassination – can see history not only in a rear-view mirror, but dead ahead, and can lead the Israeli people through the kinds of contacts and decisions needed for an historic Israeli-Palestinian peace.

A president can learn that Israelis by and large want the occupation to end, but they have lost the sense that leaders will do what is necessary to make it end. Israelis, by and large, want settlers to stop embittering their lives and tarnishing their country's name, here and in the Diaspora, while vetoing and murdering any chance for peace.

And a president can even learn something about the American Jewish community. As soon as the Prime Minister's Office signaled its all-too-revealing dismissal of Israel's Oscar nominee ("A spokesman for Prime Minister Benjamin Netanyahu," wrote *The New York Times'* Jodi Rudoren, "said the prime minister had not seen 'The Gatekeepers' and had no plans to") voices were raised in the U.S. to discredit the film, the former Shin Bet chiefs, and their message.

"The Gatekeepers," warned Phyllis Chesler in the hard right, New York-based *Jewish Press* weekly, "will cause Israel great harm, great damage." Director Dror Moreh, she wrote, "is following a lethal narrative script against the Jewish state."

To be fair, Chesler may have been influenced as much by the "ultra-liberal" Jews with whom she watched "The Gatekeepers" at Lincoln Plaza Cinema on the Upper West Side.

"And still, these safe-and-liberal Jews push and shove and behave like Jews do on a line at the Jewish Film Festival or at the Central Bus Station in Tel Aviv. This I find funny and slightly endearing," she wrote. Hmm.

President or not, whoever and wherever you may be, go see "The Gatekeepers." With whomever you choose. Keep your mind open. This film explains Israel. Let it rip your skin off.

It's hard to imagine a time when Benjamin Netanyahu was not all in for the deepest red Republican Party, not all in for End Times Evangelicals, not a man who shared his hatred for Barack Obama and the Democratic Party as a whole, with the likes of Vladimir Putin.

It's difficult to believe that in November, 2009, Netanyahu agreed to a request by Obama for a 10-month freeze on settlement construction. Or that a half year before this, he declared of the Palestinians, "In my vision of peace, there are two free peoples living side by side in this small land, with good neighborly relations and mutual respect, each with its own flag, anthem and government, with neither one threatening its neighbor's security and existence."

It soon became clear, though, that Netanyahu's May, 2009 speech at Bar Ilan University was laced with the kinds of policy landmines designed to detonate any meaningful progress toward the idyllic future he ostensibly foresaw.

With a different Israeli prime minister, Obama could have played a crucial role in forging an accord. As it was, Netanyahu could afford to tell elegant lies about wanting peace in the Holy Land, because he would see to it that, no matter who was in the White House, it was already tragically too late.

THIS YEAR FOR PASSOVER, I'M BURNING MY CYNICISM

MARCH 24, 2013

T he president of the United States came by a few days ago. Caught us by surprise. Going in, no one knew quite what to make of the visit. We had to fit Passover preparations around it. His people told us to expect very little, and I doubt if any of us expected even that.

Lord, how I love it when we're all wrong.

No matter what we think or practice, no matter where we lie on the scales of politics, religion, class or ethnicity, we're so sure of ourselves all the time. We're so very certain that things will work out badly - or, more often than not, stay fixed at the terrible level of emotional subsistence that all we've grown to call home.

Lord, how shocking it is when we're forced to deal with something good.

When the president spoke to students Thursday evening, even before the ovations finally subsided, the cynicism began. From the hard right and the hard left, from here to Seattle, a consensus: it's delusional to think that this will change anything, improve anything, be any more than one more load of pap.

Enough. Who has patience anymore for the ennui, the omniscience, the certainty of failure. The mind that can never be caught open. The eternal cynicism.

Who has the time to waste on it anymore, or the energy? Something is stirring here. The cynics can choose to ignore it or belittle it. Sure, maybe they'll be proven right, and it will all go up in smoke. But something may be stirring. A sea beginning to part.

Monday morning, when our family collects the last crumbs of bread in the house and burns them in the traditional introduction to Passover, I'm throwing in something more this year, along with it: my cynicism.

I'm not sure what it's going to feel like, looking behind and below and in dark places and hard-to-reach corners and dislodging it. I'm not sure how I'll feel, going without it. Stripped of armor, probably. Pale and pasty, naked maybe. A little stupid. But better off.

This Passover, I'm going on a fast from cynicism.

I'm going to give it a week. But I'm going to give it everything I have. And when this week is done, I'll do everything I can to give it another week. And another.

The president's speech was one step toward the sea that may be parting. The fact that an Arab Israeli woman won The Voice balloting was another. Let the hard left call this nothing, and the hard right call it enough. It was neither. But it was important. Because it was another step forward.

If it all stops here, the cynics, in their consummate tedium, can smile that knowing half-smile of theirs - the hard right which says there can't be peace because the Palestinians are all violent terrorists who want the Jews dead and the land to themselves, and the hard left, which says there can't be peace because any Jewish state is inherently unjust and illegitimately ethnocentric, and because the Israelis are all colonialist exploiters who want the Palestinians expelled and the land to themselves.

But what if there were one further step, and another? What if people come to the realization that the hard left and the hard right offer them, in the end, nothing? Nothing but the worst of what we have now.

As I was given to understand, the idea of Passover is to take the rhythms and the long-fixed furniture of life, and to upset them, shift them, clean them out – all to restore a lost sense of proportion and a lost sense of perspective, of vision. A fresh start. A Spring.

By tradition, when the Children of Israel reached the Red Sea on their way out of Egypt, out of slavery, the sea did not part for them. They began to wail and weep, suspecting they should have chosen to keep the life they were accustomed to, bitter and hopeless as it was. The cynics among them said it was delusional to think that there was a way ahead.

One person, though, Nahshon, took one step into the water, and then another. He kept walking until the water reached his waist, his chest, his neck. He took one step after another until the water was above his mouth and touched his nose, threatening to drown him. Only then did the sea part.

Something's in the air just now. If it's real, it will be scary. But if it is real, and people take one step after another, even if it takes years and years, what waits on the other side is peace.

If we don't take those steps, if we give in to cynicism, we'll be living this bad imitation of exile on and on, drowning in it, enslaving ourselves as we enslave others. If we do that long enough, the sea will come to us. And it won't stop at our mouths.

Who has time or patience anymore for the same old useless, empty fights, the way-cool faux righteousness of cynicism? There's too much waiting for us on the other side.

PART FIFTEEN:
TRUMP. A WHOLE OTHER LEAGUE

"Show me your friends," the old saw goes, "and I'll show you your future."

In Donald Trump, Benjamin Netanyahu found the political ally of his most cherished dreams. Seemingly out of nowhere, in 2013, Trump, not yet a candidate for president, released a video resoundingly endorsing Netanyahu, then fighting a race for re-election. "A terrific guy!" Trump declared. "A terrific leader! ... He's a winner, he's highly respected, he's highly thought of by all!"

Netanyahu would return the favor many times over. One example came at the height of Trump's battle with Hillary Clinton for the presidency. Netanyahu posted a video pointedly hinting that the Obama-Biden administration which Clinton had served as secretary of state, backed a sweeping future "ethnic cleansing" campaign against West Bank settlers, should an independent Palestinian state come into existence,

Netanyahu may have helped Trump much more by going altogether mum on an evident truth: Trump's rise to power constituted the greatest victory for anti-Semitism in the United States since the Lindbergh era, granting an implied imprimatur to legions of far-right bigots.

THE LAST TIME I WAS CALLED A KIKE,
I WAS A FOURTH GRADER. 'TIL TRUMP

OCTOBER 5, 2016
One month and three days before U.S. Election Day

I don't remember the first time I got called a kike as a kid. But I remember the last.

I was a fourth grader. I wound up in a short fight with a bigger kid. All I remember is that he was a guy with trouble at home and trouble inside, and harbored some grievance about our respective places in line for the movies.

The adult advice I got at the time was that anti-Semitism – of the long-ago type that had made changing our family's immigrant last name a key part of my dad's application process for college – was on the ropes. It would soon be extinct, I was assured, like polio. "Just let it go, or it'll get worse."

It was bad advice. It was bad advice then, and it's bad advice now. That fight was the last time I ever got called a kike. Until this year.

Until this presidential campaign. Until Donald Trump.

Until, that is, white supremacists and American Neo-Nazis and Klansmen and the technology-borne alt-right gleefully began to hear in Trump's dog-whistles, in his retweets of their filth, and in his belated, disingenuous, or nonexistent disavowals, the sound of a common cause, and a golden opportunity.

Actually, at the periodic "kike" and "Jew underminer" call in my inbox, I've been let off easy.

Two weeks ago, Washington Post columnist Anne Applebaum wrote a piece titled "In Poland, a preview of what Trump could do to America."

The Breitbart news site – whose on-leave executive chairman is Trump Campaign Chairman Stephen Bannon – then ran an article which said of Applebaum that "hell hath no fury like a Polish, Jewish, American elitist scorned."

The attack on Applebaum followed a torrent of online abuse directed at Jewish reporters, or reporters with Jewish-sounding names, or reporters married to Jews, whose words were seen as uncomplimentary to Trump or his wife.

The attacks began in earnest early in the year, following the February South Carolina primary, when reporter Bethany Mandel was attacked as a "slimy Jewess" and was told she deserved "the oven" for writing about Trump's relatively large number of anti-Semitic supporters.

"As any high-profile Twitter user with a Jewish-sounding last name can tell you, the surest way to see anti-Semitism flood your mentions column is to tweet something negative about Donald Trump," Mandel later wrote in the Forward.

"My anti-Trump tweets have been met with such terrifying and profound anti-Semitism that I bought a gun earlier this month. Over the coming weeks, I plan to learn how to shoot it better."

The attacks only grew in intensity, scope, and, if alt-right sites are to be believed, in organization of harassment. In April, prominent feature writer Julia Ioffe published a profile of Melania Trump in GQ.

Ioffe, who is Jewish, was barraged with death threats and crank callers, one of whom played recorded speeches of Hitler on her phone line, another who told her that her face would look good on a lampshade.

On Twitter, Ioffe was pictured as if interred in Auschwitz, with the caption "Julia Ioffe at Camp Trump."

Melania Trump later said that while her "fans maybe went too far," Ioffe had "provoked them."

Ioffe, for her part, remarked, "The irony of this is that today, when I was getting all of this horrible anti-Semitic shit that I've only ever seen in Russia, I was reminded that 26 years ago today my family came to the U.S. from Russia."

"We left Russia because we were fleeing anti-Semitism," Ioffe told the Guardian. "It's been a rude shock for everyone."

Social media-borne Holocaust imagery has been directed at countless journalists, among them Huffington Post Senior Polling Editor Natalie Jackson, pictured on Twitter locked into a gas chamber, with a beaming Donald Trump, dressed as a Nazi officer, ready to push a green button marked "GAS."

"Your clothes will be removed and fumigated. You will be held down and given a bath," the tweet reads.

For many journalists, especially millennials, the barrage of pro-Trump, alt-right harassment, threats, and mass trolling, has been their first brush with anti-Semitism.

And not only journalists.

"What Trump has brought to the surface is, in many ways, the first blatant anti-Semitic experience for the vast majority of American millennials," Ohio State sophomore Zach Reizes, 19, told Politico Magazine.

The quote is from an extraordinary report this week by Politico's Ben Wofford. In an allusion to the large numbers of Jewish organizations who have refrained from challenging Trump on the anti-Semitism issue, Wofford notes that among Jews the pro-Trump outrages of the alt-right have "heightened a divide between young and old, left and right: Progressive young Jews learning to form the words 'anti-Semitism,' often for the first time — even while they take umbrage at their right-leaning scolds who, now into October, have kept up a deafening silence on the topic of Trump."

Through it all, Jew-hating Trump supporters have reserved some of the most toxic of their venom for staunch Republicans and conservatives who happen to be Jewish. They've even coined an obscenity just for them: Kikeservatives.

As in this headline on the Infostormer website: "Kikeservative [Susan] Goldberg Defends Kikeservative [Jonah] Goldberg from Patriotic Jew Exposers."

Back in May, when former KKK leader David Duke said that white supremacists saw great promise in Trump as "our white knight, our advocate, our person," he added that the Jewish enemy within was not far off: Jewish neo-conservatives who oppose Trump.

"I think that like so often happens, Jewish chutzpah knows no bounds," Duke said in his radio broadcast. "These Jewish extremists have made a terribly crazy miscalculation because all they're really going to be doing by doing the 'never Trump' movement is exposing their alien, anti-American majority position to all the Republicans." Trump helped throw the holding tanks of anti-Semitism wide open in July, when he gave national exposure to, and then proceeded to defend, a white supremacist-designed meme in which Hillary Clinton appears flanked by a red six-pointed star on a background of a pile of hundred-dollar bills.

Rabbi Abraham Cooper of the Simon Wiesenthal Center was quoted at the time as saying that Trump's comments, even if unintended, had legitimized the kind of bigotry represented by the likes of David Duke, whom the Anti-Defamation League has called "perhaps America's most well-known racist and anti-Semite."

In Cooper's view, "The anti-Semitics, the David Dukes, and their younger supporters—they're having a field day." He added that it was important that Trump make clear to "these people who have crawled out of the sewers that he doesn't speak for you, he doesn't represent you, that's not what America is all about."

For alt-right figures like Andrew Anglin, however, that is exactly what America is all about. In response to the anti-Clinton meme, Anglin of the avowedly pro-Nazi Daily Stormer website, tweeted: "Glorious Leader Tweets Hillary Image With Dollars and Jew Star." In a piece set under a winking image of a youngish Adolf Hitler, Anglin wrote of Trump that "the evangelicals will listen to his pro- Israel statements, while we will listen to his signals. Everybody wins.

They can even report on me saying this is a dog-whistle – it doesn't matter."

The website, named for the rabidly anti-Semitic Nazi tabloid Der Sturmer, goes on to explain that under alt-right ideology and values, "Jews are behind all of the things which we are against, the diametric opposite of everything that we stand for. In a very real sense, defeating and physically removing the Jews will solve every other problem. None of this would be happening if it were not for the Jews."

Not all Jewish organizations have been silent in the face of Trump's anti-Semitic supporters. "We've been alarmed that Mr. Trump hasn't spoken out vociferously against these anti-Semites and racists and misogynists who continue to support him," Anti-Defamation League leader Jonathan Greenblatt said in July. "It's been outrageous to see him retweeting and now sourcing material from the website and other online resources from this crowd."

There's a reason why so many anti-Semites are going for Trump. It's not that he's an anti-Semite, though many of his public statements about Jews being good with money suggest that he may well be. But he's clearly also something worse. He's an influential public figure who trades on anti-Semitism, who benefits from it, who enables and tolerates and excuses and pumps it, and who, most crucially, cannot afford to lose the votes of his admirers who hate Jews.

Just as he cannot afford to lose the votes of his admirers who bear strong prejudice against women, Muslims, Hispanics, African-Americans, Asian-Americans, Native Americans and others.

He has given a podium to bigotry, an arena stage to hatred.

Donald Trump may be the grandfather to a Jewish baby. But if that baby grows up in a nation ruled by Trump, one day he may be the one Jew at that dinner table to ask why his grandfather helped make anti-Semitism American again.

Reacting to the firestorm over Trump's vulgar characterizations of women, Anglin this week held Jews responsible for the criticism. "We are being kiked so hard it'll make your head spin," he wrote. "I hate all these people. We're on the brink of a nuclear war, and these scumbags are talking about pussy-grabbing."

If we lose this election," Anglin concluded, "the Jews are going to be blamed."

For many American Jews, the surge of virulent far-right and neo-Nazi anti-Semitism unleashed by the rise of Donald Trump came as a terrible shock. Born into a post-Holocaust America, Jew-hatred seemed to have been relegated to history books, a thing very much of the past.

Israelis, among them Benjamin Netanyahu, now strongly wedded to Trump, had largely ignored mounting far-right U.S. anti-Semitism, even as they swiftly condemned attacks on the Jews of Europe, and denounced pro-Palestinian groups in America as anti-Semitic.

There was, however, one far right, anti-Jewish and anti-immigrant attack that neither Netanyahu nor Trump could ignore. For American Jews in Israel, the massacre was an earthquake, shattering long-held certainties about the place of Jews in an increasingly self-defined Christian America.

THERE WAS A POGROM THIS WEEK, LORD. IN THE UNITED STATES OF AMERICA

OCTOBER 30, 2018

El Malei Rachamim - God who is made of mercy.
El Malei Chemlah, God who is made of compassion.
El Malei Or, God who is made of Light:
God whose house has been defiled by a cruel and monstrous and
godless darkness – bless the survivors.

There was a pogrom this week, Lord. In the United States of America.

In Your house. In that congregation which is an extended family. During a prayer service. Welcoming a newborn. That very moment, Lord. Shattered in slaughter.

There was a terrible darkness in Your house, Lord. But then there was light.

It came from Pittsburgh, from Jews and Muslims and Christians standing together, mourning together, refusing to hate, refusing to surrender. In Your house. Refusing to forget.

The light has only spread, across the country and beyond.

May the One who grants healing, help to mend those who loved and lost Jerry Rabinowitz.

A doctor whom families trusted and adored. A doctor who treated HIV patients and embraced them when others would not. A doctor who, when heard shots fired at the Tree of Life congregation, rushed in from another service to help the wounded.

Jerry, who lived 66 years. Slain because he came to shul on Shabbat. Murdered for being a Jew.

Your children who survived are not broken. Their love is more powerful by far than hate. This is the meaning of these vigils, these prayers, their vows:

We who have survived this terrible darkness – we, all of us - are light.

May the One in whose image we are all created, see to those who loved and lost Cecil and David Rosenthal.

Two brothers, inseparable, who welcomed fellow congregants to the Tree of Life synagogue. Beloved, sweet, gentle. Two brothers who did not allow their disabilities to limit them.

Cecil, who lived 59 years, and David who lived 54 years. Slain because they came to shul on Shabbat. Murdered for being Jews.

The memories of Your children who were slaughtered, their good works, their giving spirits, are alive now in the hearts of all those who did not know them in life.

Their memories are, even now, a blessing:

May the One who sends angels, watch over those who loved and lost Bernice and Sylvan Simon.

Married 62 years ago in the synagogue in which they were killed. Kind. Generous. Loving. Gracious.

Bernice, who lived 84 years, and Sylvan, who lived 86 years. Slain because they came to shul on Shabbat. Murdered for being Jews.

May the One who sustains life, comfort those who loved and lost Rose Mallinger.

Rose, witty and buoyant and razor-sharp, whose family said she knew her children, grandchildren and great-grandchild better than they knew themselves.

Rose, who lived 97 years. Slain because she came to shul on Shabbat. Murdered for being a Jew.

May the One who gives strength when all strength is gone, come to the aid of those who loved and lost Daniel Stein.

Daniel, who loved nothing more than his grandson and the Tree of Life synagogue - the grandson whose bris had taken place in the very room where Daniel was slaughtered.

Daniel, who lived 71 years. Slain because he came to shul on Shabbat. Murdered for being a Jew.

May the One who repairs the world, look after those who loved and lost Joyce Fienberg.

Joyce, a researcher in the field of learning and teaching. An engaging, warm and elegant person.

Joyce who lived 75 years. Slain because she came to shul on Shabbat. Murdered for being a Jew.

May the One whose universe is constantly evolving, be a source of solace to those who loved and lost Richard Gottfried. Richard, who was a dentist, also aided interfaith couples in preparing for marriage.

Richard, who lived 65 years. Slain because he came to shul on Shabbat. Murdered for being a Jew.

May the One to whom we turn when burdens cannot be borne, support those who loved and lost Melvin Wax.

Melvin, a person of positive outlook, a quiet man who loved to tell jokes. Melvin, who was leading Shabbat services when the slaughter began. Melvin, who lived 88 years. Slain because he came to shul on Shabbat. Murdered for being a Jew.

May the One who sets in motion birth and growth and generations, watch over those who loved and lost Irving Younger.

Irving, who coached kids in baseball, and who made worshippers feel welcome and a part of services.

Irving, who lived 69 years. Slain because he came to shul on Shabbat. Murdered for being a Jew.

Your children are not forgotten, Lord. Not in Pittsburgh, and not in Jeffersontown, near Louisville, Kentucky.

May the One who created us all, who made us human, grant solace and hope to those who loved and lost Maurice Stallard.

Maurice was with his 12-year-old grandson, buying poster board for the grandchild's school project, when a terrorist, unable to enter and violate a nearby church, entered the Jeffersontown store where they were shopping, and opened fire.

Maurice lived 69 years. Slain when he went to a store to help his grandson. Murdered for being an African-American.

And may the One who to whom we turn when words fail and tragedy overwhelms, grant peace to those who loved and lost Vickie Lee Jones.

Vickie Lee, whose life work was helping veterans in need, and who had moved to Jeffersontown because she wanted to be safe.

Vickie Lee lived for 67 years. Slain because, the terrorist said, "Whites don't kill whites." Murdered for being African-American.

There was a pogrom this week, Lord. But look again. Something better is coming.

El Malei Rachamim, God who is made of mercy. El Malei Chemlah, God who is made of compassion. El Malei Or, God who is made of Light. God whose house has been defiled by a cruel and monstrous and godless darkness – bless us, the survivors.

Good will come of this. The memories of the fallen are, even now, a blessing.

The election of Donald Trump did something to us all. In the case of Benjamin Netanyahu, it freed something in him, emboldening him, unleashing forces in him he had managed, until then, to keep under relative restraint.

After an eternity in office, Benjamin Netanyahu was finally able to show us who he truly was.

THIS ISRAEL WOULD HAVE SIDED WITH THE CONFEDERACY

SEPTEMBER 12, 2017

If the American Civil War were being fought today, there's every chance that the Israel of Benjamin Netanyahu would side with the South.

I don't say this because of Israel's critics, who have often and persuasively pointed to the similarities between Israeli policies and those of the segregated Jim Crow South. Nor because of the many ways in which official treatment of the Palestinians living under occupation in the West Bank bears points of resemblance to the administration of slave states in the antebellum period.

I reached this conclusion independent of photographs showing white supremacists displaying the flag of the state of Israel alongside the Confederate battle flag or the mail-order sales of lapel pins with the Star of David alongside the Southern Cross.

No. It was none of these. It was *Israel Hayom*.

On Monday, Israel's largest-circulation daily newspaper and the authoritative house organ of the prime minister himself, published an opinion piece by Likud elder statesman Zalman Shoval, one of Netanyahu's lieutenants of the longest and most loyal standing.

There was no point in Shoval wasting a column on defending the prime minister's son Yair for having posted a meme composed of obscenely anti-Semitic images – the Monday paper had already done that in a front-page editorial by a columnist who was at one time on the payrolls of both *Israel Hayom* and the Prime Minister's Office.

So Shoval, Netanyahu's onetime ambassador to Washington and a staple of Likud's all-powerful Central Committee, turned his attention to a somewhat more unexpected topic: defending the honor and image of the Confederate States of America and of the commander of the South's main field army, Gen. Robert E. Lee.

In a jewel of revisionist history worthy of the authors of sentimental pro-South fiction and Dixiecrat segregationists, Shoval wrote: "Even though the American Civil War is usually presented as a righteous struggle to free the slaves, the reasons and motivations for the war were much more complicated, including an economic struggle between the agrarian South and the industrial North."

Here's where we begin to see how Netanyahu's Israel might see itself identifying with the sensibility and sensitivities of southern whites, the shadows of victimhood, the unacknowledged trials and virtues of the much maligned and the wholly misunderstood.

"Moreover," Shoval continues, "the war was one of principles, a struggle between two basic political views: Is the U.S. a confederacy of sovereign states as the South maintained, or is it the union itself that is sovereign, with policy being formulated by the executive, legislative and judicial branches in Washington, D.C.?"

Now it all begins to swing into view – the Israel we have come to know, the Old South we have come to resemble: a society obsessed by myth, animated by a lifeblood of slights real and imagined, rotted with denial over its oppression of minorities, unable to curb the violently racist fanatics its own side has spawned, segregated, living in mortal, paralyzing terror of a rebellion by the millions deprived of the most basic of human rights.

Criticism of Israel? The occupation as Sweet South sentimentalism thinking goes: Just whose side do you think God is on? Look at how the other side lives, thinks, sins. Our critics carp and lie about the occupation and its brutality, the settlements and their lavishly subsidized lawlessness, the anti-democratic legislative agenda, the racist pronouncements from the very top down. The fact is that they would criticize us no matter what. The critics are jealous. They can't begin to understand us, nor do they try. Theirs are the misapprehensions of hatred – not ours.

What side would Netanyahu's Israel have chosen in the war? Shoval does not raise the question, but early on, his op-ed hints at an answer.

Referring to the Charlottesville, Virginia, "Unite the Right" violence, Shoval notes that "thousands of Jews fought in the ranks of the Southern army during the American Civil War. They even earned the friendship and support of Lee, as opposed to Gen. Ulysses S. Grant, the commander of the Northern army and later the 18th American president. Grant happened to be an anti-Semite who issued General Order No. 11, which expelled all Jews from the military district under his control in late 1862."

In a statement which says more about Shoval, and Netanyahu's Israel, than it does about the flesh-and-blood Lee, Shoval declares: "Ironically, Lee was not at all a racist."

Shoval cites as proof a letter Lee wrote to The New York Times two years before the Civil War, which implied that Lee might free his own slaves within five years.

Nonetheless, in practice, "documents show Lee was cruel to his slaves and encouraged his overseers to severely beat slaves captured after trying to escape," The Associated Press wrote last month.

In a passage worthy of study – and foreshadowing hardline contemporary *hasbara*, Lee wrote in an 1856 letter to his wife that while "slavery as an institution, is a moral & political evil in any Country. . . The blacks are immeasurably better off here than in Africa, morally, socially & physically. The painful discipline they are undergoing is necessary for their instruction as a race, & I hope will prepare & lead them to better things. How long their subjugation may be necessary is known & ordered by a wise Merciful Providence."

To put Shoval's account into perspective, Georgia-born Lee biographer Roy Blount Jr. wrote in 2003 that after Lee's death in 1870, "Southerners adopted 'The Lost Cause' revisionist narrative about the Civil War and placed Lee as its central figure. The Lost Cause argued the South knew it was fighting a losing war and decided to fight it anyway on principle. It also tried to argue that the war was not about slavery but high constitutional ideals."

In Netanyahu's Israel there is something very akin to the Confederate-friendly vision of the Lost Cause. In place of a rose-hued vision of the sweet-tea antebellum South, there is a sharp longing for a lost Greater Israel, an ante-Intifada, pre-Gaza Disengagement mythical land of unfettered settlement, happy Palestinian neighbors, minimal demands for democracy and equality, and permanent, in fact, eternal, Occupation – without resort to the O word.

Recalling the plight and the politics of disadvantaged whites in the slavery-era and Jim Crow south, today's Israel is also a markedly classist society, with restricted upward economic mobility for generations of those who have enthusiastically provided the electoral and popular backbone for Netanyahu's rule – working-class Jews.

There was a time when Israelis joked, half in hope and half in reservation, that this country was becoming the 51st of the United States. No longer. Now it feels more like the 12th state – of the Confederacy.

PART SIXTEEN:
UN-JEWS AND NONE JEWS

Both in Israel and the Diaspora, the schism between the Netanyahu-adoring right and the prime minister's left-liberal Jewish critics grew ever deeper, strengthening Netanyahu politically even as the confrontations eroded Israel as a society and as a once-unifying lodestone for Jewish communities. The rift also weakened Israel's support internationally, doing significant damage to crucial bi-partisan backing from Israel's indispensable ally the United States.

Across the Jewish world, the debates often turned ugly, as in a breathtakingly nasty 2021 "pro-Israel" essay in Tablet Magazine titled "The Un-Jews." The piece, by historian Gil Troy and widely respected Israeli elder statesman Natan Sharansky, was a prolonged hatchet job on Jews who decry present-day Israel and/or Zionism, as opposed to "most actual Jews."

Under a Stalin-era Yiddish-language poster of a huge sow and a corps of piglets stretching to the horizon, the essay compares these "un-Jews" to notable Jewish traitors to their people, reaching back into history for corresponding villains. Among them: "One of the Roman generals who helped raze Jerusalem and destroy the Second Temple may have been the first un-Jew."

THE NEW SELF-HATING JEW

MARCH 24, 2011

This is no time for this. This is a war. Palestinian rockets are slamming into major Israeli cities. Israeli aircraft and armor are firing on Gaza. A bombing rocks Jerusalem. All over the south, people are taking cover and praying.

This is no time for the ruling coalition and the Knesset to squander its time in driving a wedge between Jewish and Arab citizens of Israel. This is no time for Israel to alienate its supporters abroad, by holding Knesset hearings alleging that thousands of American Jews who openly call themselves supporters of Israel, really aren't.

This is no time for Israel to pass laws which, at face value, support segregated housing and curb freedom of expression – just as Israel Apartheid Week is celebrated in a hundred cities the world over.

This is the worst of times to make friends and family into enemies. Who could possibly see the good in any of this?

Welcome to the new Zionism. Welcome to the new self-hating Jew, the legion of professed lovers of Israel who want Zionism only to themselves. And who hate the Jews who want to see Israel change.

Which is, at this point, most Jews.

The message of the new self-hating Jew is this: You don't like this the way it is? We don't need you. We don't need anybody. We don't even need Obama, so what makes you think you've got any place here at all?

This is the message: We're one big happy start-up here, and we don't need Debbie Downers to spoil the party. We take our Judaism straight-up frum or none at all. Our neighbors are, regrettably, Nazi scum on two legs, so we'll take our Israel with all of the West Bank and East Jerusalem, thank you very much.

No others need apply.

We want you gone. You Jews. And we know how to make it happen:

INCITEMENT: Take an Israeli patriot like [respected leftist elected official and then-New Israel Fund leader] Naomi Chazan, take out expensive billboards and newspaper ads showing her as a cartoon villain, Hulk green with a grotesque horn thrusting from the center of her forehead, and hang all of Israel's problems – from accusations of disproportionate military force to charges of rampant discrimination – squarely on that horn.

BOYCOTT: Take the fastest growing pro-Israel organization in North American Jewish communities and on U.S. campuses, the dovish J Street, and have Israel's ambassador shun it even as he attacks it.

Then, despite the threat of imminent war and the specter of renewed terrorism, have a Knesset committee devote an entire session to "investigating" J Street's claims to being Zionist and pro- Israel.

DELEGITIMIZATION: If a lifelong, ardent Zionist like Theodore Bikel announces that he backs an artist's boycott specifically against settlements, insist that any boycott against the settlements must be considered an attack against all of Israel.

Then decide that groups that take positions similar to Bikel's must be denied membership in the wider Jewish community.

For Jews truly interested in alienating most other Jews and having Israel to themselves, the Wednesday Knesset hearings against J Street reached new heights. Said the American Jewish Committee, whose own politics are appreciably to the right of J Street: In holding hearings on whether a voluntary American Jewish organization is indeed a pro-Israel lobby, the Knesset committee has interfered in an entirely inappropriate way in the internal affairs of the American Jewish community.

Like it or not, an ancestral homeland sets the tone for an entire people. It may provide cultural and spiritual inspiration, a richness of language and the arts, a calm, profoundly positive sense of self and self-worth which comes of quiet pride in roots.

Or it may become a *shondeh.*

"Most American Jews want to feel proud of the Jewish State, not frustrated or ashamed," Gary Rosenblatt, editor and publisher of the New York Jewish Week, wrote in a landmark opinion piece this month.

The essay, titled "When Israel becomes a source of embarrassment," is shocking perhaps less for its substance than for its centrist author and its context, the highest-circulation of all North American Jewish newspapers.

This is a primary voice of mainstream Jewish America. And the message is that Israel's actions and statements have direct consequences on the present and future of the largest community in the Jewish Diaspora.

"Federation fundraisers say that even big givers worry aloud about Israeli policies and the negative impact such policies are having on their children," Rosenblatt writes.

Gary Rosenblatt may think he's a strong supporter of Israel. And he is. But in the eyes of the new self-hating Jew, Gary Rosenblatt is expendable. He has an independent opinion, which may make him disloyal. His moderate voice is that of the majority of North American Jews, which makes him all the more suspect, all the more undesirable.

They are Jews who want to take pride in a homeland which fosters democracy, civilization, a conversation with the world as a whole. They are Jews who abhor faith-based bigotry against non-Jews. They are Jews who believe in self-determination, for Palestinians and for Jews alike.

This is the message of the new self-hating Jew: There is no place for the likes of Gary Rosenblatt in the new Zionism. Nor J Street. Nor the New Israel Fund. Nor Jews who oppose the occupation. Nor Jews who believe that non-Orthodox Judaism is valid and important.

A people which hates its own. A people which dwells alone. We are Zionism, the new article of faith has it. We don't need anyone. And we certainly don't need you. You, you liberal Zionists, you progressive Zionists, you leftists and former Zionists who for some reason still care about Israel, you're the new Palestinians. You have no right to your ancestral homeland, the place your people came from. Because we're here now, and we're not going anywhere.

But the new self-hating Jew may yet be in for a surprise. There's another generation of Jews coming up. One which has grown tired of the aging explanations for an Israel which lives for, and dies as a result of, occupation. "We love Israel unconditionally," J Street student leaders said in a recent essay.

"We have a moral commitment to a national home in which Jews can determine our own political destiny. We have a religious and cultural connection to that home. We do not, however, support Israels policies unconditionally. That is not true love."

Israel, with the self-hating right in the lead, can no longer afford to make war on its own. Not now. It is one war Israel cannot afford to win.

It served the purposes of Netanyahu and of Republican Jews abroad to entirely alienate liberal-leaning young Jews from Israel, which, in theory, would lessen dissent and leave the Jewish community to rightist leaders. For quite a while, it appeared that this approach might succeed.

THE TRIBE OF THE NONE JEW

MAY 29, 2012

Years ago, our family met a woman who had lived her entire life on the Hawaiian island of Kauai. Hearing that we were Jews who lived in Israel, she asked us, straight out and calmly, "What tribe are you from?"

I thought I hadn't heard right. She told us that she had learned in church that her people were from the tribe of Ephraim. She tried asking the question in a different way. "Who are your people?"

In one form or another, and often – as we were that day - without an answer, it's a question that's been coming up more and more. It's in the background of an American Jewish Committee study, which found that, on the average, if U.S. Jews came to "profess a faith different from the one in which they were raised," their designation of their "Current Religion" was overwhelmingly – by a factor of 59.6 percent - "None."

I would wager that if the AJC asked a representative sample of Israelis – right, left or centrist - what political parties or politicians they wholeheartedly believed in and identified with, the "None" numbers would be markedly higher.

Go ahead, ask around. Ask me. I, too, have in many ways joined what has become the newest branch of Judaism: None Jews.

This is the generation of the wilderness. This isn't post-Zionism. This is something on a much larger scale. This is a huge number of Jews bailing on what Israel stands for right now. It's bigger than the question of staying here or leaving. It's bigger than the question of loving Israel or not. It's bigger even than the issue of whether Israel will end the occupation, or vice versa.

It has to do with the Jewish People, wherever they may be, and the future of the tribal encampment we loosely group under the heading of feeling and being - and somehow not hating being - Jewish.

What many of my people, the None Jews, are saying is that while much of today's Israel and today's Judaism are unbearable, there is still much – much more – which, while it may be understated, unstated or outright denigrated, is worth cherishing, bringing forward, preserving from the wrecking balls of shut-your-trap *Hasbara* and the Judaism of moral blinders.

In one form, the conversation over bailing on Israel is a literal one. In a painful, fascinating exchange, +972 writers Yuval Ben-Ami and Haggai Matar discuss what Ben-Ami, in a play on the concept of brain-drain, calls his "Heart-drain diary: The option of leaving Israel." Despite the pull and push factors lending momentum to a decision to bail on Israel, Ben-Ami ends his piece on a wistful note, wondering if we are even constitutionally able to sever our soul-deep bonds and flee. "An eternal jetlag awaits us if we leave," he writes, "as well as an undying longing for that land of bright light."

In a reply, leftist activist and journalist Matar declares that "while this place is violent, extremist and weighs on you like a stone, while I fear the direction it's heading in and am quite aware of the price one pays for living here, it is also the place I love most and am quite happy to call home. This does not make sense. Or does it?"

It does, when Matar writes of this place, where "my family lives, where my love and her family and friends are. The streets I walk have a special meaning to me that other streets in the world cannot have. I shall probably never feel at ease with any other language the way I do with Hebrew, with all the cultural associations and nuances it holds for me."

"There is no people I can better understand and talk to than Israeli people. It is a part of me, and part of who I am, and a part that would always be empty and missing were I to live in exile."

For the None Jew, and for many an avowed anti-Zionist Jew as well, there is no escaping this place. You are in its orbit even in Kauai, a full 13 time zones away.

All in all, there is much to be said for bailing on the Israel and the Judaism we have come to know, and which many of us know that we love even as it drives us off the mental cliff. There's something healthy in stripping off the layers of clergy and clerks and ghetto-bred intolerance. Behind all of it, impossible to kill, are cultural treasures of language and wit and literature and wisdom.

I now realize that I became a None Jew when I was in Hebrew school. That American institution that I so hated, that I moved to Israel, in part, so that my kids would never have to experience it.

Born here, what they did experience, was a feeling - for the Bible, for the land of their most distant ancestors, for the staggeringly ancient and the wondrously real-time Hebrew that is at the core of a brilliant and knowingly preposterous culture, and, yes, for their people - that is so profound and rooted and a part of them, that I can only marvel at it.

When I moved from California to Israel, I figured I'd give it a year, see how it went, before making a decision whether to stay or leave. At the end of that year, I decided to give it one more year. The year after, also.

Turns out, it was the right decision. Even for a None Jew. Especially for a None Jew. Thanks to my people, people like Yuval Ben-Ami and Haggai Matar who, despite everything, still want to make this place better - and thanks to creative None Jews all over who want to make feeling Jewish a positive and healthy matter for themselves and their kids - I figure that when that date comes around again in October, I'm going to give all of this one more year.

ZIONISTS WHO HAVE FORGOTTEN WHAT IT MEANS TO BE JEWISH

NOVEMBER 14, 2017

When I was little I was taught what it meant to be Jewish. And that hasn't changed.

I was taught that the overwhelming majority of American Jews believes in social justice for all. Still does.

By a huge margin, the Jews of America believe that a female American or an African American or a Mexican American or a Muslim American or an LGBTQ American or a disabled American are, and ought to be, respected and treated as full citizens of the United States of America.

The Jews of America haven't forgotten what it means to be Jewish. But the Zionist Organization of America has.

Consider the leading lights of the ZOA's Sunday "Star Studded Gala 2017."

- Sebastian Gorka, ex-Trump White House aide, who left under allegations that he belonged to a Hungarian group with a Nazi past. He denies it.

• Jack Posobiec, an alt-right conspiracy theorist and online promoter of pro-Trump hoaxes, including the "Pizzagate" and Seth Rich falsehoods.

• David Friedman, Donald Trump's bankruptcy lawyer, and former president of American Friends of Beit El Settlement. Despite having declared that liberal Jewish J Street supporters were "far worse than kapos" in Nazi concentration camps because, as liberal Jews freely supporting a two-state solution, he wrote in May, 2016, they are "smug advocates of Israel's destruction delivered from the comfort of their secure American sofas – it's hard to imagine anything worse." Soon thereafter, Trump rewarded Friedman by naming him U.S. Ambassador to Israel.U.S. Ambassador to Israel.

• And the guest of honor, Steve Bannon.

Steve Bannon, the man who brought America its alt-right, the confederacy of fanatics which has powered the most virulent surge of U.S. anti-Semitism since the original America First movement of the late 1930s and early 1940s.

Steve Bannon, flack and puppetmaster and would-be shield of Alabama U.S. Senate candidate Roy Moore, who was accused of sexually assaulting teens while he was an assistant district attorney in his 30s. Steve Bannon, who, in his speech to a worshipful crowd in the organization's event of the year, referred to Donald Trump's boasts of womanizing and sexual assault ("When you're a star, they let you do it. You can do anything. Grab 'em by the pussy. You can do anything.") without any trace of reproach.

That is not what a Jew is meant to believe. Nor support. Nor defend. But, as Bannon proudly told the ZOA, one of them did lend his support. Sheldon Adelson. Mega-donor to both Trump and the ZOA.

"It's not about resources," Bannon insisted.

What was Adelson's moral choice? Unlike establishment

Republicans, Bannon declared, "Sheldon Adelson didn't cut and run. Sheldon Adelson had Donald Trump's back. Sheldon Adelson offered guidance and counsel and wisdom of how to get through it. He was there for Donald Trump, about how to comport oneself, and dig down deep, and it was his guidance and his wisdom that helped get us through."

Being Jewish is all about making moral choices. The leaders of the ZOA have clearly made theirs. The ZOA knows what it means to be devoutly Republican, to be piously pro-Trump, pro-Bannon, pro-Gorka. But in choosing the alt-right over the Jewish community, the ZOA's forgotten the first thing about being Jewish.

One of the guests, Harvard Law Professor Alan Dershowitz, found a way to oppose extremism without upsetting his hosts.

"I think today the hard left is far more dangerous to Israel's existence and to the safety of the Jewish community," Dershowitz said. "The right has no influence today on college campuses, which are the future leaders of America."

I hope Dershowitz is right about future leaders coming from the campus left. Because outside the hall, the future of the Jewish community, like the leftist IfNotNow organization, was making its opposition – and its Judaism – more than clear.

"The ZOA is hosting Steve Bannon, somebody who is known to represent white supremacy, anti-Semitism, sexism and misogyny," Hannah Temkin of IfNotNow told the *Forward*.

"We believe that we would like to hold our mainstream institutions accountable for the values of what makes me Jewish today, which are the values of standing up for freedom and dignity for all."

Eli Valley, who has inspired young Jews and outraged the Jewish establishment with blistering leftist comics, was seen carrying a sign reading – in a nod to U.S. Ambassador to Israel David Friedman, another honored guest of the ZOA gala – "You collaborate with neo-Nazis and call us Kapos?"

"The future is out here, of course," Valley told the Forward. "The future is inside if our future is a fascist dystopia. OK? Then the future is inside. Hopefully that is not our destiny."

If the ZOA had any historical perspective, it would know this: Those young Jewish radicals who were protesting outside the Trump adoration gala were not really being radical at all.

They were being Jews.

POST-JUDAISM: THE HEART IS TORN

MARCH 18, 2021

When I was small, not so many years after the Holocaust, I remember wondering if I would live to see a day when Judaism was over.

We had a teacher in Hebrew school, a survivor of concentration camps and of subsequent wars in Israel, who seemed to be haunted by the idea.

"*Halev nikra,*" he told us once. The heart is torn. "Your generation," he went on, to our uncomprehending ears, "May it not be the last." No Judaism left to practice. The teachings lost. The wisdom gone. The traditions and subcultures all but forgotten, disfigured out of existence, turned inside out, unrecognizable, dead.

Over time, I understood him to mean that that the State of Israel was then still terrifyingly vulnerable, that assimilation was growing among Diaspora communities. Age-old centers of Jewish life in Europe and in the Muslim world were already extinct.

The fears were real. But there was one threat to Judaism our teacher hadn't seen coming:

Benjamin Netanyahu.

Maybe our teacher would have seen it now, had he lived. You can't miss it now. In the quarter-century since he first took office, Benjamin Netanyahu has transformed Judaism more dramatically and more destructively than any other single figure of his time.

This, in the end, is his legacy. Post-Judaism.

Netanyahu first rose to power at a time of a shattering new crisis in Judaism, the events surrounding the 1995 assassination by a far-right Jew, and the subsequent wave of Hamas murders of Jews in suicide bombings of public buses in Jerusalem and Tel Aviv.

The unthinkable had become the norm. For Jews, for Judaism, the wounds were horrific, bone deep. Netanyahu was smart enough, energetic enough, talented enough, to know very well how to begin to treat the wounds, to cleanse them and bind them and heal them. But he made a radically different choice, right then and there.

He would take the wounds and bleed them for all they were worth.

And he's never stopped. He's doing it again, right now.

This week, a small country of close-knit families and families of friends, a nation in which every death reverberates in concentric shock waves of mourning, was grieving the death of the 6,000th Israeli killed by COVID-19.

Netanyahu could have devoted himself to consoling the grief-stricken, to supporting the thousands of coronavirus patients still suffering debilitating symptoms months after contracting the virus, to paying honor and material help to the medical staffs, rescue workers, teachers, essential workers and others whose heroism, self- sacrifice, and exhausting persistence helped the rest of us through this crisis.

It's what a good Jew would have done.

Instead, that day, the prime minister barnstormed the West Bank, campaigning for a fringe extremist party he himself forged into being, combining many of Israel's most openly hateful, homophobic, anti-democratic, supremacist and violence-legitimizing activists into a pro-Netanyahu slate called Religious Zionism.

Halev nikra.

Once, long ago, there was a time before Bibi. A time before his close allies branded North American Reform Jews as dogs, progressive and centrist Jews as kapos, and an Israeli woman soldier who converted to Judaism as a shiksa, unworthy of marriage to a Jew. In those days, we were taught the following in a Hebrew school in California:

All that the Lord requires of us as Jews is to do justice, practice lovingkindness and mercy, and walk humbly with our God [*Micah, 6:8*].

Do not stand idly by while your neighbor is bleeding, nor endanger your neighbor's life [*Leviticus 19:16*]

Do not take revenge nor bear a grudge against the members of your own people, but you shall love your neighbor as yourself. [*Leviticus 19:18*].

You can forget all that now.

This is how Benjamin Netanyahu, master of the grudge, translator of vengeance into votes, built his legacy. How he got where he is. How he runs his campaigns. Take the best parts of Judaism and trash them, deride them, dishonor them, make them an object of scorn and abuse and vicious attacks. Take the worst parts of Judaism and exalt them, shield them, cement them into law, put them literally into power.

And now he's running again.

Post-Judaism in one sentence? Listen to Netanyahu's newest white hope, the segregationist, gay-bashing Religious Zionism leader Betzalel Smotrich.

"There is a true religion – the Jewish religion," Smotrich declared on Wednesday. "A religion of peace, love, and tolerance. And then -" referring to Islam - "there is a religion of violence, of terrorism, of jihad."

When I was small, we were taught that humility, compassion, generosity of the spirit, integrity, and respect for all people as having been created in God's image, were essential Jewish values. We were taught that savagery against the innocent was not.

Now I turn on the news in Netanyahu's post-Jewish state. Another Jew has been attacked by Likud activists for not supporting Netanyahu. Yet another Palestinian shepherd, or farmer, or child, has been attacked for not being a Jew. Yet another husband and father has murdered a member of his family for no reason at all.

And Netanyahu, beaming, tells us all that, thanks solely to him, we're living it up.

When I was small, we were taught in Hebrew school that it was a Jewish value to bring light to the world.

What they didn't teach us was that Judaism dies in darkness. And when Netanyahu wins.

PART SEVENTEEN:
I WAS WRONG ABOUT HIM.
HE'S EVIL

Now we know. Now we know what Hamas knew. The damage this man could do. There was once a historian who wrote that "He is an enemy by essence. His personality won't allow him to compromise. It doesn't matter what kind of resistance he will meet, what price he will pay. His existence is one of perpetual war."

The historian, Benzion Netanyahu, was writing about Arabs, all Arabs. What we didn't know at the time, but what we surely know now, is that he could have been writing, as well, about his middle son. The one who became prime minister for life.

I WAS WRONG. HE'S EVIL

FEBRUARY 19, 2019

He's not Trump. You can't blame what Benjamin Netanyahu does on a serious, volatile, obvious and likely untreatable personality disorder, or on profound, doesn't-know-what-he-doesn't-know ignorance.

He's not Trump. Netanyahu is smart, knowledgeable, self-aware. He is not rash.

For decades now I've been watching Netanyahu, studying him, asking aides about him. I figured I knew him. I used to think I understood him, that his actions and words made it clear that for all his posturing, he was amoral, bereft of a sense of right and wrong, unconcerned about ethics, unhindered by conscience, devoid of a moral compass.

But now, with this election campaign, I realize I was wrong.

Benjamin Netanyahu is not simply amoral. He's evil.

This is what tells you more than you want to know about evil: Netanyahu's relentless campaign to bring into his future governing coalition the Otzma Yehudit (Jewish Power) party, led by disciples of the vicious, unabashedly racist, rabidly Jewish supremacist ideology of the late Meir Kahane.

Netanyahu has openly expressed his deep concern that as many as 100,000 or more far-right votes could be cast in vain if extremist parties like Otzma fail to clear the 3.25-percent electoral threshold.

Backed to the hilt by the bottomless-pocket media resources of Sheldon Adelson's mass-circulation daily *Israel Hayom*, the prime minister has spent much of his time and energy pressing leaders of other right-wing parties to merge with Otzma, which would then form a key part of a post-election Netanyahu coalition.

But so extreme is Otzma that even Bezalel Smotrich, a leader of the far-right Habayit Hayehudi party, and perhaps the most publicly racist and homophobic of Israeli lawmakers, initially rebuffed the pressure from Netanyahu to bring in Otzma. However, on Wednesday, the eve of a deadline for finalizing party tickets, Otzma announced it had agreed to a merger with the Habayit Hayehudi and National Union parties, in order, Otzma said, to prevent "the establishment of a leftist government, God forbid."

It later emerged that in order to seal the deal, Netanyahu offered Habayit Hayehudi the education and housing ministries - giving them effective control of settlement expansion and public school curricula - in addition to two seats in the security cabinet.

Past Likud leaders like Menachem Begin ostracized and eventually formally outlawed Kahane and his followers. Led by Begin, the other 119 legislators would leave the Knesset hall in the mid-1980s when then-MK Kahane would take the podium.

But Netanyahu, whose political legacy was cemented by his last-minute 2015 announcement to Jewish voters that massed Arabs were about to storm the polling booths, is unfazed, saying nothing about the violence, bigotry, incitement and anti-democratic pillars of the Kahanist creed.

Netanyahu has gone so far as to take time away from meetings at the recent Mideast summit in Warsaw to telephone influential settlement movement rabbis in an effort to pressure settler-dominated parties to accept Otzma.

This week, as the Thursday deadline for party mergers neared, Netanyahu turned the heat up further. The calls to rabbis now included Smotrich's father, Rabbi Haim Yeruham Smotrich. Netanyahu "beseeched him, 'Talk to your son, [get him] to unite with Otzma Yehudit,'" Israel's Channel 13 quoted the prime minister as saying.

Ironically, it was a move by hardline Netanyahu coalition rightists that originally raised the threshold to 3.25 percent, in a direct, and failed, attempt to eliminate Arab parties from the Knesset in the 2015 election.

Netanyahu and others have pointed with alarm to the 1992 race, when the far-right Tehiya party got a particularly low threshold raised, only to be eliminated from the Knesset by the terms of its own law. This, in turn, paved the way for the rise of the Rabin government, perhaps the most left-leaning in Israel's history.

The objects of Netanyahu's political ardor may be seen in ads adorning city buses in Jerusalem: the Kahane heirs who are Otzma's poster boys, graduates and spearheads of Kach, Kahane Chai (Kahane Lives) and other Kahanist offshoots.

There is Baruch Marzel, who has in the past called for the targeted assassination of leftists and a holy war against LGBTQ people.

There is Itamar Ben-Gvir, attorney for a long list of Jews suspected of anti-Palestinian terrorism and anti-Arab hate crimes, and who before Yitzhak Rabin's assassination held up a hood ornament ripped from the then-prime minister's car, declaring "we got to his car and we'll get to him too."

And, among many others, there is Benzi Gopstein, head of the extremist Lehava organization, whose protests against Arab-Jewish marriages often end in fistfights and worse.

Kahane's legacy in Israel has literally been written in blood.

In 1982, a Kahane follower, Baltimore-born Alan Goodman, wearing his IDF basic-training uniform and armed with his standard-issue M16 assault rifle, opened fire on Muslims in the courtyard of Jerusalem's Al-Aqsa Mosque, killing one and wounding 11. Goodman served 15 years of a life sentence.

In 1994, Kahane disciple Dr. Baruch Goldstein, a Brooklyn native who'd moved to the settlement of Kiryat Arba, murdered 29 Muslims in Hebron's sacred Cave of the Patriarchs, before he was beaten to death by survivors of the shooting.

Most recently, Kahane's grandson Meir Ettinger, suspected of leading an underground group of young settlers believed responsible for a wave of attacks against West Bank Palestinians, reportedly came to the aid of a group of then-fugitive teenagers suspected of an October stone-throwing ambush which killed Aisha Rabi, a Palestinian mother of nine.

Netanyahu has been pointedly silent over the attack.

Meir Kahane's one-term legislative legacy is terrifying as well.

Last week, in a *Yedioth Ahronoth* op-ed on Netanyahu's pursuit of Otzma titled "The Disgrace of Kahanism," journalist Nadav Eyal compiled a list of the bills Kahane proposed – a possible indication of what could someday be in store if Otzma reaches the Knesset:

- Revocation of the citizenship of all non-Jewish Israelis.
- Expulsion of non-Jews from Jerusalem.
- Eventual imposition of slavery on Arabs and other non-Jews.
- Prohibition of contact between Jews and Arabs, including sexual relations.
- Segregated beaches.
- Prohibition of non-Jews living in Jewish neighborhoods.
- Forced dissolution of all intermarriages.

Meantime, *Israel Hayom* is keeping up the pressure. "Without a merger, the left will win!" a blue-white banner headline read on

Tuesday. It echoed a recent op-ed in Adelson's pro-Bibi vehicle, which said of a merger with both Otzma and the anti-gay rights Yachad party, "Our lives depend on it."

Which tells us something about newspapers as well. If democracy dies in darkness, that's exactly where evil thrives.

I HEREBY RESIGN FROM THE TRIBE

OCTOBER 22, 2015

There was a time when I used to forget things, to lose things, with damnable frequency.

At some point, it occurred to me that I always lost things exactly when I was leaving one place for another. I forced myself to imagine, just before leaving anywhere, that I would never be able to return to that place, so I'd sure as anything better take with me everything I'd need for this trip.

It worked. In fact, this month, leaving Israel to visit my family in California, it worked so well that the lie-to-myself, the conscious fiction, the part about never returning, may have come true without me even knowing it.

Two weeks ago, in the middle of the night, I again told myself that lie, in order to make sure that I wouldn't forget anything before leaving for the airport in Lod. Now I'm on a plane headed back to Israel. Six miles above a Utah escarpment, I am handed yesterday's *Yedioth Ahronot* newspaper and begin to sense, headline by headline, that a million nonstop hours from now, this airplane will land in the same Ben Gurion Airport I'd taken off from - but not in the same country.

The day I left Israel, that mountaintop we'd uneasily lived with so long - the smoking summit which, we knew, capped a mountain of hatred - shuddered and blew entirely off. The ensuing eruption has claimed new victims daily, in every direction. And, with the speed and unstoppability of a volcano, its flow of fire is changing the landscape into something no one can quite recognize.

Just in the short time I've been gone, Israel's eternal, indivisible capital has been physically divided. Palestinians have slashed, hacked, shot or run over dozens of Israelis, killing many of them. Israelis have shot hundreds of Palestinians, scores of them fatally, some for having attacked Israelis, some not.

Within Israel, street mobs have severely assaulted Arabs for being Arabs, and have mistaken Mizrachi Jews and an Eritrean man for terrorists, with tragic and even fatal results.

"You're right," social activist Ronny Douek wrote in an open letter to the prime minister in that Monday edition of *Yedioth*, "that in the past we've seen terrorist attacks more severe, and that we've known more dangerous periods of time.

"But do you not see that this time, in fact, something has opened a crack inside us? That, in contrast to other periods of crisis, in which we knew how to come together and look forward, this time the horizon looks dark."

I have lived in Israel for many years, decades in fact. But I know enough about this place - and the fear and the despair in which my loved ones there are now living - to know that I am coming back to a place about which I know nothing.

I have been a member of this tribe we call the Jews for my whole life. I have been schooled in the mechanics and the horrific if periodic works of pogrom and bloodthirst and genocidal persecution from the time I heard my first fairy tales.

But this, I fear, is something different. Something somehow more permanent.

In the past, when confronted with people who wanted Israel to cease to exist, people who believed Israel was doomed, fragile, unsustainable, and/or indefensibly, immorally evil, deserving of a death sentence, I would react with a faith-based defiance grounded in optimism for a better, more just, more humane future.

I won't lie about this: For the present, my focus is elsewhere. I want my loved ones to live.

For the future though, I am left to wonder: How is my tribe to live like this? Lost. No chief. No security. No plan. No hope.

There have been times when I thought, Why not just resign from the tribe?

Truth be told, I get letters all the time from people - fellow members of the tribe - who recommend that I do just that, in one form or another. They inform me that my name's not Jewish enough, my politics not Zionist enough, my complaints about Israel such that I should leave the country, my complaints about Israel such that I should die.

Maybe it's time I listened to them. Maybe it's time to resign from the tribe that these people belong to, and to realize, at long last, that all this time I've been a member of a different tribe. Not a rival, exactly. Just different.

Maybe it's time I realized that the tribes of the Holy Land are not simply the mortal enemies we call Jews and Arabs. Maybe all the deafening, implacable, violence-espousing extremists, both disgusting sides of them, are actually in one tribe, together.

And, yes, that first tribe is winning. At this point, any kid with a cleaver, any meathead yelling for death, is a chief on his own.

But maybe there's another tribe which loves this land so deeply, that it's still willing to seek a way to share it among the people who live here. This is a tribe which wants to see human rights defeat hatred, democracy vanquish deity-based dictatorship. The tribe of humans. If that second tribe is paralyzed, demoralized, delegitimized by the current reality, small wonder. But sometimes, under great pressures, things which you're sure are lost forever, can reappear. Like love itself.

So here's my letter of resignation from that first tribe, a letter which I'm submitting here, because my tribe lacks a chief I could hand it to:

I hereby resign from the tribe that says killing unarmed people is a form of self-defense, whose practitioners are heroes.

I hereby resign from the tribe that says: We deserve everything, all the land, and we've got the Book that says so.

I resign from the tribe which says the other guys are monsters, animals, out only for our blood and our land, undeserving and disqualified from having a country of their own.

I resign from the tribe that says settlers are not civilians and are fair game for murder. I resign from the tribe that says any Jew, because they're Jewish, deserves to be stabbed.

I resign from the tribe that says Death to Arabs, the tribe which posts that hating Arabs is a virtue.

I resign from the tribe that says Palestinian kids suspected of throwing rocks should be put to death on the spot.

I resign from the tribe which blames the Palestinians for the Holocaust.

I resign from the tribe that says "We'll knock flat the homes of the relatives of suspected terrorists - but only the Palestinian ones, never the Jews." I resign from this tribe not only because this ritual is wrong and immoral and collective punishment. I resign also because it doesn't work, only making a vicious circle that much broader and that much deeper and that much more vicious.

Maybe you have to leave a place in order to know what's been lost there. But sometimes, as well, you have to come back, to appreciate what's still there, what can improbably reappear.

Yes, I'm resigning. But I still I haven't given up on all this. And, for what it's worth, I'm keeping my name.

I REFUSE TO BE YOUR ENEMY

DECEMBER 14, 2019
First Annual Israel March for Human Rights

This is where the war ends.
This is where the future goes to breathe.
It begins in a city which practices what Jerusalem preaches And
what Jerusalem, with its vicious holy men, betrays: God's work.

I have seen the future. It was last Friday, in the faces of thousands of
people marching in the street in Tel Aviv-Jaffa. In the face of a little
girl dancing on the shoulders of her father to music played on a
pensive oud and a goblet drum and to music played on a jacked
electric guitar and a trombone.

"It's true," says my wife, looking at the crowd, every color, straight
and gay and Jew and Arab and citizen and foreign worker and
refugee, devout and atheist, care giver and victim of domestic
violence. She continues:

"God doesn't make mistakes."
There was every reason to skip this march for human rights.
It was supposed to rain.
No one was likely to show up. My foot was broken.

But when the crowd began to move
From the square where Yitzhak Rabin sang publicly for the first time,
and was then killed,
What they began to chant changed everything:

"Yehudim, Aravim - M'sarvim L'hiyot Oyvim."
Jews and Arabs, Refusing To Be Enemies

This was a march about what is wrong with Israeli society
But it was an expression of what is right with it.

A woman, elderly, religious, watches the mysterious,
uncategorizable mingling of tribes straggle past her down the
street. The signs speak of the rights of lovers to marry, of Africans
who have cheated genocide to make a new home, of Gilad Shalit
to return to his. Of the right to share the Holy Land between
two peoples, for the sake of, and despite, the two peoples' many
quarrelsome sub-tribes, camps and splinters.

As we pass, the woman on the sidewalk asks
"Are you people trying to kill my country?"
My 15-year old daughter answers without hesitation.
"Has v'shalom." Heaven Forbid.

I want a word with the people - my people and theirs -
Who treat land as sacred, and people not theirs, as dirt:
My war with you is over.
My enemy today is the word Never.

This is where it begins.
Not the Jerusalem of murderous faith and a vengeful God
But in a city which faces God because it faces the world.
"This is a taste of the World to Come," my wife says,
the crowd swaying to music, other peoples and their own.

A year from now, at the second annual Israel March for Human Rights,
there will be still more people. More people who, in their songs
and their movement and in their self-respect, will be saying,
"This country is too young to die. I declare the war is over."
Next year in Tel Aviv-Jaffa.

I'M KILLING OFF PARTS OF ME. FOR MY OWN GOOD

JUNE 14, 2017

What I'm about to say will be grossly unfair.

I'm worried sick about Israel. What it's becoming, day by day. Totalitarian. Totalitarian and abusive. Totalitarian and abusive and oblivious. Totalitarian and abusive and oblivious and suicidal.

It's unfair of me to say this because I played a part in it. It's unfair of me to voice concern about this because I let it happen. I couldn't stop it. I didn't even manage to slow it down. Worse, I helped keep it going. I paid taxes. I occupied. I stayed.

There's no way around it. We screwed up. Criminally. My generation. And day by day, we find ways only to make it worse.

It's unfair of me to say this on a day when Israel, the Palestinian Authority and God knows how many other regional actors are conspiring to make the living hell that is Gaza, an even more unspeakable torture chamber, and all theoretically to pressure Hamas. They are cutting off electricity to nearly two million innocent people, including their hospitals – and all during the Ramadan holiday.

But mostly, it's unfair of me because I am coming to believe that if Israel will ever begin to change for the better, it will only be because young people, Israelis and Palestinians, Jews and Muslims and Christians – born into this morass through no fault of their own - found entirely new ways to change it, ways the rest of us were unable or unwilling to try - devising shocking and/or obvious approaches to fix the ungodly, catastrophic mess that they had no hand in making.

Doubly unfair, because those young people whom we have systematically worked to deprive of all hope, are the only hope we have left.

And because if they don't, "Death to Israel" will definitely begin at home. In fact, it already has.

Don't take my word for it. Listen to the assessment of the Israeli official responsible at the highest and most comprehensive level for evaluating threats to the nation's very existence. In March, Tamir Pardo, the recently retired head of the Mossad intelligence agency, declared publicly that "Israel has one existential threat. It is a ticking time bomb."

It wasn't Iran he was talking about. Nor Hamas or Hezbollah. He was talking about the occupation, and the threats to democracy posed by our leader's intentional inaction with regard to negotiations between Israel and the Palestinians.

Unfair as it is to urge young people to put out the fires of their elders, there are already signs that this is exactly what has begun to take place.

In the West Bank village of Sarura, south of Hebron, hundreds of Israelis, Palestinians, and diaspora Jews banded together last month to set up an unorthodox, ongoing and inspiring protest camp in support of Palestinian villagers harassed by settlers and the army.

There are signs that other joint Palestinian-Israeli initiatives will emerge.

Some of them have already changed me.

"New Voices from Palestine" was the subject of a panel during the

2017 Israel Conference on Peace sponsored by *Haaretz* on Monday.

There was something quietly but fundamentally revolutionary about the views expressed. The speakers confounded all expectations, stressing again and again that liberation was bound up with leaving behind the mentality and the comfort zone which says "I am a victim."

It's a lesson which Israel as a whole needs to take to heart, in order to do what is needed to save itself.

During another panel, which discussed ways to teach peace, Palestinian educator Prof. Mohammed Dajani Daoudi noted that his students had asked him why they should learn about the Holocaust while the Israeli government has pursued legislation to curb teaching about the Nakba.

"Because you would be doing the right thing," he replied. The right thing.

Let me get a little less unfair. Let me pledge, here and now, that I will do everything I can to kill off the parts of me which say "I'm a victim." And to kill off the parts of me which despair. The parts of me which say, "It's already too late."

From this day on, I refuse to be a victim. And I refuse to be a perpetrator. From this day on, I will be empowered by hope.

I deeply thank these Palestinians for their wisdom. I refuse to consider it unfair to apply it.

From this day on, I refuse to believe that it's already too late. And one other thing I learned this week:

Once you stop bending and breaking and remaking yourself in order to change for the better – once, that is, that you stop learning from your mistakes – it's at that very moment that you begin to die.

PART EIGHTEEN: STARTING OVER

We are all starting over. Every one of us. The horrors of October 7, 2023 and its aftermath have left every one of us stricken, beaten down, sleepless, transformed in ways we ourselves cannot imagine.

At this writing, in ways unique in modern history, a people without a government is conducting a war, seeing to the needs of a quarter-million people evacuated from homes under attack, seeing to the needs of a third of a million military reservists and their families, seeing to the needs of families and individuals in anguish over loved ones murdered, missing, or taken hostage.

No one knows where the government is. Or how its members, cowardly, paralyzed, fearing for their positions, can sleep at night when no one else is. At this point, no one has the time and energy to care. More than half of adult Israelis not in uniform or left homeless or in unbearable fear or grief, are volunteering to help those who are.

Today is the fourth of November. This year, for the first time in 28 years, there will be no commemoration of the assassination of Yitzhak Rabin.

We are starting over. What happens from now on will determine whether Israel will end here, or begin again in a new direction.

There is no rational reason to hope for the second.

But just as the war has changed everyone, I am not the person I was before. For no reason whatsoever, I have come to believe in a God who is made of hope. And Who made us, all of us, in that exact image.

HEADLINE:
NETANYAHU MARKS RABIN MURDER WITH
NIGHTMARE PROPHECY OF ISRAEL'S FUTURE

OCTOBER 27, 2015

Twenty years ago this November 4, we had a young family, and hope.

Twenty years ago this November 4, when we loaded the old car with the kids and a stroller to drive down the mountain to go hear Yitzhak Rabin speak in Tel Aviv, we lived in a country with a future.

It was a young country then. But only for a few more hours.

We could not have known it at the time, but on that long-ago Saturday night, our future was about to be placed, over and over again, in the hands of Benjamin Netanyahu.

And this week, as Israel marked the 20th anniversary of the assassination of Yitzhak Rabin, Netanyahu finally revealed what our future was about to be. A permanent nightmare.

"These days, there is talk about what would happen if this or that person would have remained," the prime minister told the Knesset

Foreign Affairs and Defense Committee, in a clear but unusually callous reference to the slain Rabin, and to the goal to which Rabin's final years were dedicated, a peace with the Palestinians and all of Israel's neighbors.

"It's irrelevant," Netanyahu continued. "There are movements here of religion and Islam that have nothing to do with us."

Then, turning to Rabin's ideological heirs on the committee, supporters of negotiations with the Palestinians, the increasingly testy Netanyahu set out his dark vision of our futures as Israelis:

"You think there is a magic wand here, but I disagree," he told them.

"I'm asked if we will forever live by the sword — yes".

Twenty years ago, we had a young family, and hope.

Like most of the people who were moving toward Tel Aviv's central square that night, we were skeptical and somewhat guarded in mood, concerned that no one would show up. Concerned that the threats in the air, the acid in the protests against Rabin, the current of implied violence in the chants against negotiations with the Palestinians, in the catcalls of Rabin the Traitor and Rabin the Murderer, would deter people from coming, would turn them despondent, shorn of hope, intimidated.

We could not have known it at the time, but there would be two earthquakes that evening.

The first came when we noticed people pouring into the square, flooding in, people from far away in Israel, gratifyingly diverse, young and old, Jew and Arab, a surprising number of them religious.

When Rabin began to speak, you could feel the earthquake in that huge crowd, an electricity which no one could have anticipated. There was an abrupt momentum to their reactions, an unaccustomed and unexpected exhilaration, to which Rabin, a painfully undemonstrative man, clearly responded.

"Allow me to say, I am also moved," Rabin began, looking into the square. *«I want to thank each and every one of you who stood up*

here against violence and for peace.

"This government, which I have the privilege to lead, together with my friend Shimon Peres, decided to give peace a chance. A peace that will solve most of the problems of the State of Israel."

Twenty years ago, Rabin's was a very different Israel, a very different government than any the country had known – or would.

The nation was taking substantive, unprecedented steps toward reversing decades of discrimination against its Palestinian and other citizens. It was actively working with the Palestinians, the Americans, the UN, Europe and an ever-expanding list of nations, on the first stages of a plan meant to lead to Palestinian independence alongside Israel, and eventual normalization of relations with all of our neighbors.

"I have always believed that the majority of the people want peace, are prepared to take risks for peace."

Israel was opening itself to the world, and the world - significantly including countries which had long shunned and boycotted and quarantined us - had begun to embrace Israel with openness.

"I was a military man for twenty-seven years. I fought as long as there were no prospects for peace. Today I believe that there are prospects for peace, great prospects."

We stood on a small lawn at the rear of the immense peace rally, our younger daughter, 20 months old, asleep in the stroller.

We wondered if peace could possibly come before our elder daughter and her classmates, then turning 12, would be drafted to serve in the army. Surely, we dared hope, that by the time our toddler was 18, the horrors of war would be behind us.

"Violence is undermining the very foundations of Israeli democracy. It must be condemned, denounced, and isolated. This is not the way of the State of Israel."

We thought, this is the kind of speech, the kind of crowd, the kind of occurrence that can change history.

And, just then, when we turned to leave, history changed.

The second earthquake hit. It took nothing larger than a handgun to set it off. It made barely a sound. But its effect was vastly larger, an earthquake that is still taking place, to this very day.

Now, all these years later, I have to force myself to remember that nothing is forever. Not even Netanyahu.

This Saturday night, not knowing entirely why, we'll be going back to the square, as we have every year since our family was young. Much has changed - our family has grown, and is growing still, thank God. But some things haven't changed.

I still take Rabin's view over Netanyahu's. I still believe that the great majority of people here, Arabs and Jews both, want to see peace here, and true democracy, and social justice.

I have no illusions that I will live to see it come to pass.

But I believe that our children might. And I believe that their children will.

And that's more than a good enough reason to work for that future.

We are all starting over. Lately, I've been hearing talk about what will happen when the war is over. What will happen if Netanyahu decides to keep his throne rather than accepting responsibility for the worst catastrophe in the history of this tragedy-worn country.

Militant settlers, some of whom who claim to love the Land of Israel more than life itself, are taking advantage of the war by trying to set the Land afire. One of their representatives in the government just said that one way to destroy Hamas is to drop an atomic bomb on Gaza. Then what? Send in the settlers. To stay.

As for Israelis of good hearts and good will, the endless year 2023 has changed them. They are waiting, but they are seething. And they know how to go into the streets and change this place for the better.

In times past, there was a sense that a revolution was necessary. But Netanyahu found ways to defuse it, divert it, suppress it.

This time around, the magician of Balfour Street may reach yet again into his magician's hat, only to find nothing left there but lint.

IN ISRAEL, THE FUTURE CAN COME DOWN TO JUST ONE NIGHT

SEPTEMBER 2, 2011

How can you tell if a revolution is real? When this all started, I had no idea. But I kept going to the tent camps and to the marches until I learned. It took just three words. An Arab Israeli, speaking to thousands of demonstrators two days after the recent terror killings near Eilat, said it all:

"*Anachnu Am Echad.*" We're one people. In this society of tribal fractures and chronic rage, those three words were as radical and transformative and moral and direct a statement as any revolution could spawn. One people, Jew and Muslim and Christian and Druze, one people right and left, observant and secular, straight and gay, woman and man, infant and aged.

How can you tell a revolution is real? When it holds up a mirror that lets you see the back of your mind. In less than two months, this movement has changed the way people of all walks of life see each other, treat each other, and view their own lives. A week ago, our family marched in a demonstration behind a man who held up a sign reading "I'm a human being, Goddammit. My life has value."

How can you tell a revolution is real? When time after time, you suspect that no one will go to the demonstration this week, but you go anyway, because you believe that there is something vital in this, and its only when you get there that you realize that thousands and thousands and even hundreds of thousands of people were feeling the exact same thing.

What makes a revolution real? When the future of an entire country can come down to just one night. Saturday, for example.

From a distance, the idea of a revolution in an ostensibly modern, statistically prosperous country may seem suspect, outmoded, puzzling. Imagine one of eight American men, women and children, some 40 million in all, taking to the streets of major cities, chanting a demand for social justice.

Fair enough. This is not the Israel you're used to. This is not the Israel you knew two months ago. These are not the same Israelis. These people have come alive, just as the peculiar culture that has poisoned Israel for years and years and years has begun to die.

This is not a revolution against the current government. It's a revolution against the bullying behavior that is the overwhelming plague of day to day life here. Government after government.

In a culture which for decades has granted standout bullies management positions in government, business and unions, there is no act more radical than the phenomenon of people gathering to listen, actually stop and shut up and listen, to one another's experience and opinions.

No wonder the ordinary people who keep this country afloat have been made to feel shame, made to feel like losers. In this Israel, this Elbonia with an H and M, graft and law-bending and cronyism have long trumped talent and aptitude and honest, caring, hard work. In this Third Temple of mega-wealth, there was no room for a trickle-down effect. The backbone of the country, people who work, pay their taxes, do their reserve military duty and raise families, have been pushed to realize they have a choice: change this country, or look for another one.

No wonder, with corporate and bureaucratic functionaries rewarded for bleeding and bilking and misleading and milking and ultimately discarding the customers and clients they were meant to be serving, that the burdens of everyday life have for so long persuaded people that they could do nothing about them.

This is the structure that says: never question, never apologize, never take responsibility. This is the structure that created Israel's ills.

This is the structure that fosters, cements, eternalizes, destroys us with occupation, segregation, discrimination, humiliation, and, at the same time, saps the will and the means to do anything about it.

No more. It either ends here, or Israel does. Saturday night. Be there. Go ahead, make your future.

GIVE THE PALESTINIANS THE VOTE

APRIL 12, 2016

Having lived in the Holy Land for a number of years now, I've come to understand a few things. Here is one:

Dreams here die in one of two ways.

We've all watched many of our dreams here die a violent death.

Others, more tenacious perhaps, manage to expire of old age.

And then there's the one about Two States. Dead of both causes. An immense number of people here, Arabs and Jews alike, along with a surprising number of supporters of BDS, and even some settlers, are in agreement about Two States. They will tell you:

1. It's what I would like to see happen here." And also:
2. "It can't be done."

A few years ago, it became fashionable on the right to declare a final, irreversible triumph over the two-state solution.

Leading the victory lap was the then-head of the settlement movement's YESHA leadership council, Dani Dayan, just named consul general to New York.

"We are standing on the edge of a historic victory against the left, since soon the situation will be irreversible, and a Palestinian state would not be able to be established."

"So the two-state solution is both unfeasible, and if it is feasible, it is a catastrophe," Dayan told *The Atlantic* in 2012. "So yes, I think it's a great thing that we are preventing it from happening."

Let's say Dayan was right. Bearing in mind that many Israelis once used the word "irreversible" in connection with the Oslo diplomatic process and the goal of two states, and barring the unforeseen, let's go with this.

Let's say that the terrible, volatile, universally unsatisfying reality of occupation - the violence, the fundamentalist extremism, the inequality of both human rights and basic privileges - is all we can expect for the foreseeable future:

One State, indivisible, under a Jewish God, with relative liberty for Jews, and injustice for all others.

What happens to the dream, the goal, the value, of democracy in Israel?

The One State reality certifies that there is no difference between Israel on the one hand, and, on the other, the parallel, separate and grossly unequal systems of law, human rights, social services, and self-determination under which Jews and Palestinians live in the West Bank and East Jerusalem.

It is the One State reality which truly invites comparisons to an apartheid state. And more than any other single element, it is the disenfranchisement of Palestinians which clinches the comparison.

Can anything be done to change this? There is one thing. One thing which could change everything:

Give the Palestinians the vote.

Offer Israeli citizenship and equal rights to all of the Palestinians of the West Bank.

In a groundbreaking 2010 article, journalist Noam Sheizaf

surveyed the many figures on the Israeli right who supported such a move. Prominent among them was President Reuven Rivlin, then speaker of the Knesset.

"We're living in a political reality that requires answers," Rivlin told Sheizaf in a shocking, and startlingly logical, interview.

"When people say that the demographic threat necessitates a separation, my reply is that the lesser danger, the lesser evil, is a single state in which there are equal rights for all citizens."

According to Rivlin, "As a rule, whenever I hear about a demographic threat, it comes first of all from a type of thinking that says the Arabs are a threat. And this leads to thinking of transfer, or that they should be killed. I am appalled by this kind of talk."

One of the most vociferously hardline of settler ideologues, the late former YESHA chairman and onetime chief Netanyahu aide Uri Elitzur, writing a year before in the settlers' journal *Nekuda*, argued for a process which would culminate in Palestinians having "a blue ID card [as do Israelis], yellow license plates [as do Israelis], National Insurance [social security] and the right to vote for the Knesset."

"The worst solution," Elitzur wrote, "is apparently the right one: a binational state, full annexation, full citizenship."

Elitzur – and this is in 2009 – dismissed other alternatives to the two-state solution as "softened or newspeak variations of apartheid." He predicted that the grace period which the world has allowed Israel to take definitive action to end its "temporary" occupation of the West Bank, would run out on the occupation's 50th anniversary – just over one year from now.

Other significant voices on the Israeli right who have spoken in favor of granting West Bank Palestinians the vote and full rights and citizenship are former foreign and defense minister Moshe Arens and Netanyahu's current Deputy Foreign Minister Tzipi Hotovely.

Rivlin said in the 2010 interview that new ways of governing and sharing the land could be found, in marked contrast to the current system. Solutions based on separation of the two peoples have acted to increase hatreds, not heal them, he said.

"I go into schools, and when they hold mock elections, [pro-transfer, anti-Arab politician Avigdor] Lieberman gets 40 percent of the vote, and I hear kids saying that Arabs should be killed. It seems to me that many of the belligerent Jewish movements that were built upon hatred of Arabs and I'm not only talking about Lieberman, but within the Likud as well, grew out of the patronizing-socialist attitude that said 'They'll be there and we'll be here.'"

At some point, all of us will need to deal with the uncomfortable realities of the history of this land. There are Israeli children being born on settlements who are the third generation of their families to live there. They did not go there by choice. They know it only as their family home.

And there are Palestinian children being born in the United States who are the fourth generation of their families to live in exile. Their families did not go there by choice. Some will doubtless want to come to live here.

"There is a conflict in the Middle East between two entities, and they're both right, each in their own way," Rivlin stressed five years ago.

"This is our only home, and therefore all kinds of solutions can be found."

ISRAEL WILL BE BETTER OFF
WHEN MY GENERATION IS DEAD

AUGUST 19, 2014

G enerations eventually pass. Thank God.
　　Someday, a new generation will arise in Israel, look at what we've been doing for the last 18 years or so, and say to my generation: You had your chance. You blew it. You're done.

And not a moment too soon. Israel will be better off when my generation is dead.

We had our chance. In the early 1990s, when Israel held its fire in the face of Iraqi ballistic missile strikes on Tel Aviv, the Shamir government, with a young press spokesman named Netanyahu, went to a landmark peace conference in Madrid which brought it face to face, for the first time, with Arab adversaries like Syria, Lebanon, and the Palestinians.

Then, two years later, in order to preserve democracy in Israel, and mindful of the precedent that gave birth to the state, a successor coalition began the process of partition and recognition of the concept of a people and a state of Palestine living alongside Israel.

This was not my generation. This was the already aging generation of Yitzhak Rabin and Shimon Peres, who had been young leaders in 1948. But within a few years, a combination of assassination, terrorism, left-center complacency and religious rightist election meddling would put the once-boy wonder Netanyahu into power. And later, with the best of intentions, Israel voted in the once-boy wonder Barak. And that, as it turned out, would be that.

The people wanted partition. The polls were clear. What they got was the veiled, knowingly illegal government enterprise that made partition impossible: settlements. And all because of a dominant minority of powerful members of my generation, and their vision of a revolutionary change in the shape of a Jewish state, and a revolutionary change in the nature of Judaism.

My generation commandeered Judaism itself, inculcating the idea that Torah-true religion is not a system of allegiance to law and ethical ways to live with others. Rather, the new Torah-true Judaism is overwhelmingly about the conquest of land, the primacy of the rights of the Jews over all others, the flouting of all law, all authority, all ownership, all opinion that stands in opposition to the permanent conquest of territory.

My generation is the era of state-paid, indictment-immune rabbis counseling hatred, preaching racism, inciting bloodshed, exalting war, degrading democracy, sanctifying inequality, forbidding compromise, undermining solutions.

My generation is the era of the blockhead genius, of leaders like Benjamin Netanyahu (MIT, '77), and Ehud Barak (Stanford, '78), whose borderline pathological lack of basic social skills, coupled with superhuman egos, translate into grand promises of peacemaking, followed by down-in-flames failures to deliver.

In running this country, my generation has sinned, we have transgressed, we have done perversely. Look no farther than the self-cast curse that is the siege of Gaza, Israel's standout wrong call of the entire last decade.

The siege made the entire population of Gaza dependent on Hamas. And, as a direct result: It made Hamas rich, it made Hamas indispensable, dominant, the sole arbiter of which materials would go for sorely needed home construction, and which would be diverted for use in the manufacture of rockets and tunnels.

It made Hamas the efficient weapons importer and manufacturer that it quickly became, allowing it to securely stockpile thousands of missiles and their launchers, as well as build a network of tunnels which to this day baffles and eludes the best minds and means of one of the world's premier intelligence communities.

Hamas did all that. All that, except protecting the people of Gaza from us. Not an issue for them. On the contrary.

When my generation fails, it fails big. We can't make peace. At this point, we cannot even successfully make war. We have tainted Israel's reputation abroad, we have endangered Israel's ties with its most important allies, we have jeopardized our bonds with Jews abroad, particularly in the United States.

But for the leaders of my generation, failure begins at home. Mine was the generation of leaders which blazed the trail of privatization, taking much of what was good about Israel, and systematically junking it.

These were the visionaries who took one of the world's best public healthcare systems, and bombarded it, starved it, and crushed it to the very brink of collapse. This was the generation of leaders who took deadly and unflinching aim at public education, social work, affordable housing, all the while sending the public an unmistakable message:

If you're not rich, you will sink. Your children will sink further. There will be no one left to catch you. No social net. And if you happen to be neither rich nor Jewish, you will sink faster, and much farther.

We've shown the younger generation what we can do. And, like all younger generations, they already know, all too well, what we cannot, what we are truly awful at.

When I was their age, in an America chewed up and torn to pieces by an endless war in Vietnam, at some point, my generation – despite years of cultural and educational brainwashing about the greatness and superior morality of democracy in the USA - came to the collective conclusion that our parents had been idiots.

May our children here in the Holy Land come to the same conclusion.

In failing ourselves, we have failed them. It's time for a new generation to take over.

May they kick us out soon.

THE MONSTER UNDER YOUR BED

JUNE 16, 2014

You've got to be taught To hate and fear,
You've got to be taught, from year to year, It's got to be drummed
in your dear little ear You've got to be carefully taught.
— *"South Pacific," Rodgers and Hammerstein, 1949*

It wasn't always this way. It wasn't always true that the Holy Land is divided into two kinds of people – those who fear peace, and those who hate it.

You're not born this way. You have to be taught, because there is something unnatural about the idea that peace should be considered dangerous, treasonous, defeatist, lily-livered.

But we've been carefully taught. All of us, Israelis and Palestinians, as one. A rare consensus, which lands all of us, the peoples of the Holy Land, each in our own pain and our own grief and our own bitterness, each in our equally and oppositely legitimate aspirations and hopes and claims for justice, in the same mire.

It wasn't always true that a majority of people – Israelis and Palestinians both – want to see a peace based on two states, yet are terrified of what haters of peace are capable of doing in response. But it's true now.

There was rejoicing by both Palestinians and Israelis that September in 1993 when the Oslo Accords were announced. But much has changed. And the people who changed it, the extremists in our midst, have coined an entire Orwellian dialect to explain why peace is to be hated. More than war.

We know how they work. They intimidate us into silence and inaction, they guilt us into tolerating their intolerance, they blackmail us and hold us hostage with political machinations and obscene religious pronouncements, and because it's so hard to just live here – and try to live a decent life – we've lost the strength and the faith we need to stand up to them.

We know that many of the extremists are willing to literally die to keep us from that peace. And we know that they are willing to take many, many of us - children, the elderly, the pregnant and infirm included – with them when they go.

They have taught the rest of us well. They have incinerated rush- hour buses and assassinated a prime minister and rocketed residential neighborhoods and massacred worshippers at prayer. They have carried out drive-by shootings and attacked children and uprooted whole orchards, all to get us to fear the peace they so despise.

They have taught us that there is only one thing certain about peace in the Holy Land: It will hurt.

In many ways, extremists made our children, the generation that grew up after the signing of the Oslo Accords, what they have become – distrustful of the idea that peace is possible, the concept that democracy is desirable, the hope that the future can possibly be at all better.

Fear is, after all, its own best engine. Fear makes us hesitate to take the very actions that can address our fears. Fear lulls and fools us into believing that things are so fragile and darkly hazardous that any step forward that we take to address them is a step into cataclysm and abyss.

Fear can make smart people stupid.

Fear teaches us that No is a word of might and clarity and self-esteem and stature, while Yes is a word of vulnerability and uncertainty and deference and submission.

How do you fight fear? How do you deal with the monster hidden and lurking out of view under the bed, the shadow behind the closet door?

Maybe, for us, the first step is to open our eyes. Let there be sight. For our part, as Israelis, under our covers on this side of the walls we have built, we've only now begun – and not entirely of our own free will, to look at Palestinians, and at ourselves.

Recently, thanks in part to peace activists and a new world of available technology, we have begun to see on the evening news what happens when we send our soldiers, that post-Oslo generation, past the separation barrier and into occupation duty. We have watched as our soldiers – themselves fearful - have opened fire without apparent cause, arrested small children without legitimate cause, killed people without just cause.

We need to see this. We have to find ways to see what we are afraid of. We have to know. We have to know what lack of peace is like. And what it takes to keep it going.

We need to see more of this. Let a hundred cameras blossom. A thousand. Let there be sight.

Yes, we have every reason to be scared. Because all of us, Palestinians and Israelis both, know the extremists in our midst. We are, after all, family. We know with what passion our madmen and women hate that idea of a peace.

After all this, though, two other things are true:

If you still believe in the possibility of peace, you are as much a true believer as the fiercest extremist.

You fight fear by not being alone. We're not alone. Incredibly, among Israelis and Palestinians both, there are still many more of us, than there are of them.

LOOK AGAIN. RIGHT NOW

APRIL 24, 2018

It's no stretch to suspect that in his heart of hearts, Benjamin Netanyahu would like to be Israel's prime minister for life.

The question is, though: Whose life - Netanyahu's or Israel's?

In Israel, North America, the world over, many Jews are going through something unfamiliar these days, something disturbing on a level which is both new and profound:

Thanks to Netanyahu, the Israel you know – or thought you knew - is fast disappearing.

In fact, Netanyahu's every move may be propelling the Holy Land into a future which just a short while ago seemed impossible – and to Netanyahu's own vision, distinctly undesirable: The replacement of a single independent Israel with a confederation in which Israel and Palestine are self-governing, co-equal, co-existing, culturally distinct, independent, self-governing entities.

In all of his proud intransigence, Netanyahu may be creating the very conditions for a radical new Holy Land, a future Israeli-

Palestinian confederation.

As public opinion analyst Dahlia Scheindlin has shown, a majority of Israelis may support the general approach of confederation.

It won't happen any time soon. But given present realities, a confederation may one day prove inevitable.

The government's entire direction is not only rendering the Oslo- model two-state solution impossible, it is making untenable and unsustainable the present one-state/no-state reality of a monstrous form of triceratops rule (literally, a "three-horned face" - one entire body of law and enforcement for pre-1967 Israel, a second for West Bank settlers, a third for West Bank Palestinians).

If Israel can no longer realistically move settlers – or, for that matter, Palestinians - out of the West Bank, if Israel refuses to give the millions of West Bank Palestinians the right to Israeli citizenship and the vote, then the government is itself creating the conditions under which a confederation may be the only sustainable option.

And what of the meantime? As the prime minister desperately treads water, every solemn national observance in Israel has become a malleable, exploitable, intentionally and obviously divisive campaign stunt for Netanyahu and his Likud-primary-obsessed lackeys, up to and including the memorial day for the Holocaust and resistance to the Nazis.

Love it or hate it, the Israel you know in your kishkes and have grown so accustomed to defending or excoriating, is passing, right before your eyes.

Look again. Right now.

Is it a homeland for Jews? A refuge? A soft place to land? Not any more. Not if you're the wrong color, or you're not Orthodox, or if you support an independent judiciary, or you actively oppose settlements, occupation, forcibly deporting African asylum seekers, or shooting unarmed demonstrators on the other side of a border.

Or if you simply, actively, publicly oppose Benjamin Netanyahu.

Or, maybe you're a major in the IDF reserves. Someone like

journalist Yoav Keren, 44, who last year took to video to tell his fellow Israelis something he probably never thought he'd hear himself say: "This was the first Independence Day in all my 44 years, that I felt that I did not belong to this place."

He is abashed that, in the current toxicity of an alt-right political climate, he feels that he must, before all else, justify himself by presenting his credentials as an authentic Israeli (a second generation paratrooper, "five years regular army, 18 years reserves. Lebanon. Gaza."

"True, I'm not a Likud voter," he said in the *Yedioth Ahronoth* video Op Ed. "True, I'm Ashkenazi. True, I'm secular. But, hey, I'm a major in the reserves. And, besides, my daughters are half-Mizrachi. That also counts, doesn't it?"

Apparently not.

Not, he suggests, when Minister of Culture Miri Regev speaks of 'exterminating the old elites'. And Keren realizes that, despite his relatively modest means, Regev is including him in the 'elite' worthy of extermination. In the same vein, attacks by the prime minister and hard right Education Minister Naftali Bennett against supposedly disloyal and effete leftists, target him by extension.

And then there is the social media far-right.

"When people write me [calling me] 'scum,' 'sleaze,' and 'piece of shit' just because I criticized the Culture Minister in a Facebook post, I know that they mean every word."

Last week on Memorial Day for the fallen of Israel's military, Keren laid a wreath on the grave of an acquaintance, air force pilot Yonaton Begin, who died in a crash in the course of a training flight in 2000. Yonaton Begin was the grandson of Likud founder Menachem Begin and the son of Likud MK Benny Begin, who has paid a severe political price for opposing anti-democratic moves by party leader Netanyahu.

"As I stood beside the grave, Section 8, Row 1, I thought about The Shadow [firebrand far-right rapper Yoav Eliasi], the right-wing activist and Likud member who recently cast blame at bereaved father Benny Begin, saying 'He taught his kids to be haters of Israel."

Keren said he would not attend the alternative Israel-Palestine memorial day ceremony organized by the Bereaved Parents Circle and Combatants for Peace, at which right-wing activists have jeered, cursed, and assaulted participants.

"But when right-wing activists call bereaved parents 'Nazis' just because they chose to take part in a Jewish-Palestinian ceremony, when they write 'All the leftists must be annihilated,' I feel they're even trying to take Memorial Day away from me.

"I love the country," Keren said. "But apparently it no longer loves me."

This is Israel, 2018. This is the Israel whose leader goes on record – on Independence Day - as effectively declaring to his base: "My party colleague, Yuli Edelstein - who survived KGB persecution and expulsion from university, and then hard labor and injury in a Soviet Siberian prison, and who was willing to endure all that in order to move to Israel, only to rise to become speaker of the Knesset – is, in the end, nothing but a dumb immigrant. And, for the sake of winning an election, you, as my base, along with my Culture Minister and me, can publicly humiliate him all we want."

As the bubble of Netanyahu supporters grows ever tougher, ever more racist, ever more exclusionist, ever more anti-democratic, authoritarian, ever more supportive of violence in word and action, ever more isolated from the rest of the Jewish people, a new, entirely unintended reality, is emerging as a consequence.

Netanyahu's aversion to peace talks and a two-state solution, his whole-hog backing for settlement expansion, his creeping but accelerating annexation of the West Bank, and his having earned the increasing enmity and mistrust of the Diaspora's largest Jewish community have actually laid the groundwork for new concepts of an Israeli-Palestinian confederation.

Netanyahu, being Netanyahu, will do what he does best – stall.

But how long will Israelis follow a leader who rules by persuading an activist minority that all the Palestinians really want is to see all the Jews dead?

Not a decent life with basic rights and reasonable opportunities and a fair share in determining their own fate, no – they want you dead.

How long will Israelis follow a leader who promises them that "we will forever live by the sword."

Forever, he says.

Forever, that is, your children – and theirs - will serve in the army and, if I, as your indispensable leader say so, will be ordered to shoot other children.

But even Netanyahu, knows, in his heart of hearts, that nothing is forever.

And no one knows better than Netanyahu, the way things actually work here. Just when you think nothing will ever change, the inconceivable turns overnight into the inevitable.

A WORD OF THANKS

From 'A Farewell Column,' April 22, 2019

It is an honor to be a journalist. It has been, and is to this day, my privilege to work with wondrous people, people of rare bravery and inextinguishable fire and heightened senses and hardened exteriors and open hearts and fingertips touched by God.

I prize them. I love them. They help save the world from itself.

I am thrilled by the younger writers now taking their rightful place at the heart of this profession. They are what real journalists have to be: warriors.

I've been at this for a long, long time, and still I marvel about what journalists have to do, what they have to go through, to practice what has become the most dangerously maligned necessary job there is on earth.

Journalism remains necessary because, even in the age of social media, perhaps especially in the age of social media, the vulnerable and the victimized are all too often unseen and unheard and unaided until their plight is made public. By the press.

I am proud of the place I work. It preaches freedom and practices it. It sheds light. It keeps alive a flame which has grown more and more rare, more and more fragile, more and more a target in an environment which has turned darkness into a cult, and intimidation into law.

Haaretz has been around for a hundred tough years. *Haaretz* is a lighthouse.

There is nothing in this world like it. It is part NGO, part pain in the ass, part virtual congregation for those who feel they have been, at least in part, excommunicated. May it continue to rain holy hell on those who so richly deserve it.

The person who owns it is a quiet man who is, in many respects, the most courageous of all of us. In a profession of unimaginably stubborn people, he stands his ground as no one else. He is unafraid of being unpopular, of speaking his mind, and of printing the unpopular views of others. He is not of the present century. He is one of a kind.

It's an honor to have known the people I've worked alongside. Some of the best of my colleagues, my teachers and my friends, are gone now. In particular, David Twersky, David Landau, Robert Rosenberg, and Merle Gould, who all passed away much too soon, maybe of having lived all that much.

I sometimes wonder how they would have dealt with this time of high-test evil and the exceptional success authoritarian rulers have found in scapegoating and inciting against news outlets they don't already control as a pillar of their rule. With the growth of authoritarianism, many of my colleagues have been wounded, some left disabled, in the course of their work. More and more are being jailed for doing their job. More and more, for the same reason, are being killed.

I pray for the safety of my colleagues. I wish them strength. I wish them the appreciation they so wholly deserve.

I will them my optimism. May they be ferocious when appropriate and kind when kindness is called for. May they continue to support and shield and come to the aid of one another.

They are heroes. Their loved ones are heroes tenfold, for putting up with all of this.

As for me, I've had my say. It's been an astonishing privilege, something I never expected to have happen in my life. Every so often I'll file another piece. But only when I'm good and furious, or intensely moved.

In the end, if authoritarians are to be defeated, it will be in part because the endangered species called journalists refused to roll over and be domesticated or eradicated, because newswomen and newsmen were willing to take the heat inherent in committing the crime of just doing their job. Accurately. Fairly. And despite their real fears, fearlessly.

Prize them. They're your best shot.

ACKNOWLEDGMENTS

The inspiration for many of the ideas expressed here, certainly for the best of them, stems not from me, but from my person, the exceptional writer, the boundless soul who makes this life full and afire and so entirely worth living, Varda Spiegel.

I fell into journalism with more foolhardiness than knowledge and more desperation than skill. I owe my trade wholly to the help and friendship of immensely talented colleagues.

The wonderful people who put together underground newspapers a lifetime ago got me started in this, at North Hollywood's *Incubator* and the *Jewish Radical* in Berkeley, along with the network of other Jewish student newspapers of my college years. My thanks and love to David and Rachel Biale, Ken Bob, David DeNola, Susie Dessel, Miri Gold, J.J. Goldberg, Joanne Jarr, David Lichtenstein, Mark Linton, David Leichman, Jonathan and Michael Medved, Lorrie Oreck, Carrie Rickey, Steve Rosen, Sherman and Melodie Rosenfeld, Shelly Schreter, Elaine Schlackman, Ellie Shapiro, Robin Sohmer, and to Arnie Druck and Buddy Timberg, of blessed memory.

A special shout-out to Rina Castelnuovo and Jim Hollander and to my beloved comrades at Reuters, among them Sami Aboudi, Howard Goller, Christine Hauser, Jim Hollander, Paul Holmes, Rob Mahoney, Jack Redden, David Silverman, Stephanie Fried, and Taher Shriteh.

And to Amos Schocken and my extraordinary colleagues at *Haaretz*. The courage, vigor, moral compass and professional excellence of the people of *Haaretz* never cease to astonish me – of Zvi Bar'el, Gila Babich, Aluf Benn, Omer Benjakob, Larry Derfner, Natasha Dornberg, Akiva Eldar, Avirama Golan, Jonathan Gorodischer, David B. Green, Charlotte Halle, Yishai Halper, Adrian Hennigan, Peter Hirschberg, Jillian Jones, Dina Kraft, Amy Levinson, Gideon Levy, Judy Maltz, Sara Miller, Matti Milstein, Nirit Mitrany, Anshel Pfeffer, Alon Pinkas, Shira Philosof, Adar Primor, Ben Samuels, Karen Saul, Cliff Savren, Hagar Shezaf, Allison Kaplan Sommer, Simon Spungin, Aliyana Traison, Amir Tibon, Leevi Winter, Noa Yachot, Rutie Zuta, and, of course, of blessed memory, David Landau, Yoel Marcus, Robert Rosenberg, Yossi Sarid, and Ze'ev Schiff.

My gratitude to the invaluable Skyler Kratofil, whose design made this book. And for their vital help producing some of these stories, thanks to Joel Greenberg, Jill Jacobs, Ray Hanania, Edo Konrad, Susan and Steve Lax, and Sarah Tuttle-Singer.

Special blessings to Lani Burston Silver and Shane Silver.

I'd like to close with a word about the future. I want to mention six people whose exceptional strength gives me strength every single day, whose joy in living showers me with joy in living every moment, and whose stark originality and creativity lend me pure hope for the years to come: to Yotam and Be'eri, Timna and Tzafrir, and Kessem and Layli. Thanks, more than words can ever express.

ABOUT THE AUTHOR

Bradley Burston, a longtime columnist for Israel's *Haaretz*, is a recipient of the Eliav-Sartawi Award For Mideast Journalism, presented at the United Nations in 2006.

His columns have been quoted in The New York Times, Foreign Policy, the New Yorker, The Nation, Politico, and Dissent. He has appeared as a commentator on the BBC, NPR, ABC Nightline and CNN.

A native of Los Angeles, he moved to Israel after graduation from Berkeley. He was part of a group which established Kibbutz Gezer, between Tel Aviv and Jerusalem. He served in the IDF as a combat medic, later studying medicine in Beer Sheva for two years before turning to journalism.

During the first Palestinian uprising of the late 1980s, he served as Gaza correspondent for the Jerusalem Post, and was the paper's Military Correspondent in the 1991 Gulf War. In the 1990s, he covered Middle East peace talks and Israeli politics for the Reuters news agency. In 2000, he became a founding editor of *Haaretz* newspaper's online English edition, writing a column called A Special Place in Hell, from which this collection was compiled.